In keeping all the bo attention to context and retrieving the so-called 'difficulties' for the teacher (the lists of lists and the bloodshed) from any sense of apology and showing how they fit with the faithfulness of God and the purposes of the book. With its clear headed sanity, God-centred focus and nourishment for the Christian believer, this is an essential tool for any teaching on Joshua.

Nick Hiscocks
Vicar of Christ Church, Westbourne, Bournemouth

The primary task of a faithful Bible teacher (and an honest Bible reader) is to understand the Bible *as it actually is*, the words of God that are able to make us wise enough to trust in the Lord Jesus Christ and so be saved. How do we do that with the Old Testament book of Joshua? Doug Johnson's excellent book provides a careful, thoughtful and reliable guide that will help many to do this well. Highly recommended.

John Woodhouse
Former Principal of Moore College, Sydney, Australia
Author of several books

This is a book for preachers. Many of our modern congregations are fragile and uncertain in their faith because they are not well-nourished from the pulpit. The Lord's army needs a clear blast from the trumpet if it is to know how to do battle in today's world. Doug Johnson's careful study of the book of Joshua, based on many years of deep acquaintance with the text, will put strength into our preachers. It will deepen their confidence in the power of the Word of God to equip the church for its work.

Edward Lobb
Director of Training, The Scottish Cornhill Training Course, Glasgow

This commentary on Joshua by Doug Johnson makes me want to preach on this book of the Bible. It is a perfect preaching and teaching tool for ministers and Bible study leaders. His handling of the text is matched by his application of the text to give us an excellent commentary on a book of the Bible that reveals the God who makes and keeps promises.

Mark Jones
Senior Minister at Faith Vancouver PCA

TEACHING JOSHUA

From text to message

DOUG JOHNSON

SERIES EDITORS: JON GEMMELL & DAVID JACKMAN

PT RESOURCES

CHRISTIAN FOCUS

Unless otherwise marked, Scripture is taken from *The Holy Bible, New International Version*®, NIV® Copyright © 1973, 1978, 1984, 2011 by Biblica, Inc.™ Used by permission. All rights reserved worldwide.

Scripture marked 'ESV' taken from *The Holy Bible, English Standard Version*, copyright © 2001 by Crossway Bibles, a division of Good News Publishers. Used by permission. All rights reserved.

Scripture marked 'NASB' is taken from the *New American Standard Bible*®, Copyright © 1960, 1962, 1963, 1968, 1971, 1972, 1973, 1975, 1977, 1995 by The Lockman Foundation Used by Permission (www.Lockman.org).

Scripture marked 'NET' is taken from the *New English Translation Bible*® copyright ©1996-2006 by Biblical Studies Press, L.L.C. http://netbible.com Used by Permission. All rights reserved.

Copyright © Proclamation Trust Media 2019

ISBN: 978-1-5271-0335-1

10 9 8 7 6 5 4 3 2 1

Published in 2019
by
Christian Focus Publications Ltd,
Geanies House, Fearn, Ross-shire,
IV20 1TW, Scotland, Great Britain

with

Proclamation Trust Resources,
Willcox House, 140-148 Borough High Street,
London, SE1 1LB, England, Great Britain.
www.proctrust.org.uk

www.christianfocus.com

Cover design by Moose77.com

Printed and bound by
Bell & Bain, Glasgow

All rights reserved. No part of this publication may be reproduced, stored in a retrieval system, or transmitted, in any form, by any means, electronic, mechanical, photocopying, recording or otherwise without the prior permission of the publisher or a licence permitting restricted copying. In the UK such licences are issued by the Copyright Licensing Agency, Saffron House, 6-10 Kirby Street, London, EC1 8TS www.cla.co.uk

Contents

Series Preface 7
Author's Preface 9
How to Use this Book 11

Part One: Introducing Joshua 15
    Getting our Bearings in Joshua 17
    Why Should We Preach and Teach Joshua? 43
    Ideas for Preaching or Teaching a Series on Joshua 57

Part Two: The God who Makes and Keeps Promises 93
    1. Confirming the Promise (1–2) 95
    2. Witnessing to the Promise (3–4) 129
    3. Realising the Promise (5–6) 165
    4. Responses to the Promise (7–8) 207
    5. The Power of the Promise (9–12) 249
    6. Receiving the Promise (13–21) 289
    7. Life in the Promise (22–24) 335

Further Reading 379
PT Resources 383

Series Preface

The book of Joshua is an epic within the Bible. We are familiar with many of the famous stories but often give up studying the whole book after the first 12 chapters except for maybe a one-off from Joshua's farewell speeches at the end. Our hope is that this volume as part of our Teaching the Bible series will halt this pick and mix, purple passage approach and see all of Joshua being preached and taught profitably to congregations. Doug Johnson has produced this remarkable book to try and help preachers, teachers and students of the Bible do just that. Within these pages Doug has comprehensively studied the book of Joshua and distilled excellent scholarship into accessible, rich and invaluable chapters. The sheer amount of thought, reading and experience that Doug brings to this book will not only save the pastor hours in the study but will hopefully bring greater clarity to their sermons, talks and Bible studies.

This volume, like all in the series, are written with the Bible teacher and Bible student in mind. Part One, the introductory section, contains lots of important information to help us get a handle on the book of Joshua, covering aspects like structure, place in the biblical story and also great assistance on how you would go about planning a preaching series. Then Part Two works through the book systematically giving insight into the text as well as suggesting sermon outlines, key applications and also Bible study questions. These are not there to take the hard work out of preparation but to be a helping hand as people invest their time, efforts and gifts in preparing to teach the Bible to others.

Teaching Joshua brings the number of published volumes in this series to twenty-one. We are encouraged by how this series is developing and the comments we hear from people involved in regular Bible teaching and preaching ministry. We long for these books to help people to keep working hard at the Word in order that they might proclaim the unsearchable riches of Christ ever more clearly.

Our thanks go to Christian Focus for their continued partnership in this project. Without their faith, expertise and patience none of these books would ever make it on to the bookshelf. Thanks must also go to Geraldine Sparks and Charlotte Bailey in the PT office who took the editorial scribbles of Jon Gemmell and transferred them skilfully to the manuscript.

Jon Gemmell and David Jackman
Series Editors
London, 2019

Author's Preface

The first time I preached on the book of Joshua is a somewhat distant memory now. It was, in fact, the first sermon I ever preached in a 'formal' church setting. I owe that opportunity to Ian Barclay. His encouragement in my first attempts at preaching and, later, towards training and full-time ministry is gratefully remembered. His insistence on which college I should go to meant that I spent three fruitful years learning the Old Testament from Alec Motyer. Alec's clear teaching, enthusiasm for Scripture and his extreme patience in our weekly Hebrew text tutorials remain among my warmest memories from that time of my life. Although, I should say, the birth of my son Daniel on my first day as a theological student has to take pride of place!

Two other men deserve thanks for helping my thinking on Joshua develop in the way that it has. John Woodhouse's lecture notes from a PT Fairmile conference are still in my 'archive' and show signs of much use. Ralph Davis came to my rescue as I sought to preach a series on Joshua at the then infant church-plant, Dundonald, in Wimbledon. His book, *No Falling Words* (originally published by Baker in 1988) is still on my shelf and remains invaluable to the preacher. Alongside my thanks to these two men, I must add a disclaimer on their behalf – they must not be held responsible for the way I have used or developed their thinking!

As well as preaching through the book a number of times, 'Joshua' has accompanied me on several preaching conferences in East and West Africa. Five or six years of Cornhill students have also had a close encounter with much of this material. I am particularly grateful to David Jackman for the opportunity to have been part of Cornhill for twelve happy years.

There have been a number of occasions when, first Adrian Reynolds, and then Jon Gemmell, have had to remind me that I had promised to write this book. My thanks to Adrian for encouraging me to take it on; and to Jon for seeing it through to completion.

My final and greatest thanks must be reserved for my wife, Ann. Her encouragement and support, as well as her willingness to make a manuscript into a typescript, have made producing this book possible.

My hope is that preachers and teachers will be encouraged to proclaim afresh 'the God who makes and keeps His promises' through the pages of the book of Joshua. And, that through that teaching, the Lord of the Covenant will be glorified.

Doug Johnson
Yeovil, 2019

How to Use this book

This book aims to help the preacher or teacher understand the central thrust and purpose of the text in order to preach or teach it to others. Unlike a commentary therefore, it does not go into great exegetical detail. Instead it aims to help the teacher engage with the themes of Joshua, to keep the big picture in mind, and to think about how to present it to their hearers. It has been deliberately written so that it can serve a number of different kinds of people; each will, hopefully, get what they need from the volume:

- For those starting out in ministry and for whom expository preaching is a new idea, the book presents a 'start-to-finish' process of preparing a sermon, talk or study, including some suggested questions for a group.

- Those with more experience may find the sections which work through the text and suggest preaching/teaching units the most helpful parts of the book. These sections form the first half of each chapter on the Bible text. The later sections of those chapters suggest lines of application and group study questions. These are intended to supplement and affirm a teacher's own work rather than replace it.

The chapters in Part One (the introductory section of the book) should help every preacher and teacher.

'Part One: Introducing Joshua' examines the book's themes and structure as well as some of the context. This material is crucial for our understanding of the whole book, which in turn will shape the way we preach each section to our congregations. Part One also suggests a number of divisions of Joshua's twenty-four chapters into preaching/teaching units.

Part Two then contains separate chapters on each of these preaching units. The structure of each of these chapters is the same: there is a brief introduction to the unit followed by a section headed '**Listening to the text.**' This section outlines the structure and context of the unit and takes the reader through a section-by-section analysis of the text. All good Biblical preaching begins with careful, detailed listening to the text and this is true for Joshua as much as for any other book.

Each chapter then continues with a section called '**From text to message.**' This suggests a main theme and aim for each preaching unit (including how the unit relates to the overall theme of the book) and then some possible sermon outlines.

All these suggestions are nothing more than that – suggestions, designed to help the preacher think about his own division of the text and structure of the sermon. We are great believers in every preacher constructing their own outlines because these need to flow from our personal

How to Use this Book

encounter with God in the text. Downloading other people's sermons or trying to breathe life into someone else's outlines are strategies doomed to failure. Doing this may produce a reasonable talk, but in the long term it is disastrous to the preacher himself. If a preacher is to speak from the heart of God to the hearts of his congregation, he needs to live in the Word and the Word needs to live in him.

However, these 'Text to message' sections will provide the preacher or teacher with a number of starting points for their own studies. They give a few very basic ideas about how an outline on some of these passages might shape up. There are also some bullet points suggesting possible lines of application, with particular focus on how lines to Christ may be drawn.

Each chapter on the Bible text concludes with some suggested questions for a group Bible study. These questions are grouped into two types: questions to help *understand* the passage and questions to help *apply* the passage. Not all the questions would be needed for an individual study but they aim to give a variety of ideas for those who are planning a study series.

The aim of good questions is always to drive the group into the text to explore and understand its meaning more fully. This keeps the focus on Scripture and reduces speculation and the mere exchange of opinions. Remember, the key issues are always 'What does the text say?' and then 'What does it mean?' Avoid rushing quickly to the 'What does it mean to you?' type of question. Everyone needs to be clear on the original and intended meaning of a text before thinking about personal applications. Focusing on the intended meaning of a text will keep the Bible in the driving-seat of your study. It will stop the session being governed by the participants' opinions, prejudices or experiences!

These studies will be especially useful in those churches where Bible study groups are able to study a Bible book at the same time as it is preached, a practice I warmly commend. This allows small groups to drive home understanding and especially application in the week after the sermon has been preached. It ensures God's Word is applied personally and specifically to the daily lives of the congregation.

Finally, many have found this series of books a useful aid in personal devotions, making use of the study questions to help understanding, application and prayer. Though they are not primarily designed for this purpose, we are delighted that they are used in such a way, for wherever God's Word is faithfully proclaimed and taught, there God's voice is clearly heard.

May you know God's help and strength as you dig deeply into the book of Joshua for yourself and on behalf of others.

Part One:
Introducing Joshua

I

Getting Our Bearings in Joshua

Introduction

Many people today immediately think of the book of Joshua as simply being about battles and bloodshed. It is a view popularised by the so-called 'New Atheists' in their attempt to discredit and undermine Scripture. A classic example is Richard Dawkins who writes:

> The ethnic cleansing begun in the time of Moses is brought to bloody fruition in the book of Joshua, a text remarkable for the bloodthirsty massacres it records and xenophobic relish with which it does so.[1]

And yet, only six chapters (6-11) of Joshua's twenty-four actually contain stories of the battles Israel fought. Where it does so, it uses more restrained language than Richard Dawkins. To focus solely on the battles is to miss

---

1. R. Dawkins, *The God Delusion* (London, UK: Black Swan, 2007) p. 280.

the broader perspective of the book and many of its key themes, including:

- the possibility of mercy for the outsider
- the justice meted out to the unfaithful insider
- the establishment and unity of a nation
- the demands of loyalty to Israel's God
- the faithfulness of God to His people and to His promises

Nonetheless the issue of massacre and genocide raised by Dawkins is one that we must face. We will consider it in some detail in chapter 3 and at other appropriate points as we look at the text of Joshua. It is important to note that the New Testament simply accepts these events without embarrassment or qualification (See Acts 13:18-20 and Heb. 11:32-34).

This acceptance by the New Testament is part of its recognition that Scripture (in this case the Old Testament) is authoritative and given to teach, rebuke, correct and train us in righteousness (see 2 Tim. 3:16). As preachers and teachers, therefore, we need to take seriously its place in the great sweep of the biblical narrative – Genesis to Revelation – as the saving purposes of God are unfolded.

The book of Joshua helps us in that journey. As the book closes, Joshua focuses the people of Israel's attention on the action and purposes of God. In just twelve verses (Josh. 24:2-13) God recounts through Joshua several centuries of history, and His fundamental actions on behalf of His people. From the call of Abraham to the settlement in the land, the first person statements in these verses make clear the initiative and activity of God. Many of these actions are also a reflection of a prior Word of God – demonstrating a fulfilment of His promise. This is the major theme that echoes throughout the book.

Joshua in its setting

In the ancient world

The period in which the book of Joshua is set – the Late Bronze Age (c. 1550–1200 B.C.) – was a period dominated by three major powers, the Hittites, Egyptians and Mitanians (replaced by the Assyrians in the mid 14th century). This competition created something of a power vacuum in Canaan, and a whole series of independent city-states vied for dominance. By the end of this period the power of Egypt had declined and had little influence over the area. The Amarna Letters written around 1350 B.C. describe how these power struggles were unfolding, with pleas to the Egyptian Pharaohs to intervene. It is clear from reading Joshua that some Canaanite cites were well fortified but the land as a whole was vulnerable to a well organised and determined invasion force. It was into this situation that the nation of Israel under Joshua made their advance.

The actual date of the Israelite entry into Canaan has been a matter of dispute and determining it is linked, necessarily, with the date of the Exodus.

The main options are:

1. An early date (c. 1406 B.C.). This fits best with the biblical chronology – 1 Kings 6:1 states that there were 480 years between the Exodus and Solomon's fourth year as king (966 B.C.).

2. A late date (c. 1250 B.C.). This infers that the date in 1 Kings 6:1 is symbolic – 12 generations of 40 years each. The archaeological evidence is said to be more in accord with this dating.

3. An intermediate position is proposed, locating the entry in the mid-1300s B.C.

None of these proposals are completely without difficulty, and although I am working from the early dating which seems most logical, the treatment of the text that follows is not materially affected by this decision.[2]

Another issue needing to be considered briefly, with regard to the historical context, is the nature of the conquest. There are four basic models of conquest hypothesised, three of which have serious implications for the historicity of the book of Joshua.[3]

These models are:

- **Conquest** This model takes the text of Joshua at face value and has been the accepted model through the history of interpretation into the 20th century. Sometimes the conquest has been misread or over-emphasised to make the book speak of a wholesale destruction of the land. The book itself, however, only describes the complete destruction of three cities: Jericho, Ai and Hazor. Conquest involving both

---

2. For further discussion see: R. L. Hubbard, Jr, *Joshua NIVAC* (Grand Rapids, USA: Zondervan, 2009) pp. 35-42; and I. Provan, V. P. Long & T. Longman III, *A Biblical History of Israel* (Louisville USA: Westminster John Knox Press, 2015) pp. 190-201.

3. Again see Provan et al. and commentaries listed in Further Reading pp. 379 below.

invasion and subjugation seems to be in accordance with the biblical account.

- *Infiltration* In the first half of the 20th century, a new model was suggested. This involved the gradual (and peaceful) movement of nomadic people and tribes into the land. These people were mainly pastoralists and linked together by tribal bonds. Over the course of a century or more they came to dominate the land.

- *Revolt* Unlike the first two models that are based on a movement of people into the land, this model (and the next) considers the 'takeover' of the land as arising from the inside. The 'revolt' is that of the peasant population against the overlords of the land, who particularly occupied the cities. The suggestion is made that the common denominator for the various groups in revolt was their religion – a common faith in Yahweh.

- *Evolution* This is also based on the idea of change from within the land and its existing communities. It suggests, however, that the change was peaceful. By a variety of means a gradual change occurred, the end product being a new and more unified people with a common religious allegiance – the nation of Israel.

The three models of infiltration, revolt and evolution have received a great deal of academic attention in recent decades, but are all built on a high level of scepticism concerning the biblical account. They have also employed clear ideological presuppositions as to how the development of Israel happened. They either use principles derived from other cultures (infiltration) or from 20th century sociological or political thinking (revolt and evolution).

In rejecting these three models, we must be careful not to buy into an exaggerated form of the conquest model that misreads the text (as noted above). The text must govern our approach; the conquest must be seen and preached as it is portrayed there.

Following his review and evaluation of the four models, David Howard wisely concludes:

> ... that the biblical picture of an "Israel" descended from Abraham entering Canaan from without and engaging and defeating various Canaanite forces, but without causing extensive material destruction, is the most reasonable and defensible model, and the one that is assumed here.[4]

The accusation often levelled against the text of Joshua and those who take it seriously, is that it is ideologically or theologically biased. This same criticism can be used against the accusers also. No interpretation of Joshua, or of history in general, is or can be entirely objective; all history is to differing degrees subjective. Recent research has shown that the book of Joshua fits well in its context. Its style and content show an affinity with other ancient Near Eastern conquest accounts. This strengthens its claims of historicity and shows that the book is written in a genre appropriate to its time and place.[5] And so, it is to Joshua as a piece of biblical literature in its Old Testament setting to which we will now turn.

---

4. D. Howard, *Joshua* NAC (Nashville, USA: Broadman & Holman, 1998) p. 40.

5. See Further Reading p. 379 and books noted there.

In the Old Testament

One way of locating the book of Joshua in its Old Testament setting is to ask the question: 'Is Joshua among the prophets?'[6] It may seem an odd question to ask, but it helps us to recognise both the character and purpose of the book.

In our English versions of the Bible, Joshua is classified among the history books (as against law, poetry and prophecy) of the Old Testament. Although there is truth in this classification, it is not the whole story. The divisions of the Hebrew Bible, as Jesus and the first Christians would have known it, were threefold. It was divided into the Law, Prophets and the Writings. The Prophets were further sub-divided – the Former and the Latter Prophets. Within this structuring of the Hebrew Bible, Joshua is the first book of the Former Prophets. This is important to remember because *all* of the books that are categorised as 'Prophets' are not just history but also give an interpretation of history. To be an interpretation does not mean that the historicity of the book is therefore eroded. All history writing involves some interpretation. It is written from a particular perspective and context, which helps to determine how people, motives and events are understood. An example would be the way in which events in the New World of the 18th century are reported by writers. Events either take place in the War of Independence or in the American Revolution, depending on which side the writer's loyalties lie.

The prophetic books of the OT, both Former and Latter Prophets, bring a 'bird's-eye' perspective to what

---

6. This question is also asked by Ralph Davis, *Joshua – No Falling Words* (Fearn, UK: Christian Focus, 2000) p. 11.

is happening – or to what is going to happen. Through the Prophets – whether by historical narrative, present command or warning, or by predictions concerning the future – God is revealing His will and acting in the midst of human history. This kind of activity is attributed to Joshua himself in 1 Kings 16:34. Joshua's particular contribution is to bring before us 'the God who makes and keeps promises'.[7]

Among the key features in the OT's way of telling the story of God's dealings with Israel are two that surface time and time again in the book of Joshua:

- the history recorded is selective, as it is in all history writing. The events recorded are not an exhaustive record of what happened to Israel, rather they are selected to show the progress of the nation (or lack of it on occasions) in possessing the Promised Land.

- The events are generally accompanied by an explanation. The defeat at Ai (chapter 7), for example, is not simply recorded as purely an important military episode registering the strategy, army size, result and casualties. The writer also gives the reason for that defeat as well as spelling out the remedy.

The book of Joshua is among the prophets as it explains the events of the conquest in the light of the promises and action of God. This should make us wary of pursuing an overly rigid approach to the historical sequence of the narrative. As stated earlier, we do not have an exhaustive record of what happened during the conquest of Canaan.

---

7. I owe this expression to Alec Motyer – first heard in lectures nearly 50 years ago!

Getting Our Bearings in Joshua

Seen in the broader context of ancient conquest accounts, Joshua follows one of the conventions of that genre. This convention is the technique of telescoping events, where a narrative is delivered in compressed, packaged form. What happens in this telescoping is that a number of related events spread over a period of time, are brought together into a single statement or episode. A simple illustration of this comes from the lips of Joshua himself. In 24:7 he sums up the forty years of wilderness wanderings in a single sentence – 'Then you lived in the wilderness for a long time.' Such a simple statement, however, would be laden with meaning for the people who experienced first-hand some of that period, the memory of those wilderness days would be alive and well among them.

A further classic case of this kind of telescoping is found in the relationship between the people of Israel and the city of Shechem. The city features as the location for the renewal of the covenant in both 8:30-35 and 24:1-28. The city is not named in the narrative of chapter 8, but it is situated between Mount Ebal and Mount Gerizim – important locations in that chapter. It is on these two mountains that Israel gathers to rededicate itself after the defeat and subsequent victory at Ai. At the end of his life Joshua calls the people together again at Shechem to renew their commitment to the covenant, there is, however, no account in the book of Joshua of the subduing or conquest of the city. The only other times the city is mentioned is as a boundary marker for the tribe of Manasseh (17:7) and as a city of refuge (20:7). Shechem was of historical importance, linked to the Patriarchs (see e.g. Gen. 12:6-7, 33:18-20 and 37:12-14); yet how and when the city comes into the hands of the Israelites is not recorded. The city itself is, therefore, not the primary focus of the writer's attention. The greater concern is to include the theological importance of what happens in this location. So, the people are called to remember God's actions on their behalf and to commit themselves to obedience to God's work in both the present and the future. Or, as Paul House puts it, these '… theologically interpreted events should create the impetus for the nation's future.'[8] This perspective of the book of Joshua clearly places it among the prophets. It also has implications, therefore, for the way in which we read and teach it.

Two other features of the book in its Old Testament setting are worth noting. The first is that it naturally takes its place in the narrative flow of Scripture. There is a sense in which the story recorded in the Pentateuch only reaches a climax in the account of the entry into the Promised Land.

Think of the narrative as it focuses on the people of Israel:

- it begins with the promise to Abraham (Gen. 12).
- the rest of the book of Genesis sees the slow gradual growth of his family/clan.
- Exodus introduces us to the threat of extinction that hangs over the people.
- God's intervention on behalf of the people and His confirmation of them as *His* people is recorded.

---

8. P. R. House, *Old Testament Theology* (Downers Grove USA: IVP, 1998) p. 212. See also Hubbard, *Joshua* p. 549f on the significance of Shechem.

Getting Our Bearings in Joshua

- both Exodus and Leviticus show how the people are to live in relationship with God, with each other and before the world.

- having been formed as a people and established in their relationship with God, the book of Numbers takes them on a journey to the fulfilment of God's promise – the land God is giving them.

- Deuteronomy prepares the new generation for entry and life in the Promised Land.

And then ... the book of Joshua; which completes this part of the story. The Pentateuch forms the backdrop to the account of Israel's possession of the Land, and conditions (as we shall see) the way they conduct themselves, their warfare and their division of the Land.

This foundational nature of the Pentateuch is underlined by a second feature concerning the book of Joshua's setting in the Old Testament. The first five books very quickly became established as the Torah – the title given to them in the Hebrew canon. The most basic meaning of the Hebrew word is 'teaching'. It is often translated as 'law' but is used in a much broader sense than simply 'legislation'. The Torah is the bedrock of all that is to come in the remaining sections of the Prophets and the Writings. And through its teachings the people of Israel, and we, are introduced to the Lord – His character, power and purposes – the one who is sovereign in creation, history, salvation and who calls on His people to live for Him. In both of the subsequent sections of the canon, the Prophets and Writings, this God and His demands are not left behind. Significantly, both of these sections open with the call to meditate on the 'Law of the Lord' – the Torah. So:

- Keep this Book of the Law always on your lips; meditate on it day and night, so that you may be careful to do everything written in it (Josh. 1:8).
- Blessed is the one... whose delight is in the law of the Lord, and who meditates on his law day and night (Ps. 1:1-2).

The people of God never 'grow out' of the Word of God; the whole of life ('day and night') are governed by it. The literary setting of the book of Joshua places it firmly in the onward flow of the biblical narrative. It does not mark a new beginning so much as a further step in the continuing story.

In the 'Big Picture'

Earlier, we focussed briefly on the story of the people of Israel as it is traced through the first five books of the Bible. Although the promise to Abraham is a fundamental part of the story it is not the whole story. To see Joshua in the light of the greater story of scripture, we need to stand back and take in a sketch of the 'Big Picture'.

- The creation story in Genesis 1 makes clear the absolute sovereignty of God. God's purpose is brought about simply by His speech. That purpose is seen in the formation of a habitat (a place to live) and inhabitants (people to live there). The people who are formed have a special nature; they are 'in the image of God'. Out of all the created order only humanity has this special

Getting Our Bearings in Joshua

relationship with God – summed up in the word 'blessing'.

- The fall and downward spiral of sin in Genesis 3-11 seems to undo this web of relationships. The people are alienated from the land (the place), from each other (the people) and from God. The relationship of blessing is replaced by curse.

- The purpose of the sovereign God cannot be destroyed. It is restated in the form of a promise to Abraham. The chief elements of that promise express God's creative purposes – a place to live (land), a people to live there (offspring) and blessing.

- These three elements are clearly portrayed and developed in the remainder of the Pentateuch – the beginnings of the people (Gen. 13-50 and Exod. 1), the blessing theme is developed in terms of relationship and rescue (Exodus & Leviticus) and there is progress to and preparation for the land – (Numbers and Deuteronomy).

- At vital stages in this narrative God repeats these aspects of His purposes. In Exodus 6, for example, all three are there; and the new element (stated for the first time in Scripture), which will make the fulfilment of His purposes possible, is God's redeeming activity.

- In the story which runs from the entry into the land to the exile from it (Joshua to Kings) there is both a partial fulfilment of the promise/purpose and a confirmation that the promise still stands despite the failure of the people (see 2 Sam. 7). They receive the land (Joshua), are a unified people (for the most part), especially under

David and Solomon. And they have the great blessing of God living with them (see 1 Kings 8:56-61, which again reflects the threefold promise/purpose).

- The promise does not end with the failure of the people. As the exile approaches, and during it, the prophets direct our attention to the future. One of Isaiah's main themes is that of the place. The corrupt city of Jerusalem will become the renewed city, often called Zion. Indeed, there is the promise of a new heaven and earth (Isa. 65). Jeremiah speaks of a renewed people and his book moves from a people who are worse than the pagan nations (Jer. 2), to a people with new hearts and forgiven sins (Jer. 31). The theme of the blessing that comes through relationship with God is a major part of Ezekiel's prophecies. The book moves from the abandonment of Jerusalem to the return of the Lord in glory after the punishment of the exile and the renewal of the people. Significantly the book closes with the city being given a new name – 'the Lord is there' (Ezek. 48:35).

- At the same time these three 'major' prophets (and others as well) speak of a 'new covenant'. They are looking forward to a time when God will permanently establish this new situation. It has continuity with what has gone before – at its heart is still the great promise/purpose of God summed up as, 'I will be their God and they will be my people' (Jer. 31:33; Ezek. 37:23; cf. Isa. 54:5-10). But, this time it will be different; there will be a permanent dealing with sin and an everlasting establishment of the new order.

- The gospels and epistles clearly see the death of Jesus as establishing this new covenant and explicit mention of it is made in the records of the Last Supper in Matthew, Mark, Luke and 1 Corinthians. Echoes of the three themes we traced above are also clearly to be seen. In very broad terms we can say that the New Testament sees the theme of the place focussed on Jesus. Where, for example, there was once the land (the people of God's place of rest) now that 'place' is Jesus. Where once the people were those in 'Israel', now they are those 'in Christ'. And where once the blessing of God (particularly forgiveness of sins) was ministered through Temple and priesthood, now it is only in and through Jesus.

- The next-to-last chapter of the New Testament points us to the completion, the fulfilment of these themes. In Revelation 21, God's purpose comes to its final and eternal realisation. Here we see a new heaven and a new earth focussed on the New Jerusalem. This is the place where the people of God will dwell forever. Revelation 21:3 recalls the great biblical theme of God dwelling with a people He had made His own. And if this is not wonder and blessing enough, the penalty and effects of sin will have been wiped away, banished for ever (21:4)

It is in the context of this great sweep of the history of God's creative and saving purposes that Joshua finds its place. As we will see, the book opens with reminders and restatements of the three great themes we have traced – a place to live, a people to live there and blessings to enjoy in relationship with God.

Joshua – the book itself

As the book of Joshua opens, we learn that the first great leader of the people of Israel, Moses, is dead. He has been centre stage in the story so far, in Exodus, Numbers and Deuteronomy. His death and Joshua's succession as leader raise some questions concerning the future of the nation and the purposes of God. How does the book of Joshua resolve these issues?

Two questions will help us formulate an answer.

Is this book about a man?

The book, very obviously, bears Joshua's name. Although he features in many of its chapters we are told almost nothing about him as a person. In some ways, the brief interlude involving Caleb is more revealing at a personal level (Josh. 14:6-15), than anything said about Joshua. If you want to learn more about Joshua the man, you have to look outside of the book for that information. There are some twenty-seven references to Joshua in the books of Exodus, Numbers and Deuteronomy. Some of these are incidental, but some give an insight into the developing role of the man.

Below are some of the more significant references:

- Exodus 17:8-13 – Joshua makes his appearance on the scriptural scene as he leads the Israelite army in defeating the Amalekites.

- Exodus 24:13 – Joshua is designated the assistant or minister of Moses. He accompanies Moses when he goes up Mt Sinai.

Getting Our Bearings in Joshua

- Exodus 32:17 – Joshua is the first to hear the noise coming from the Israelite camp as he and Moses come down Mt Sinai. They discover the people worshipping the Golden Calf.

- Exodus 33:11 – After the Lord had spoken to Moses at the Tent of Meeting, Joshua would stay by the Tent when Moses returned into the main camp.

- Numbers 14:6-9 and 30 – Only Joshua and Caleb bring back a positive report from the spying trip into Canaan. They believe God can overcome the difficulties and enemies to be encountered – they are both promised a place in the land.

- Numbers 27:18-23 – Joshua is recognised as 'a man in whom is the spirit' and he is appointed as Moses successor.

- Numbers 32:12 – Of all Israel, only Caleb and Joshua are said to have 'followed the LORD wholeheartedly.'

- Deuteronomy 31:23 – The Lord commissions and encourages Joshua for his task of leading Israel into the Promised Land.

- Deuteronomy 34:9 – Joshua is 'filled with the spirit of wisdom.'

These, and many other references, serve to show that Joshua had a long apprenticeship before he assumed the role of leader of the people of Israel. And, although the book that bears his name confirms the information gleaned from the other books, it does not add anything particularly new about him. The focus of the book is not to give a 'biography' of Joshua, or investigate his character or paint him as a great example of leadership – although there are lessons to be learned about those things. The book's focus lies elsewhere.

So to our second question:

Is it about a nation?

Once again we may say that the nation of Israel features prominently in this book. One of the great repeated refrains concerns *all Israel*. But, if we focus only on Israel the nation, a problem immediately faces us. The problem is that the book presents a very mixed picture of Israel. It certainly does not present a clear model to follow or attitude to copy. The nation moves between success and failure; faithfulness and faithlessness; and between obedience and rebellion.

This is, in many ways, a reflection of Israel's history to this point in the Bible's narrative. To return to the outline of the biblical story, we have already seen that the foundational promise to Abraham – that God would make of him 'a great nation' (Gen. 12:2) – is the beginning of Israel's story. This promise was repeated and confirmed as the story unfolds through the book of Genesis. At the close of that book there are enough people of Abraham's family to make them worth counting. Seventy go down to Egypt (Gen. 46:27, see also Exod. 1:5). The silent years (centuries!) between Genesis 50 and Exodus 1 see their numbers grow – 'the Israelites were fruitful and multiplied greatly and became exceeding numerous so that the land was filled with them' (Exod. 1:7). This growth, however, brings with it a great threat. Pharaoh sees their increasing numbers as a danger to his own nation, Egypt. So begins a systematic policy to wipe out Israel. But, the attack on

Getting Our Bearings in Joshua

Israel is picking a fight with Israel's God – on the basis of His promise, God intervenes.

On meeting with Moses at the 'burning bush' God declares His intentions:

> ... I have come down to rescue them from the hands of the Egyptians and to bring them out of that land into a good and spacious land flowing with milk and honey – the home of the Canaanites, Hittites, Amorites, Perizzites, Hivites and Jebusites (Exod 3:8).

The book of Exodus proclaims that great rescue. Through the defeat of Pharaoh and his gods in the plagues, by the overcoming of physical barriers (e.g. the Red Sea and the great hunger) and hostile forces (e.g. Pharaoh's army and the Amalekites), Israel comes to meet with God at Sinai. Here the rescued people of God are declared His 'treasured possession' (Exod. 19:5). And here they receive the gracious signs of God's continuing presence with them. Both the journey to Sinai and onward to the Promised Land proves not to be a smooth process. Exodus and Numbers both record the failure of Israel to trust the Lord completely. Only by the faithfulness of God do they arrive on the border of the land. They have a new leader, Joshua, and they are still together as a nation. The book of Joshua will emphasise their need to remain as united nation. The nation is not, however, the principle actor on the stage of the book.

The heart of the book

There is an almost universal acknowledgement by commentators that the main theme of the book of Joshua can be summed up in the book's own words:

> Not one of the LORD's good promises to Israel failed;
> every one was fulfilled (Josh. 21:45).

The two preceding verses prepare the ground for this statement by the threefold repetition of God's action on Israel's behalf. We are told that **God gave** them the land, rest and victory. When Joshua makes his final address to the nation this idea is central to what he wants them to understand and remember. Further, he emphasises the peril of forgetting this great fact (see 23:14-16). Calvin comments on this closing speech saying; 'How careful Joshua was to provide that God be glorified after his death.'[9] God, not Joshua and not the nation, is the chief actor, the primary focus of the book. Some of the major themes of the book, often identified by commentators, need to be seen specifically in relation to God. The Lord's character and actions are revealed in Joshua the following ways:[10]

God's gift From the outset of the book, the initiative is wholly with God – the benefits that come to the people come purely as a gift. This is true both for the land,

> Now then, you and all these people, get ready to cross the River Jordan into the land I am about to give to them – to the Israelites. I will give you every place where you set your foot... (1:2-3).

and for the rest, the peace and security of the people,

> The Lord will give you rest by giving you this land... all your fighting men... must cross over ahead of your fellow

---

9. J Calvin, *Calvin's Commentaries Vol IV Joshua*, (Grand Rapids USA: Baker Books, 2003) p. xxiv n 1.

10. This list is not exhaustive; other aspects will be developed as we 'listen to the text.'

Israelites. You are to help them until the LORD gives them rest, as he has done for you (1:13-15).

These two ideas are interwoven through the book; one depends on the other. There will be no true 'rest' for the people of Israel until the land is firmly in their possession. But, time and time again, the text underlines the fact that the land is God's and comes to them only by His gracious gift. Similarly, the 'rest' will only be theirs because the Lord will overcome their enemies and make them secure.

God's Word The occupation of the land and the security of the people are dependent on them responding to the Word of God. The necessity for them to do this is made clear once more from the outset of the story.

Remember the command that Moses the servant of the LORD gave you.... Then they answered Joshua, 'Whatever you have commanded us we will do and wherever you send us we will go. Just as we fully obeyed Moses, so we will obey you' (Josh. 1:13, 16, 17).

Obedience to the Word of God is to be reflected in every area of the Israelites' life. Not only do they have the Book of the Law written down for their guidance, they also have many things that show them the need for dedication/ consecration in their lives as they move into the land. Examples are: the distance they must keep between themselves and the Ark (chapter 3), the circumcision of the males, the Passover and Joshua's encounter with the commander of the Lord's army (chapter 5).

As the leader of the nation, Joshua is also a man under God's Word.

> Be careful to obey all the law my servant Moses gave you;
> do not turn from it to the right or to the left, that you may
> be successful wherever you go. Keep this book of the law
> always on your lips, meditate on it day and night, so that
> you may be careful to do everything written in it (1:7-8).

Although these words are addressed to Joshua personally, they set the tone for his leadership. Joshua is to model obedience and trust in God's Word to the people. When Moses was still with Israel, the people would go to him for guidance, for the commands of God for daily living. Now, they do not go to the new leader, but to the book that Moses has written. And this is true for Joshua himself – they are all now people of the book.

God's promise The fact that God has spoken and continues to speak through His Word brings us to the central theme of the book – the promise of God. We have already noted that the pivotal text of the book is 21:45. It brings the story of the occupation of the land to a climax. It is followed by a narrative which, despite a possible problem, ends with the people of Israel as a unified whole. Finally the book closes with a covenant renewal that binds the people to God in grateful response to all His mercies. In this way, fundamental elements of the purpose and promise of God, which were sketched earlier form a kind of backbone to the book and our approach to it. This will become clearer as we engage with the text.

God's sovereignty A promise is only as good as the person who makes it. Joshua has much to say about the nature of the one promising – about the Lord. The main way the book does this is to show the sovereignty of God in action.

Getting Our Bearings in Joshua 39

From the giving of the land to the victory over all Israel's enemies, the initiative and accomplishment are God's. As the story unfolds we see God's sovereignty in a variety of ways:

Sovereignty in the physical realm: A single example will suffice for now, others will be noted in context. The most obvious example in the early chapters of the book is the stopping of the flow of the River Jordan (chapter 3). The text is careful to point out the time of year that this happens. It is the time when the Jordan is in full flood. The narrative is brief and undramatic – 'the water from upstream stopped flowing…it piled up in a heap a great distance away' (3:16). The 'how' of this event is not discussed; it is simply assumed to be the sovereign act of God, to allow His people to cross the Jordan.

Sovereignty in the historical realm: In a number of places Scripture speaks of God's rule over the affairs of the nations and of His appointment, not just of their places in history, but also their times.[11] The book of Joshua as a whole bears witness to this idea. The settlement of Israel in the land is not just about this one nation; it has consequences for the life and history of the seven nations who are occupying the land (see e.g. 3:10). The timing of Israel's entry into the land is determined from the outset. The plan and purpose of God in human history is being worked out. It has its origins in God's promise to Abraham, which expresses something of God's timetable in human affairs and history (see Gen. 15:16).

Sovereignty in salvation: We have already seen that the land and subsequent rest for the people of God comes

---

11. See e.g. Deuteronomy 32:8; Amos 9:7; Isaiah 40:23-24; Job 12:23.

as a gift from the hand of God. Although the people are required to fight, victory is won by 'YHWH the Warrior'. At a number of crucial points in the story we hear that 'the Lord fights for you' (see e.g. 10:14, 23:10). If not stated in such a specific way, there are many indications that victory is only possible because the Lord is with them. Rahab's testimony sets the story of Israel's victories in the context of, 'the Lord dried up the water of the Red Sea' (2:10); and 'the Lord your God is God in heaven above and on the earth below' (2:11). Robert Hubbard Jr points to two subthemes under the idea of 'YHWH the Warrior'. Both are already present in Rahab's confession – the overwhelming power of God and His personal presence with His people.[12] Again, these themes will be developed in their appropriate context as we work through the narrative.

Author, date and shape of the book

The book comes to us without any attribution of authorship. The various scholarly theories remain simply what they are – theories. It would seem entirely unnecessary to deny at least some of the books to Joshua himself. As Moses had written the Book of the Law (Deut. 31:9-13), so Joshua is said to have added to it, 'Joshua recorded all these things in the Book of the Law of God' (24:26). So, whoever put the final book together after Joshua's death (24:29), had firsthand testimonies to draw on. Although Calvin mentions a couple of possible writers, his conclusion is sound; 'As to the author of this book, it is better to suspend our judgement than to make random assertions.'[13]

This judgement on authorship is probably the best one to make concerning the date as well. David Howard Jr

---

12. See Hubbard, *Joshua*, p. 55.

13. Calvin, *Joshua*, p. xvii.

Getting Our Bearings in Joshua 41

points to a repeated refrain in the book that sets the limits for dating it. The phrase 'to this day' appears approximately twelve times and most of them suggest, at the very least, a time before David. 'The reference in 6:25, however about Rahab still being alive "to this day" would seem to indicate a date much earlier.'[14] As a working assumption, the one offered by Ralph Davis seems the most plausible.

That is:

> ... that Joshua, substantially as it stands, would prove potent preaching material to the Judges generation (Judg. 2:6-10) who were slack about driving out the remnants of the Canaanites (Judg. 1:2-2:5; cf Josh. 16:10; 17:12-18; 18:3) and therefore created a climate for apostasy to occur in a most predictable way (Judg. 2:11-3:6; cf Josh. 23:6-7, 11-13).[15]

One of the most common ways of viewing the structure of the book of Joshua is to see it in four major sections, these sections are based on an analysis of the main words and concepts of the book. This analysis, taken up and used by several commentators, was originally suggested by H. J. Koorevaar and acknowledged in a number of commentaries.[16]

The sections are:

- Crossing the Jordan: 1:1–5:12

---

14. Howard, *Joshua*, p. 30.

15. Davis, *Joshua*, p. 166.

16. I am following the summary of his work (originally written in Dutch) that can be found in J. R. Vannoy, Joshua, [Theology of], *New International Dictionary of Old Testament Theology and Exegesis* (Grand Rapids USA: Zondervan 1997) pp. 810-819.

- Conquering the Land: 5:13–12:24
- Dividing the Land: 13:1–21:45
- Keeping the faith with one another and with YHWH: 22:1–24:33

Not only does this fit with the chronological sequence of the book but also with the dominant concepts in each section. The high profile words in each division are:

- going over
- taking
- dividing
- worshipping

This structure can be used and developed for preaching and teaching the book. An alternative is to analyse the book in terms of its central and overriding theme. This alternative will be outlined and considered in the next chapter.

Why Should We Preach
and Teach Joshua?

Carl Trueman once posed the question as to who would be considered the most influential thinker in the modern evangelical church. Having suggested some of the more obvious names, he goes on to voice his own opinion:

> I would like to suggest, however that there is one whose influence is perhaps much greater than we are aware of, yet whose thinking all but pervades the modern evangelical church: Marcion ... You never see his books on the shelves in your high street Christian bookshop; you never see him advertised as preaching in your local church; but, rest assured, his spirit stalks those bookshops and pulpits.[1]

While notionally we might reject Marcion's heresy – his discarding of the Old Testament and of 'Jewish' elements of the New Testament – in practice we unwittingly follow in his footsteps. Rather than ignoring or avoiding Old

---

1. C.R. Trueman, *The Wages of Spin* (Fearn UK: Mentor 2004) p. 165.

Testament books like Joshua, we need to preach them well. And, there are good reasons for doing so.

Joshua *is* Scripture

The fact that direct references to Joshua (the man) are limited in the New Testament, cannot be made into an argument from silence. That is, because it only mentions him twice, we can safely ignore the book bearing his name. In their context Acts 7:45 and Heb. 4:8 both have great historical and theological significance. Both, in their own way, are reflections on the record of God's saving action and enduring promise.

An obvious but important reminder concerning books like Joshua is that neither Jesus nor Paul give any cause to consider them as books that can be excluded from the canon of Scripture. Jesus offers no exceptions from the 'the Law of Moses, the Prophets and the Psalms'. They all convey everything that 'must be fulfilled that is written about me' (Luke 24:44). Similarly, Paul offers no exceptions, no embargos on particular books. He sees 'all scripture as Godbreathed' and 'useful for teaching rebuking, correcting and training in righteousness' (2 Tim. 3:16).

We must not let historical, cultural or supposed moral distance between us and the book of Joshua lead us to neglect or reject it. Although books such as Joshua may be situated in the distant past, they have, according to Paul, a present meaning and purpose.

> For everything that was written in the past was written to teach us, so that through the endurance taught in the Scriptures and the encouragement they provide we might have hope (Rom. 15:4).

And Paul practises what he preaches. He has quoted from Psalm 69:9 in the previous verse and will go on to quote four more Old Testament texts in verses 9-12. The truth about Christ is prefigured in the Old Testament and is a model for the church in every age according to Paul.

James Aageson rightly says,

> Paul understands scripture as having the ability to sustain him and his readers. The value and authority of the things that were written in the past continue to prevail in the present. In other words, time had not rendered scripture obsolete. It still functions as a voice for the instruction and edification of the community.[2]

Indeed, more than this can be said – it is the believer's source of hope and model for endurance. It is not just 'a voice for the instruction and edification of the community'; it is **the** voice. In the light of this, a legitimate question is 'How far does Joshua, as scripture, do this in particular?' We consider next some of the specific reasons for preaching and teaching the book of Joshua.

Joshua and the nature of God

As we have already seen, the chief actor on the stage of the book is not Joshua but God. The words and actions of God reveal His nature, His character. This will be seen in some detail as we listen to the text. Here we can only point out some of the major elements in the book's portrayal of God.

---

2. J. W. Aageson, *Written also for Our Sake* (Louisville USA: Westminster/John Knox Press, 1993) p. 47.

God's sovereignty

The conquest of the land only becomes a reality for the people of Israel because of the sovereign action of God. It is not won through force of arms, but through divine intervention. God's sovereignty is shown in a number of ways. It is not simply in the overthrow of other nations – it has, literally, a cosmic scope. God's sovereignty over the physical world is demonstrated in the drying up of the Jordan, in the timely arrival of hail and lightning and in the sun stopping in the middle of the sky. God's sovereignty over the moral order is clearly displayed as well. This can be seen for example in the conquest as an act of judgement and in the Achan incident when judgement occurs within God's own people. Closely linked to the book's view of the sovereignty of God is His power and commitment to keeping His promises.

God's faithfulness

Only the God who is truly sovereign can fulfil His promises. And those promises are fulfilled because God is faithful. The certainty of God's Word is guaranteed by the completeness of His rule. There will be many times in our exploration of the text when we will see the way, and the extent, to which God's promises are fulfilled. A very particular and public way this is emphasised is in the two renewals of God's covenant with Israel (chapters 8 & 24). These two incidents however, are simply outcrops of the underlying bedrock of the book. As the book opens we learn that the first great leader of the people of Israel, Moses, is dead. Indeed, a whole generation has died out; of all the adults who left Egypt at the time of the Exodus only two remain alive – Joshua and Caleb. A new generation

Why Should We Preach and Teach Joshua? 47

with its leader stands on the border of the Promised Land. This is testimony to God's faithfulness to His Word of promise *and* His Word of judgement to a rebellious and faithless generation of Israelites. As we will see in Joshua chapter two, the scope of God's promise reaches beyond the boundaries of Israel and includes Gentiles. In this God is faithful to His Word to Abraham that through Him blessing would come to all nations (see Gen. 12:3).

God's holiness

In his last address to the nation, Joshua declares that God 'is a holy God, he is a jealous God' (24:19). This statement serves as both a warning and a demand for the Israelites. It is a warning, in that the people must not presume on their relationship with God – it is exclusive – there can be no other gods. At the same time, it is a demand, requiring the absolute allegiance of the people. Other things, whether they be people, places or things, are only holy because of their relationship to God – they are set apart for Him. This emphasis on holiness is seen in many places in the book. Amongst the examples that may be given are:

3:5 – the people and their need of consecration

5:15 – the land on which Joshua is standing

6:19 – the gold, silver and other metals 'set apart' for God

20:7ff – the six cities 'set-apart' as places of refuge.

Further, the role of the Ark in the story also indicates the holiness of God. The people have to keep a considerable distance between it and themselves (3:4). Another outworking of the holiness of God in the book is God's acts of judgement. Anything that contradicts or diminishes God's holiness comes under His perfect and richly deserved judgement. This will be seen in the Achan story (chapter 7).

God's grace

Some elements of this have been mentioned already, particularly the gift of the land. It is God's land and He gives it freely in His grace to His people. It is not theirs by right, but by God's promise and gift. The wilderness record of the people's behaviour and, especially their lack of trust in God, is sufficient witness to show they do not deserve it. The Lord's gracious gift of the land, however, is not simply about territory. It is bound up with the idea of rest. Joshua makes this link clear as he speaks to the two-and-a-half tribes who will occupy the East bank territories:

> Remember the command that Moses the servant of the Lord gave you after he said, "The Lord your God will give you rest by giving you this land" (Josh. 1:13).

The Old Testament has a rich theology of 'rest', which is picked up in the New Testament – especially in Hebrews.

John Oswalt paints a vivid picture of some of the essential elements of the idea:

> This promise of land (and thus of rest) is a promise of permanence... One generation gives way to another but the land will remain... Here is a place of continuity in the midst of the endless changes that characterize a world where death reigns. Culture and customs may change, but geography has a way of remaining the same. Here is place to which the heart may return again and again...

This link between the land and rest has many other facets according to Oswalt. There is the assurance of security, of freedom from bondage, of serenity and tranquillity. And all come as gifts of God's grace.[3]

The achievement of rest is also dependent on the grace of God. Two elements of the book of Joshua make this clear – ***divine initiative*** and ***divine presence***. Not only does God give His people the land, He also goes before them in the conquest. God's role is often characterised as God the warrior – the one who fights on Israel's behalf (see e.g. 3:10; 10:10,14; 23:10). The battle for the land is under God's control and depends on God's *initiative*.

The necessity of God's *presence* with His people is also emphasised throughout the book. Beginning with God's promise, 'the Lord your God will be with you wherever you go' (1:9) to Joshua's summary of the personal intervention of God in Israel's history (24:1-13); the presence of God is at the heart of the story. This presence is often symbolised by the Ark and the role that it plays. Again both of these elements – God's initiative and presence – are picked up by the New Testament and are intimately connected with the achieving of God's rest.

Joshua and the people of God

With any historical narrative there is always the danger of simply drawing straight lines from the past to the present.

To put it simplistically, we can easily preach:

The people of old did this – and so must we.
or

---

3. J Oswalt, 'Rest' in *New International Dictionary of Old Testament Theology and Exgesis vol 4* (Grand Rapids USA: Zondervan, 1997) p. 1133. The whole article is very helpful on the topic of 'rest'.

The people of old did this – and we must not!

We do, of course, want to honour Paul's words that 'everything that was written in the past was written to teach *us*', but we need to be careful that we do not draw simple or naïve analogies. What is happening to the people of God and what they are doing, occurs in a particular set of contexts – chiefly, for us, the historical and the biblical context. There are a number of themes in the book, which focus on God's people. Some of the main ones have a degree of overlap and we will review them below. Other relevant material will be commented on as we work through the book.

Unity and the people of God
The emphasis throughout the book is on 'all Israel'. God's first word to Joshua is a command to him and the people as a whole – 'this people' – to prepare to cross into the land.[4] As the book closes Joshua 'assembled all the tribes of Israel at Shechem' to renew the covenant. It is, in fact, the covenant that is the 'glue' that binds the people together. God's action on their behalf giving them the land, fighting their battles is the foundation of their unity. Whatever the perceived divisions or differences there may be between them, these must not affect their unity. No geographical separation (West and East bank tribes), ethnic distinctions (native-born or foreigner, 8:33) no generational differences (past, present or future, 24:6, 19, 13) are considered to be barriers to unity. In New Testament terms the people of God are viewed as 'one body'.

---

4. See comments on 1:2 below.

Why Should We Preach and Teach Joshua?

Other themes arise from the fact that Israel is the covenant people. The first is the need for the people's ***obedience***. Once again this can be seen by the way the need for obedience opens and closes the book (with many examples in between).

The Lord's command to Joshua is:

> Be careful to obey all the law my servant Moses gave you; so do not turn from it to the right or to the left... Keep this Book of the Law always on your lips; meditate on it day and night, so that you may be careful to do everything written in it (1:7-8).

This need for obedience obviously does not simply apply to Joshua alone. This is the key to their success from a human point of view. The land may be a gift to them, but they have a responsibility as well. And so do the succeeding generations – as Joshua makes clear in his final address to the nation.

> Be very strong; be careful to obey all that is written in the Book of the Law of Moses, without turning aside to the right or to the left (23:6).

Clearly the obedience required is to the Book of the Law, what God had said through Moses. This emphasis on the Word of God represents a significant change for Israel. While Moses was still alive, he was the main source of knowledge concerning God and His ways. The people went to Moses for instruction, wisdom – we may even say revelation. But as Moses approached the end of his life, he committed to writing all that the Lord had communicated through him (Deut. 31:9, 24) even the song that God had commanded him to teach the people (Deut. 31:19).

After the death of Moses, did the people go to their new leader for a definitive word concerning the Lord and His commandments? No, they went to the book Moses had written as their source for understanding God and His way. Naturally God had more to communicate to Joshua during the course of the conquest but the foundation of His revelation to and for His people had already been laid.

Joshua's obedience to God and especially His Word highlight a further theme in the book – that of *leadership*. As was seen above, Joshua's own devotion to the 'Book of Law' (1:7-8) was the key to his success. David Howard Jr. rightly observes:

> God instructed him [Joshua] that he was to be rooted in the law, and therein would be his success (1:7-8). In this regard, Joshua was to *be* a leader in the model of godly things, for whom the key to success was also in rootedness in the law, not a dependence on their own wealth or military might (Deut. 17:14-20).[5]

Joshua's relationship to the Lord, following the example of Moses, warrants the loyalty of the two-and-a-half tribes who have already received their inheritance.

The book, however, does not disguise the fact that all is not necessarily well during the course of the conquest. It does not make false heroes out of the people of God, but is prepared to uncover the *fallibility of human nature*. At a number of places through the book, the people of Israel are given physical reminders of what God is doing for them. Some of them look back and show the people their continuity with previous generations and the work of God

---

5. DM Howard Jr, *Joshua – The New American Commentary* (Nashville USA: Broadman & Holman, 1998) p. 63.

among them (e.g. circumcision and Passover). Sometimes they are commanded to build monuments, heaps of stones, and these act as reminders of particular events or actions that they have experienced (see e.g. 4:19-24; 7:25-26). The fallibility of human nature is highlighted in the book in terms of the failure to remember what God has done and said. The book closes with an obvious example of the need to guard against this kind of failure. The interplay between Joshua and the people in chapter 24, acts as a means of underlining the gravity of what the people are promising and their fallibility in keeping promises. Linked with this theme is the issue of *faith and unbelief* in the book. Models of this are found, for example, in Caleb (14:6-15) and the tribes of Joseph (17:12-18).

Joshua's place in Salvation history

We have already looked briefly at Joshua as the natural climax to the narrative flow of the Pentateuch (see pp. 26-28). The place of Joshua 'In the Big Picture' has been outlined as well (see pp. 28-31). In summary, we can say that God's response to the catastrophe of the Fall was not only an act of judgement but also a promise to put everything right. Abraham, in particular, was the recipient of the great promise, based on God's creational purposes. In Genesis 12:1-3 God spoke to him of a land, a people and blessings not only for him and his descendants but reaching out to the whole world. These promises are clearly seen in the opening verses of chapter 1, as we shall see. Also, these promises and this out-working of them express the purposes of God from the very beginning. In answering the question: Is the Old Testament (and we may add is Joshua) for all Christians? Graeme Goldsworthy helpfully answers in this way:

> The most compelling reason for Christians to read and study the Old Testament lies in the New Testament. The New Testament witnesses to the fact that Jesus of Nazareth is the One in whom and through whom all the promises of God find their fulfilment. These promises are only to be understood from the Old Testament; the fulfilment of the promises can be only understood in the context of the promises themselves.[6]

The book of Joshua plays a clear and important part on helping us to understand this context.

Joshua points us to Christ

Some may question why considering how the book of Joshua speaks of Christ has been left to this point. Surely, we should start with the premise that all scripture speaks of Christ (see Luke 24:27)? Without doubt this is fundamental to our understanding and teaching of the Old Testament. The problem is that we often move to speaking of Christ without a proper consideration of the text before us. Instead we must realise that all Christ means to us and all that He has done for us receives it richest and fullest explanation when it is seen in the context of the Old Testament witness.

As Alec Motyer succinctly put it:

> Now this Old Testament, above all else we might say about it, is designed to prepare us for the Lord Jesus

---

6. G. Goldsworthy, *Gospel and Kingdom* (Exeter UK: Paternoster Press, 1981) p. 18.

Christ. Or putting the matter more bluntly, without the
Old Testament we could not know Jesus properly.[7]

So, we need to focus on the text before us, seeking both to understand it in its own right and also for the part it plays in the 'cumulative' revelation of Christ.[8]

There can be the temptation, for example, to work on the assumption that because Joshua and Jesus bear the same name, we can automatically draw direct analogies between the two. This may well lead to a misuse of the text of Joshua.

What Adrian Reynolds observes concerning the book of Numbers can be equally applied to Joshua:

> Some older commentaries, in particular, saw such allusions [to Christ] in all sorts of places. Better I think to make the connection where Scripture does and let the Scriptures be the best interpreters of themselves.[9]

And the New Testament does not really make a direct connection. As stated earlier there are only two references to Joshua the man:

> Acts 7:45 – this is purely descriptive using Joshua as part of the time sequence in the story of the Tabernacle.

> Hebrews 4:8 – highlights a discontinuity between Joshua and Jesus. Joshua did *not* give the people rest, But Jesus does give His people rest.

---

7. JA Motyer, *A Christian's Guide to Loving the Old Testament* (Fearn UK: Christian Focus Publications, 2015).

8. See *ibid* pp. 55-56.

9. A Reynolds, *Teaching Numbers* (Fearn UK: Christian Focus Publications, 2012) p. 37.

This, of course, is not to say that the New Testament writers were unaware of the story of Joshua; rather it should caution us against making simple analogies. We will certainly see a number of connections that can be made as we work through the text of the book. If the totality of the Old Testament witness points to Jesus, as He Himself said (Luke 24:27, 44), our task is to discern how this particular part of the story does just this. And this will not mean adding on a 'gospel appendix' to our exposition, as this opens up the possibility of our expositions all sounding the same.

As Graeme Goldsworthy wisely says:

> Far from taking the rich variety of the Old Testament and squeezing it through a narrow mold of superficial Jesus piety, preaching Christ from every part of the Bible should mean expanding this great variety into the endless riches of Christ the fulfiller.[10]

In our teaching of Old Testament narratives we are not simply seeking to inform minds (though, surely, we will do this), but we also want people to hear the voice of God and respond to it. To present people with the *Living Word* is what the Bible and our preaching and teaching of it is for – because only through Him and in Him can we relate to God properly and live for Him.

---

10. G. Goldsworthy, *Preaching the Whole Bible as Christian Scripture* (Leicester UK: IVP, 2000) p. 126.

Ideas for Preaching or Teaching a Series on Joshua

Structuring a series

Most of us will find ourselves attracted to the opening few chapters of the book of Joshua with all the action that they recount. We will not ignore the book's grand finale (chapter 24) with its clear challenge. However, to ignore some of the more difficult (or apparently boring) sections, makes an unintended statement about our view of Scripture. We obviously need to take seriously what has been given to us, in the text of Joshua itself, by the Holy Spirit.

One possible way of approaching this is to try to give people a grasp of the book as a whole. In this way we can help them see its overall purpose and how it fits together. Below are two possible ways of doing this in a relatively brief series.

1) Using the fourfold division outlined in chapter one, preach on a key text from each division that expresses the main idea and allows you to summarise the story of that section.

For example:

1:1–5:12	*Crossing the Jordan*
Key text:	4:19-24
Key ideas:	arrival in the Promised Land
	the action and faithfulness of God
	remembrance and reverence
5:13–12:24	*Conquering the Land*
Key text:	5:13-6:25
Key ideas:	God's holiness and sovereignty
	God's presence (the role of the Ark)
	the people's obedience
13:1–21:45	*Dividing the Land*
Key text:	21:43-45
Key ideas:	God's faithfulness to His promise
	verse 43 summarises chapters 13-21
	verse 44 summarises chapters 1-12
	verse 45 summarises the whole book
22:1–24:33	*Keeping faith with God*
Key text:	24:1-15
Key ideas:	God's grace
	God's demand
	the only response

2) The book can also be surveyed in terms of the great initiatives of the Lord and the response of the people.[1]

---

1. Again I am following the suggestion of Koorevaar as summarized in JR Vannoy, Joshua, [Theology of], *New International Dictionary of*

Ideas for Preaching or Teaching a Series on Joshua

1:1-9   *The call and gift of God*
Key ideas: new leader – same God
the promise and presence of God
the need for obedience

5:13–6:5   *God's presence the only guarantee*
Key ideas: recognising God's holiness (5:15)
following God's direction (6:2-4)
the key to success

13:1-7   *Inheritance assured*
Key ideas: land to be possessed
victory is from God
a secure inheritance

20:1-6   *Gracious provision*
Key ideas: 'when they had finished dividing the land' (19:49)
the place of safety appointed by God

22:1–24:33   *'Your true and proper worship'*
Key ideas: 'serve him with all your heart and soul' (22:5)
'love the Lord your God' (23:11)
'choose… this day whom you will serve' (24:14)

There are a number of ways in which the suggested fourfold division may be broken down into smaller units. Each section could well be developed as a mini-series. In working through the book, however, we are going to pursue a somewhat different scheme. While literary analysis

---

Old Testament Theology and Exegesis (Grand Rapids USA: Zondervan, 1997) pp. 810-819 [NIDOTTE].

is of undoubted value, it is just that – analysis. It is not proclamation. And if Scripture is 'God preaching God'[2] then we must focus on what the book as a whole proclaims. If the central idea of the book is summed up in the key verse of 21:45, which is the almost universal opinion of the commentators, then our job is to work out how the whole book makes clear, proclaims, the faithfulness of God to His promise. With this in mind we will approach the book with 'promise' as the dominant theme and suggest the following way of tracing the trajectory of the promise and fulfilment through the book.

> 1–2   *Confirming the Promise*
>
> 3–4   *Witnessing to the Promise*
>
> 5–6   *Realising the Promise*
>
> 7–8   *Responses to the Promise*
>
> 9–12 *The Power of the Promise*
>
> 13–21 *Receiving the Promise*
>
> 22–24 *Life in the Promise*

It is possible to preach or teach this series in these seven basic units. To do so, we obviously need to be selective with the biblical material, making sure the central idea of each section is carefully explained. Suggestions about how to do this will be offered at the end of each section dealing with the text.

---

2. An often repeated idea of J I Packer in lectures I have heard.

Handling the text

It is worth reminding ourselves at this point that the text we are handling is a narrative.[3] This type of biblical literature can present the unwary with a number of pitfalls.

Briefly, here are some of them:

Personalising Some people approach the Bible with the question, 'Where am I in this text?' They look for a lesson that puts them in the story. Out of good motives many have been encouraged to look for a message for themselves in the text. With OT narrative this approach often leads to disappointment and sometimes self-deception.

Moralising We have already mentioned this approach to Scripture it says: 'he/she/they did this, so must we'. Or 'he/she/they did this and we must *not*'. Thinking in this way is based on two cardinal mistakes. The first is to treat narrative as law. Rather than read it as it is, an unfolding story, the temptation is to turn it into a set of propositions or principles to be followed. The second mistake arises from the first. It ignores the wider context of the narrative. The story of the people in the book of Joshua is not a self-contained story. It is the outcome of the prior saving action of God. To simply look out for some moral principle in the text without considering it in the light of, and as a response to, the grace of God is a misreading of the book. The old principle that narrative is generally descriptive rather than

---

3. In this section I have been greatly helped by D. Ralph Davis, *Word became Fresh* (Fearn, UK: Christian Focus, 2006) and Chris Wright, *Sweeter than Honey* (Carlisle, UK: Langham Preaching Resources, 2015).

prescriptive remains a valid one. What Scripture describes is not necessarily what Scripture recommends or commands.

Spiritualising It is very easy to make the jump from Joshua leading the people into the Promised Land to Jesus leading us to heaven. But, if that's all we do with the story we ignore so much of what it has to say to us about 'the *real* things that happened to *real* people in *real* history and what God's involvement in these realities tell us.'[4] This approach so often ignores the context in which the 'lesson' is thought to be found. Richard Pratt illustrates this perfectly with a story of a young man seeking guidance over attending seminary. He went to one of the professors and said:

> 'God told me what to do yesterday,' he said with joy. 'I read 1 Samuel 14:12, "Come up to us and we'll teach you a lesson".... God told me through this passage to go to seminary to learn my lessons from you'.

But the passage he cited had little to do with learning lessons in seminary. In the context of the verse, the Philistines were mocking Jonathan as he approached them in battle. They planned to teach him a lesson by killing him.

'I didn't know what to think,' the professor said... with a smile. 'He was either calling me a Philistine or a murderer.'[5]

Allegorising This is linked to the spiritualising, in that it seeks to uncover alleged spiritual truths behind the more prosaic details of the story. The classic example of this can be seen in innumerable interpretations of the story of David and Goliath. Goliath is often used to represent the sins

---

4. Wright p. 102.
5. R. Pratt, *He Gave Us Stories* (Philipsburg, USA: Presbyterian & Reformed Publishing, 1993) pp. 385-386.

or difficulties we need to overcome in our Christian life. David's weaponry includes the sling of faith; the five stones of obedience, service, Bible-reading, prayer and fellowship. The question is 'which of these actually killed Goliath, or did David let fly with all five at once?'[6]

All four of these pitfalls, and others besides, can only be avoided by paying proper attention to the text. A series of questions will help us explore the meaning and significance of a particular passage.

When? This question is asking about the time it describes, the period of history in which it is situated. A further 'when' question is about the time that the story was actually written down or included in its particular book of the Bible (see comments on the date of Joshua above).

How? We need to know how it is written – what kind of writing we are studying. With a variety of genres in Scripture, it would be a mistake to treat them in an identical way. Poetry and narrative, for example, work in different ways.

Where? This is one of the most important questions we can ask – the question concerning context. We need to see what comes before and after our passage. The wider context is important as well – how does it fit into the book? And how does it fit into the Old Testament and the 'big picture'? It is good to think in terms of at least three levels – the immediate (the story itself), the national (the story of Israel) and the story of salvation (the whole Bible story).

---

6. G. Goldsworthy, *Gospel and Kingdom* (Exeter UK, Paternoster Press, 1981) p. 10. See Wright p. 104 for a further elaboration of this.

What? The content of the passage is being addressed by this question. Key words and ideas, important or difficult concepts, all need to be examined carefully. This, however, must not be done at the expense of the story itself. It is important to remember that stories have a shape – a beginning and an end! They often feature particular characters and their role in the story needs to be assessed – particularly if the writer adds an additional comment or evaluation about them. If there is any dialogue in the narrative, we need to see what part it plays. What is **said** is often of vital importance, as sometimes the action is ambiguous or opaque and the dialogue adds clarification. Also worth noting is the shape of the story – what tensions and resolutions occur. Is there an intervention by God or His agent (heavenly or human) that leads to a resolution of the tension and governs the outcome of the story?

Why? With this question we focus on the writer's intention. Why is he writing this and why now? If we can begin to grasp the reason behind the text, why it has been recorded, we will have a way in to the meaning and significance of it. The writer makes his intention known in a variety of ways; in the manner he describes God's actions, in the speeches contained in the narrative, for example. Some simple inclusions such as the mention of dates in Joshua 4 and 5, serve to underline the faithfulness of God to His Word. A concern with the author's intention may be considered outdated, or 'dinosaur hermeneutics' to use Ralph Davis' own words. But as he goes on to say: 'It is hard to get away from the suspicion that someone meant to mean something with a text. Sooner or later folks will recognise that again.'[7]

---

7. Ralph Davis, *The Word Made Fresh* (Fearn, UK: Christian Focus,

Ideas for Preaching or Teaching a Series on Joshua

That is why the 'why' question is so important – it is not just 'someone', but the Spirit of God that has caused this to be written.

Who? It is also worth asking the question, 'Who was it written for?' What do we know about the first readers? How has it been written to help them? It is obvious, for example, that the writer of 1 & 2 Kings is in exile writing for the nation that is experiencing the ultimate disaster. As the author traces the ups and downs of that nation through his book, he shows the underlying problem of the people – their rejection of God and His ways. He also points to the future saying: 'Never again'.

The story that is traced through the book of Joshua, with its emphasis on the faithfulness of God and His demands on His people makes the date suggested earlier a viable proposition. It was not just written for them, however. It was also **written for us;** but only once we have seen it in its proper setting, will we be able to learn from it as well.

Facing the difficulties

Lists and more lists

At first glance chapters 13–21 seem to be rather impenetrable and interminable lists of places and people. We may be tempted to skip over these to get to the more interesting and challenging conclusion of the book. But, before we give in to that temptation, we need to ask ourselves: What makes this section important enough to be included in the Bible? The difference in style of 13–21, compared to 1–12 and 22–24, is generally acknowledged

---

2006) pp. 4-5.

by commentators. To dismiss these chapters simply as lists is, however, to miss their point and function.

Richard Nelson says:

> A major turning point in the book is signalled by a renewed command by Yahweh. Just as the command of 1:2-9 initiated chapters 2–12, so the directive of 13:1-7 launched/launches chapter 14–21. The notice of Joshua's advanced age (v 1a) leads one to expect a farewell situation in which the aged leader will deliver a testament or final words of advice before death... Yet the reader discovers that before there can be a farewell, the task of dividing the land has to be completed.[8]

But again, it is not just a simple record of the dividing of the land. There is, according to Nelson, a theological function underlying the text. What he says of 18:1-10 is true of the whole section; it asserts that:

> ... the geographical shape of Israel in the land was not the result of human will or historical contingency, but Yahweh's will and of Israel's obedience.[9]

This can be restated in terms of the overall theme of the book as resulting from the sovereign promise of God and the believing acceptance of His people.

When we come to this section of the book, therefore, we need to exercise some imagination. Rather than seeing these chapters as an ancient gazetteer of the land, we need to stand in Israelite sandals – to see it from the first readers' perspective. The people had been promised that

---

8. R. Nelson, *Joshua* (Louisville USA: Westminster John Knox Press, 1997) p. 164.

9. Nelson p. 209.

'every place where you set your foot' will be given to them by the Lord. Now, the narrative leads them step by step, as it were, around the Promised Land. These lists were, for them, the stimulus to worship and thanksgiving for God's faithfulness to them.

The way this section is structured also suggests that it is more than 'just lists'. H. J. Koorevaar's work on the structure of the whole book has already been referred to. His analysis of chapters 13–21 is followed, at least in part, by some commentators. Others agree, at least, with his main focus on 18:1-10 as the central point of the whole section. This analysis bears some fruit for the preacher when it is seen in the light of the theme of promise running through the whole book. If we include two further elements omitted by Koorevaar the whole section is formed of six concentric circles each of which add a particular emphasis to the threefold promise we developed earlier – of land, people and blessing (see p. 68).

Starting with the outer circle we see the following elements that restate and illustrate the nature and fulfilment of these promises.

Back to the future   (i) 13:1-7   (ii) 21:43-45
The opening seven verses (13:1-7) revisit the promise, God is still present to secure the land. The closing three verses (21:43-45) speak of the promise received, they can now look forward to being at 'rest' in the land.

Guaranteed provision   (i) 13:8-33   (ii) 20:7–21:42
In both of these sections the land or city is not allocated simply by the drawing of lots. They are appointed directly as part of the promise or command of God. So, the East Bank tribes receive what has been promised by Moses (13:8-22,

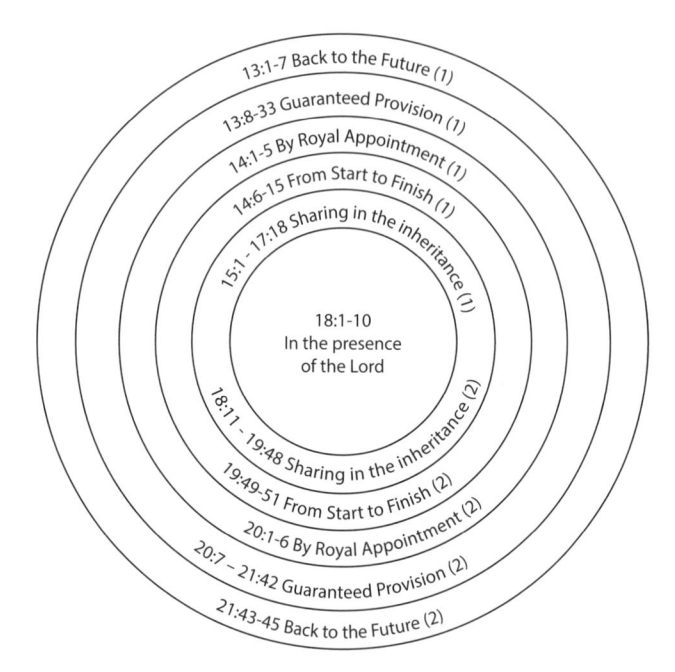

[Concentric circles diagram, from outermost to innermost:]

- 13:1-7 Back to the Future (1)
- 13:8-33 Guaranteed Provision (1)
- 14:1-5 By Royal Appointment (1)
- 14:6-15 From Start to Finish (1)
- 15:1 - 17:18 Sharing in the inheritance (1)
- 18:1-10 In the presence of the Lord
- 18:11 - 19:48 Sharing in the inheritance (2)
- 19:49-51 From Start to Finish (2)
- 20:1-6 By Royal Appointment (2)
- 20:7 - 21:42 Guaranteed Provision (2)
- 21:43-45 Back to the Future (2)

cf. Num. 32 and Deut. 2:26–3:17); and the cities of refuge and the Levitical cities are designated in the second section (20:7–21:42).

By royal appointment   (i) *14:1-5*   (ii) *20:1-6*

Once more, the Lord's sovereignty over the land and its possession as a gift from Him is emphasised – 'the Israelites divided the land, just as the LORD had commanded Moses.' Places of safety, giving concrete expression to elements of the Law previously given, are also appointed following God's commands.

From start to finish   (i) *14:6-15*   (ii) *19:49-51*

Before the larger sections describing the actual land allocated to the remaining tribes, this 'circle' records the

Ideas for Preaching or Teaching a Series on Joshua

inheritance of the two great post-Exodus figures: Caleb and Joshua (see Num. 14 in particular). Their allocations of land 'top and tail' the distribution of land and in many ways they represent 'ideal Israelites.'

Sharing in the inheritance *(i) 15:1–17:18   (ii) 18:11–19:48*
The final division of the land is recorded in these two parts of the narrative. The basic movement is from South to North in the country. The language has moved now from being mainly about conquest to chiefly about inheritance (see below).

In the presence of God   *18:1-10*
These verses represent the centre of the whole section of Joshua 13–21. They are, in a sense the fulcrum on which the story turns. Here the most important element of God's promise to His people – the blessing of His presence among them – comes to a realization.

The great function of these concentric circles is to underline some of the main emphases of the book. Working from the outer circle in, we see:

+ the certainty of God's promise
+ the land as a gift and inheritance
+ the solidarity of the people – 'all Israel'
+ the ultimate blessing of relationship with God

An alternative approach to this structure of these chapters is to view them as a mountain, with the summit as the presence of God in the middle of the people. The ascent to this summit is reached by a series of equivalent steps, from whichever side of the mountain you approach it.

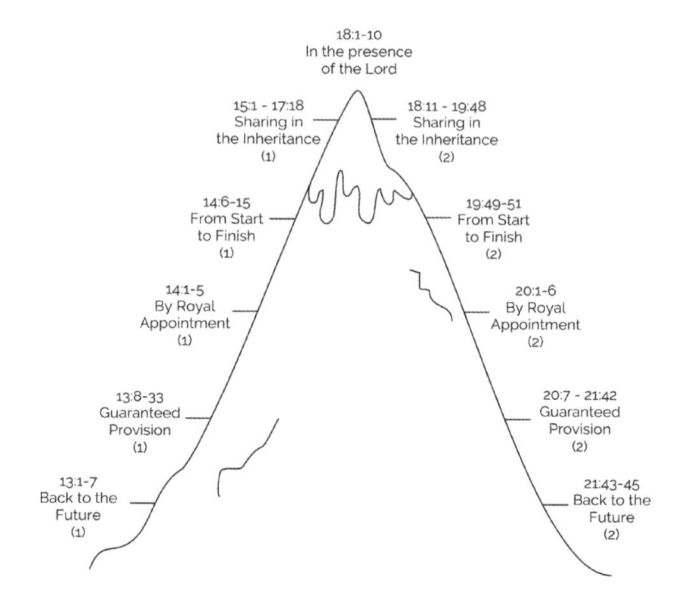

```
                    18:1-10
                In the presence
                  of the Lord
    15:1 - 17:18  /\   18:11 - 19:48
    Sharing in  —    — Sharing in
   the Inheritance    the Inheritance
       (1)                (2)

    14:6-15                19:49-51
   From Start  —       — From Start
    to Finish            to Finish
      (1)                   (2)

    14:1-5                 20:1-6
    By Royal              By Royal
   Appointment          Appointment
      (1)                   (2)

    13:8-33              20:7 - 21:42
   Guaranteed            Guaranteed
    Provision             Provision
      (1)                   (2)

    13:1-7                21:43-45
   Back to the          Back to the
    Future                Future
      (1)                   (2)
```

As 'gift' is a key term in the early part of the book, so 'inheritance' is a crucial term in Joshua 13–21. David Howard helpfully summarises the main ideas behind the concept of inheritance, concluding that:

> Israel's inheritance of the land meant that they owned legal title to it. This was possible because the land was Yahweh's, who gave it to them ... The land's importance was such that it was carefully parcelled out with Yahweh guiding the allotments by the lots that were cast. Each tribe's inheritance was a matter of great importance, so much so that the process of the allotments, and their boundaries are recounted in great detail in the book of Joshua.[10]

---

10. D. Howard, *Joshua* NAC (Nashville, USA: Broadman & Holman, 1998) pp. 306-307. Both the excursus on 'inheritance' (pp. 300-307)

The importance of this concept of inheritance can be seen throughout the history of Israel. An example of this is Naboth's refusal to give up his land, whatever price is offered. His reply to King Ahab is highly significant: 'The LORD forbid that I should give you the inheritance of my ancestors' (1 Kings 21:3). The fact that the land is both 'gift' and 'inheritance' is a vital part of the context for understanding the interpretive difficulties we face when dealing with the nature of the conquest as described in the book of Joshua.

Battles and bloodshed

The kind of criticism offered by people like Richard Dawkins does not come from a morally or philosophically neutral foundation. And neither, of course, do any responses to that criticism. Nicholas Wolterstorff puts it like this:

> Everyone who weighs a theory has certain beliefs as to what constitutes an acceptable *sort* of theory on the matter under consideration. We can call these *control* beliefs.[11]

These 'control beliefs' are instrumental in our rejecting some theories and enabling us to devise and accept others. Whatever issue we face, we all approach it from a particular perspective. If your mindset is already predisposed to a particular view of the Old Testament and the God portrayed in it, this will inevitably condition the way you interpret its narrative. It is helpful, therefore, to be clear

---

and the earlier one on 'The giving of the Land' (pp. 77-81) are valuable in understanding the whole process of the 'Conquest'.

11. N. Wolterstorff, *Reason within the Bounds of Religion* (Grand Rapids, USA: Eerdmans, 1984) p. 67.

about and develop a biblically based point of view. The presuppositions, or 'control beliefs', which undergird our dealing with the 'battles and bloodshed' in the book of Joshua, need to be rooted in a biblical view of God.

In particular, some elements of His sovereignty are of great importance.

God's sovereignty in revelation In the first place, what I have in mind here is God's absolute freedom to reveal what He wants to reveal of Himself and His ways. We are reliant on His telling us what He thinks we need to know, rather than telling us what we want to know. Our responsibility is to deal with, and act on what He has revealed. Deuteronomy 29:29 is a key text that makes this clear:

> The secret things belong to the LORD our God, but the things revealed belong to us and our children for ever, that we may follow the words of this law.

We are called to deal with what has been sovereignly given to us in the pages of Scripture. This is sometimes an uncomfortable process at both the emotional and intellectual level, but it is a necessary one if we are to honour the integrity of the text before us. It is a relatively simple thing to airbrush out elements of revelation that are said to offend our 'modern sensibilities'. An example of this is given by Peter Enns who says that '… Israel's' depiction of God vis-à-vis the nations, unmistakably and understandably reflects the ubiquitous tribal culture at the time.'[12] His problem is that he cannot reconcile what he

---

12. P. Enns, 'Inerrancy , however defined, does not describe what the Bible does' in *Biblical Inerrancy*, ed. J. Merrick & S. M. Garrett (Grand rapids USA: Zondervan, 2013) p. 112.

perceives as glaring contrasts between the Old Testament and New Testament's attitude towards enemies. But, this is a problem of his own making. For the moment it is sufficient to notice Kevin Vanhoozer's response to Enns' statement:

> I am all for seeing development in the history of redemption, but I dispute any suggestion that the Old Testament reflects an inferior doctrine of God because its authors were part of a tribal culture. Talk about chronological snobbery.[13]

Once again the spirit of Marcion is abroad and the danger is that we make ourselves sovereign over revelation, deciding what is acceptable to contemporary ears and minds.

God's sovereignty in the physical world From the majestic opening of scripture (Gen. 1) to the poetic, and sometimes playful, images of Job 38–41, there is an insistence that God is the absolute maker, owner and governor of every aspect of the physical world.

Psalm 24:1-2 sums this up perfectly:

> The earth is the Lord's and everything in it,
> the world and all who live in it,
> for he founded it on the seas
> and established it on the waters.

In the light of God's absolute sovereignty over the world, the Old Testament regards the nations as residents in their allotted lands not as owners. A further consideration arises from this: God can order the lives of nations according to

---

13. K. Vanhoozer, 'Augustinian inerrancy, literary meaning, literal truth, and literate interpretation in the economy of biblical discourse' in *Biblical Inerrancy* p. 134.

His will and in line with His own character. Each part of this statement is also an outworking of God's sovereignty.

God's sovereignty over nations The movements and affairs of the nations are not the outworking of blind historical forces. Neither are they simply the exercise of human will. Both God's own people and the surrounding nations are under the sovereign control of God.

As Amos expresses it:

> Are not you Israelites the same to me as the Cushites?
> declares the LORD.
> Did I not bring Israel up from Egypt,
> the Philistines from Caphtor
> and the Aramean from Kir? (Amos 9:7)

Implicit in His rule over the nations is ***God's sovereignty over their history***, indeed over **all** history. So, through the word given to Jeremiah, he is appointed:

> over nations and kingdoms to uproot and tear down, to destroy and overthrow, to build and to plant (Jer. 1:10).

The nations' rulers are viewed by the Old Testament as the instruments of God's purposes (see e.g. Isa. 45:1; Jer. 25:8-9; Prov. 21:1). All of this is the outworking of God's sovereignty over the course of the world's history.

So Isaiah could say:

> I am God and there is no other;
> I am God and there is none like me.
> I make known the end from the beginning,
> from ancient times what is still to come.
> I say, 'My purpose will stand, and I will do all that I please' (Isa. 46:10).

God's sovereignty in the moral world Whether Nebuchadnezzar was sincere or not, his statement about God is nonetheless true:

> He does as he pleases with the powers of heaven
> and the peoples of the earth.
> No one can hold back his hand
> or say to him: 'What have you done?' (Dan. 4:35)

There is no judge above God the Judge – He is sovereign in the moral world. If anyone or anything can pass judgement on God or even dictate the rules He should follow, they have attempted to dethrone God. They have certainly made Him less than the LORD portrayed in Scripture. It is valuable to consider the way E. J. Carnell speaks of God as the Lawgiver. The Sovereign issues laws to humanity – the Ten Commandments are the supreme expression of His law. Yet, it is worth considering which of these commandments apply to God Himself? Here are some of Carnell's suggestions that are relevant to our discussion of the book of Joshua:

> (6) You shall not kill. All life belongs to God; He cannot kill. He merely calls in that which is rightfully His.
>
> (8) You shall not steal. From whom? All belongs to God.
>
> (10) You shall not covet. God is the King. The gamut of reality is His. What is there left to be wanted?
>
> In short the decalogue is of force only where *sinners* are concerned; but God is the *Holy One*.[14]

---

14. E. J. Carnell, *Christian Apologetics* (Grand Rapids USA: Eerdmans, 1952) p. 310. I owe this reference to G K Beale, see next footnote.

Many of the objections to the bloodshed in the book of Joshua approach the issue from what is, I would argue, the wrong perspective. There is a tendency to reflect the laws of God back on Him, rather than acknowledging that,

> ... there is no judge above God to proclaim that God has done wrong. God decides what he will do, and whatever he does is considered right for him because he is the ultimate judge.[15]

We will return to many of these ideas as we now consider the way the conquest of Canaan was achieved. It is often called 'the Canaanite Genocide' or something similar; but, as we will see, that is an inappropriate term at many levels.

Some hard facts of life (and death)
There are a number of conflicts scattered through the Old Testament narrative in which Israel is involved. But these are not simply demonstrations of Israelite 'machismo' – a lust for power and violence. Indeed, war is not particularly glamorised. David, a warrior himself, calls on God to 'scatter the nations who delight in war' (Ps. 68:30). The prophetic voice is often raised for the ending of war and the establishing of peace, when:

> They will beat their swords into ploughshares
> and their spears into pruning hooks.
> Nation will not take up sword against nation,
> nor will they train for war any more. (Micah 4:3)

But that day seems barely a possibility as we open the pages of Joshua. It would seem that the warfare here is of

---

15. G. K. Beale, *The Morality of God in the Old Testament* (Philipsburg USA: Presbyterian & Reformed Publishing, 2013) p. 16.

a different – and to many, objectionable – order. This war is directly at the command of God. It also seems to involve the total annihilation of a people-group. So, what is going on? While a full answer would demand a whole book (see further reading p. 381), a sketch of the approach this book is taking follows.

A war like no other
It would be wrong to assume that the conquest of Canaan is a model for the way all generations of Israel should act. This war was designed to achieve a very particular set of purposes in the history of Israel and the flow of the biblical story. Having asserted that not all the wars in the Old Testament are '… *portrayed in the same way as the conquest of Canaan*', Chris Wright goes on to say:

> It is a caricature of the Old Testament to portray God as constantly on the warpath or to portray the conquest as simply 'typical' of the rest of the story. It is not. The book of Joshua describes one key historical event, but it was finished. It should not be stretched out as if it were the background theme music for the rest of the Old Testament.[16]

The conquest of Canaan is a war like no other because of its place in the history of salvation. Earlier we reviewed that plan from the creation to new creation on the basis of a place to live, a people to live there and a relationship to enjoy. As a temporal fulfilment of that plan, as part of the restoring promise of God, the occupation of Canaan has a special and singular place. It is, therefore, in terms of what

---
16. Chris Wright, *The God I don't Understand* (Grand Rapids USA: Zondervan, 2008) p. 90, emphasis in the original.

God has revealed of that promise/plan that the conquest must be understood.

The revealed consequences for Israel

The primary consequence for Israel as revealed in the book of Joshua is that they receive the tangible objects of God's promise. By the end of the book they have a settled place to live after four decades of wilderness wandering and centuries of slavery in Egypt before that. They also have experienced life as a united people directed by one human leader and under the guidance of the One God. The great blessing of the whole period is that the Lord has been with them in their struggles (10:42, 24:16-18) and is the centre of their national life (18:1).

The promise of God is not exhausted simply by gaining possession of a piece of real estate. The land means so much more. It is a source of provision for them (5:10-12). They can now feed themselves, but a proper understanding of the Law will mean that they should never become self-reliant. It is significant that once they are settled, they are to make an offering at harvest-time saying '… I have come to the land the Lord swore to our ancestors to give us' (Deut. 26:3). They do not say, 'to the land I have fought to conquer and obtain.'[17] Further, the possession of the land should mean peace for the people – it is now their fixed inheritance (11:23). From the slavery in Egypt, through the uncertainty of the wilderness, the people now have the security of clear borders and a settled home. This also means that the preservation of the nation, its growth and long-term stability are established. They have been given a place in which they can bring up their children.

---

17. *Ibid.*

The greatest consequences of all for Israel is that the land offers the possibility of an abiding relationship with God. Free from the distractions of the gods of Egypt, Moab and Canaan, here they can learn to ' ... fear the LORD and serve him with all faithfulness' (24:14). Aspects of all these features (and many more) will be seen as we move through the text of Joshua.

God had already made it clear to Israel through Moses that possession of the land was not because of any superior righteousness on their behalf (Deut. 9:4-6). Also if they adopted the idolatry and morality of the Canaanites they too would be banished from the land (Lev. 26).

The revealed consequences for the Canaanites
Of Jericho, it is said that:

> They devoted the city to the LORD and destroyed with the sword every living thing within it – men, women, young and old, the cattle, sheep and donkeys (6:21).

This total destruction cannot be read in isolation from its wider context in the Pentateuch in particular and with wider Old Testament. Both have much to contribute to our understanding of the actions of Israel and the reasons for them.

This 'war like no other' needs to be put alongside the rules and commands in the Old Testament for 'regular' warfare. Deuteronomy makes clear that annihilation is **not** always the right or necessary course of action. There can be the offer of peace (Deut. 20:10-11), women and children should be spared (Deut. 20:12-14). These rules are particularly to be applied to nations and cities beyond the borders of Israel (Deut. 20:15). Even the environment of a city had to be considered – there could be no 'scorched earth' policy (Deut. 20:19). Later in Israel's history, Elisha restrains the King's desire for the destruction of his enemies, by implying that it would be contrary to normal practice (see 2 Kings 6:22). The question still remains, why the unprecedented level of destruction in **this** war? One answer the Old Testament gives, is, that it is the means God uses to execute judgement on the people of the land. The war of conquest was not an unprecedented action by a malicious deity. It was the considered response to a sinful nation by a just and patient God. In the first instance this is made clear in the expanded promise concerning the land that was made to Abraham. Predicting first the time Abraham's descendants will spend in Egypt, God goes on to say:

> In the fourth generation your descendants will come back here, for the sin of the Amorites has not yet reached its full measure. (Gen. 15:16)

Bruce Waltke's comment on this verse is worth quoting at length:

> ... it is not until the nations become totally saturated with iniquity that God dispossesses them (Lev. 18:24-28; 20:23). So he does not send the Flood until the earth is fully corrupt (Gen. 6:5, 12) and he does not destroy Sodom and Gomorrah until he has satisfied himself that not even a quorum of righteous are left in the city. Israel's conquest and settlement of Canaan is based on God's absolute justice, not on naked aggression.[18]

---

18. B. Waltke, *Genesis: A Commentary* (Grand Rapids USA: Zondervan, 2001) p. 244.

Waltke points us to God's sovereignty in the moral world with examples of the Flood and Sodom and Gomorrah. These are acts of judgement on a rebellious world, acts that occur in history. They also point to the final judgement at the end of the world according to the New Testament (see e.g. Matt. 24:37-39; 2 Pet. 2:5-9, 3:5-7).

Some of the particular evils perpetrated by Canaanites and which resulted in the defilement of the land were idolatry (Lev. 20:3 refers to Molech), child sacrifice (Deut. 12:31, part of the worship of Molech) and a variety of illicit sexual activities (Lev. 20:13-21) that were commonly practices among the Canaanites.[19]

The conquest was not only the temporal exacting of the appropriate penalty on an evil nation, it was also a 'disinfecting' of the land. Deuteronomy 20:17-18 makes this clear:

> Completely destroy them... as the LORD your God has commanded you. Otherwise, they will teach you to follow all the detestable things they do in worshipping their gods, and you will sin against the LORD your God.

We will see when we come to the story of Achan, it is very possible for an Israelite to identify as Canaanite – and put himself under the same judgement.

Both justice and mercy are revealed

This is not the place to attempt a full explanation of the justice of God or of judgement. The actions of God – and they are primarily His in the book of Joshua – do reveal

---

19. See, C. Jones, 'Killing the Canaanites: A Response to New Atheism's "Divine Genocide" Claims' www.equip.org/articles/killing-the-canaanites

significant aspects of His character and work. Drawing on the work of Fleming Rutledge, Jason Micheli writes:

> The wrath of God is not an antiquated belief to be explained away; it is the always timely good news that the outrage we rightly feel over the world's injustice is 'first of all outrage in the heart of God'. Wrath is not a contradiction of God's goodness but an integral part of it .... 'The wrath of God,' she writes,' is not an emotion that flares up from time to time ... it is a way of describing his absolute enmity against all wrong and his coming to set matters right'. Understood rightly, it's actually the non-angry God who appears morally distasteful ...[20]

God who is sovereign over the world must, because of His character, act against evil in His world – in His appointed way and at His appointed time.

The exercise of justice is met by the exercise of mercy. Even in the context of God's decree to cleanse the land of evil and evil-doers, mercy was available to those who sought it. And in the book of Joshua, Rahab is an outstanding example. Although she is truly a 'Canaanite of the Canaanites', she recognises and responds to all she hears of Israel's God. The 'outsider' becomes an 'insider', as we will later see. The opportunity that was open to her, was surely open to others if they were prepared to take it – as it had been to all Canaanites for four hundred years since God had made His promise to Abraham.

The New Testament – further or different revelation?

Those who wish to polarise the Old Testament God as wrathful and the New as loving, have to do violence to

---

20. J. Micheli, 'A Wrathless God has Victims', *Modern Reformation* Vol 27 No 2 (March/April 2018) p. 48.

Ideas for Preaching or Teaching a Series on Joshua

the evidence. On the issue of whether Moses and Joshua completely misunderstood the will of God or the writers of the Old Testament were mistaken about what God wanted to accomplish – Chris Wright says: 'There is no indication that Jesus took such a view of the Old Testament and much that suggest the contrary – that he accepted it at face value.'[21]

The two references to the conquest previously mentioned (Acts 13:18f and Heb. 11:32-34) accept it as a fact without embarrassment or qualification. Although Jesus does not make a direct reference to it, He does clearly accept the fact of judgement. Melvin Tinker develops two examples in his book *Mass Destruction* from Luke 12:49–13:29 and Revelation 6. His conclusion is clear:

> Both Testaments portray God who, in his holiness, is implacably opposed to all sin which issues in judgement, and yet in his love shows mercy which calls for repentance.[22]

As noted above, the New Testament does not deny or soften this element of judgement. Indeed, it is amplified – no longer is it to be seen in mainly temporal terms, now it is seen in its full and eternal perspective. Rightly does Derek Kidner say, 'These events were the shape of things to come.'[23] That is, as with all of God's acts of judgement up to this point and beyond – the Flood, Sodom and Gomorrah, or Egypt and rebellious Israel in the wilderness – the conquest points to the greater judgement to come. In

---

21. Wright, *The God I don't Understand*, p. 91.
22. M. Tinker, *Mass Destruction* (Welwyn Garden City UK: Evangelical Press, 2017) p. 85.
23. D. Kidner, *Hard Sayings* (London UK: IVP, 1972) p. 43.

that final judgement, all other acts of judgement find their complete explanation and justification.

Melvin Tinker puts it like this:

> ... what we also see in the conquest story is, as it were, a reflective echo backwards in time of the final judgement which will take place at the end of time. The judgement in time is provisional and to some extent 'rough', the final judgement will be perfect and precise.[24]

As the Old Testament makes clear, the conquest was a unique event – not the way war was normally to be conducted. Likewise, the New Testament gives no sanction to those who would wish to use it as a mandate for Christian action. Military crusades of any kind and in any era are not to be legitimated in this way. Jesus certainly forbids this to His disciples (see Luke 22:47-53 and Luke 9:51-56). The rest of the New Testament confirms this, seeing the battle Christians are to engage in as a spiritual one, using spiritual weapons (see e.g. Eph. 6:10-17 and 2 Cor. 10:4). And Scripture closes with great rejoicing over the end of the battle against evil and the establishment of the new creation. Revelation 19 depicts the threefold (i.e. perfect) exultation of heaven that sin and the powers of evil have been destroyed and the victor, whose robe has been dipped in blood, has conquered. God's true attitude towards evil will be finally and conclusively revealed. And as a result all heaven will rejoice.

In the light of all the above considerations, it would seem inappropriate to label the conquest as 'genocide'. It has none of the ethnic and immoral characteristics that mark the genocides of the last century or so. It serves rather

---

24. Tinker, p. 92.

to underline the seriousness of God's action against sin and to stand as a warning to every generation that rebellion cannot be perpetrated with impunity.

> # Further thoughts on ...
> # battles and bloodshed
>
> There has been a continuous stream of literature on this issue of violence in the book of Joshua for many years. We are unable to deal with every aspect of it, but there are two issues in recent books that deserve further comment.
>
> ## 1. Reappraising the language of the text
>
> It is often suggested that the reports of battles and victories as recorded in the book of Joshua are couched in the language of hyperbole. A number of comparative studies of other ancient Near Eastern battle accounts have shown that this is a common way of expressing victories in particular. Paul Copan and Matthew Flanagan give a sample of these accounts and conclude:
>
> > The hyperbolic use of language similar to that in Joshua is strikingly evident. Though instances could be multiplied, the point is that such accounts contain extensive hyperbole and are not intended to be taken as literal descriptions of what occurred.[1]
>
> The comparative study most often cited concerning the use of hyperbole is that of K. Lawson Younger Jr. His work shows the similarities between the Bible accounts
>
> ---
>
> 1. Paul Copan & Matthew Flanagan, *Did God Really Command Genocide?* (Grand Rapids, USA: Baker 2014) p. 98.

and those of other nations. One of his conclusions is as follows: 'It would seem that a similar ideology is underlying both the ancient Near Eastern and biblical texts.'[2]

He also rightly warns:

> The fact that there are figurative and ideological underpins to the accounts should not make us call them into question *per se* – it should only force us to be cautious![3]

This is a caution that needs to be heeded. A tendency in some recent literature has been to privilege ancient Near Eastern thought at the expense of the biblical approach. While there is much to be learned from the wider context, the biblical context must take priority. It can be acknowledged that the Bible does use the language, literary and thought forms of its day, but it is based on a completely different 'ideology' (i.e. theology). In many places, for example the creation account, it may use some of the language of its day and context, but the striking feature of that language and its use is the difference it indicates between its own view and that the surrounding cultures. It is, therefore, the dissimilarities in the use to which the Bible puts these concepts (despite using the same 'transmission codes'[4]) that is often of greatest importance. John Oswalt is happy to argue, 'The writers of the Bible have

---

2. K. Lawson Younger, *Ancient Conquest Accounts* (Sheffield, UK: Sheffield Academic Press, 1990) p. 253.

3. Ibid p. 266.

4. This is Younger's term.

consciously (and perhaps unconsciously, since they were part of their world) utilised language concepts and even practices of the world around them to make the points they are trying to make.'

But, he continues:

However, that they did so is not evidence that the Bible is really saying the same things that the world around was saying. I have argued that the similarities are not essential to what the Bible is saying. Rather, the Bible is using these things allusively, illustratively, and sometimes pejoratively to say something that is in fact radically different from the world around.[5]

That the Old Testament books must be read in their ancient Near Eastern context is not being disputed. But as Sidney Greidanus judiciously notes:

… just as sermon illustrations using Little Red Riding Hood do not thereby teach that this fairy tale is literally and historically true, so the biblical authors' use of ancient Near Eastern stories does not mean that they taught that these ancient stories were literally and historically true.[6]

It is clear, as we will see from our study of the text, that there is a tension in the book of Joshua between a complete and a partial conquest. When we view some of the statements about the victory, we must see them in both the book's context and in the wider biblical context.

---

5. John Oswalt, *The Bible among the Myths* (Grand Rapids, USA: Zondervan 2009) p. 107.

6. Sidney Greidanus, *From Chaos to Cosmos* (Wheaton, USA: Crossways, 2018) pp. 21-22.

In the process of conquering and cleansing the land we read:

> So Joshua subdued the whole region, including the hill country, the Negev, the western foothills and the mountain slopes together with all their kings. He left no survivors. He totally destroyed all who breathed, just as the Lord, the God of Israel had commanded (10:40).

This cannot simply be dismissed as hyperbole; it is the command of the Lord. Although that command was relayed through Moses (Deut. 20:16-17), we cannot assume that Moses was engaging in hyperbole as well. The commands he relayed are all part of God's instruction to His people when they enter the land (Deut. 10:12-13 sets the context for these instructions). Reading the Bible on its own terms, we must recognise that the command to Joshua is not inconsistent with the holy character of God. The flood story, an early act of God's judgement, includes these words:

> Everything on dry land that had the breath of life in its nostrils died. Every living thing on the face of the earth was wiped out (Gen. 7:22-23).

As we argued above, we are not in a position to maintain that our moral sensibilities can override the justice and holiness of God. He alone is the arbiter of what is right.

It is also difficult to dismiss the ban as being hyperbole when it is in fact imposed within Israel itself. The seriousness of the sin committed by Achan, means that the Israelites camp is polluted by the things of Canaan. The result of that sin issues in the complete destruction of Achan and all that is his. While heeding Younger's plea for caution, we must also seek the biblical balance as best we can.

2. Rewriting the history of the Canaanites

John Walton and his son J. Harvey Walton have recently argued that the conquest was not intended to be a punishment of the Canaanites for their sin. At the risk of oversimplifying their argument, I want to suggest that the heart of it can be summed up as:

> Those outside the covenant cannot commit this crime [idolatry] because they have no covenants to break.[7]

This approach allows them to offer the following two propositions: The depiction of the Canaanites in Leviticus and Deuteronomy is a sophisticated appropriation of a common ancient Near Eastern literary device, not an indictment (Proposition 12). Behaviours that are described as detestable are intended to contrast with ideal behaviour under the Israelite covenant, not to accuse the people who did them of crimes (Proposition 13).

There is not space here to offer a detailed criticism of these two propositions. Suffice it to say, the caution raised above concerning the privileging of ancient Near Eastern literature applies here. A greater focus on the biblical context and meaning, which can be illustrated or amplified by the literature of the surrounding cultures, does indicate that God has pronounced a

---

7. John Walton & J Harvey Walton, *The Lost World of the Israelite Conquest* (Downers Grove, USA: IVP 2017) p. 81.

judicial sentence on the Canaanites. Once again there is the need to examine carefully, not just the similarities, but also the dissimilarities. Elsewhere, John Walton has recognised this fact himself concerning various creation accounts.

He says:

> Most of the elements of the cosmos are personified in the rest of the ancient Near East but they are not personified in Genesis: in the case of the *ruah*, however the converse is true.[8]

And it is the dissimilarity that makes the difference.

It is difficult to see how the various actions of the Canaanites are not to be seen as crimes and offences against God, just because they are outside of the covenant. This seems to carry with it the implication that God is unconcerned about these actions. The Bible testimony concerning the character of God makes a view like this completely untenable. This view is confirmed by the work of James Bruckner who has carefully investigated the role of law in the Abraham narratives.

His conclusion is:

> In the pre-Sinai narrative, legal referents are presented within the ebb and flow of the lives of characters who have not yet received the God declared laws of Mt Sinai. Biblical law is thereby set in the context of creation in relation to the broader Hebrew canon.... Legal referents in the pre-Sinai narrative do not have covenantal contexts

---

8. John Walton, *Genesis 1 as Ancient Cosmology* (Winona Lake, USA: Eisenbrauns 2011) p. 146.

but are simply applied and assumed as part of the created order.[9]

Later texts of the OT also witness to the fact that there will be judgement for those outside of the covenant. For example, a major premiss of the book of Jonah would be invalid without the concept of God's judgement on a pagan nation. This is also clear in Lamentations 4:22 and Zechariah 14:19.[10]

Despite the Waltons' approach to this issue and their re-reading of Genesis 15:16, there is, I believe, no reason to revise the approach outlined above in *The revealed consequences for the Canaanites*. The conclusion of Koowon Kim, in his review of the Waltons' book, gets to the heart of the matter:

> ... even when accepting the thesis of this book, the reader is still left wondering why God allowed 'innocent' Canaanites to be 'caught up' in the destruction of the land (p. 131). Although the authors may not intend to answer this question definitively, appealing to God's mysterious purpose or asserting that the Bible is not intended to give us universal moral principles (p. 100) comes dangerously close to moral relativism or agnosticism.[11]

---

9. James Bruckner, *Implied Law in the Abraham Narrative* (London, UK: Sheffield Academic Press 2001) pp. 207-208.

10. I owe these two references to Koowon Kim, see footnote 11 below.

11. See http://themelios.thegospelcoalition.org/review/the-lost-world-of-the-israelite-conquest-covenant-retribution-fate-canaan

Part 2:
The God Who Makes and Keeps Promises

I

Confirming the Promise (1–2)

Introduction

The people of Israel, having arrived on the plains of Moab, spend some time there being instructed by Moses. He teaches them the Law of God and its particular relevance for the new situation into which they are about to enter – 'East of the Jordan in the territory of Moab Moses began to expound this law ...' (Deut. 1:5).

This was a vital part of their preparation for the occupation of Canaan. But Moses is not to be the person to lead Israel into the land (see Num. 20:12). A new leader has to be appointed – that leader is Joshua (see Deut. 31:1-8). As the book of Deuteronomy closes, there is no doubt as to what is to happen next:

> Now Joshua son of Nun was filled with the spirit of wisdom because Moses had laid his hands on him. So the Israelites listened to him and did what the Lord had commanded Moses (Deut. 34:9).

As we read straight on from Deuteronomy into the book of Joshua, we are conscious of an unbroken sequence of events and purposes.

Chapters 1 and 2, though they are written in a narrative style, are a record of some important dialogues, which set the tone for the whole book. These dialogues reach back into Deuteronomy – God reiterates to Joshua the commission given to him by Moses (cf. Josh 1:1-9 and Deut. 31:1-8). They reach back into Numbers and the allocation of East Bank lands to the tribes of Reuben, Gad and the half tribe of Manasseh (cf. Josh. 1:12-18 and Num. 32). Indeed, the dialogues reach back as far as the Exodus (cf. Josh. 2:10 and Exod. 14 :19-31). The original foundation on which these dialogues are built is, in fact, God's promise to Abraham (Gen. 12:1-3). They are about to enter the land as a united people and they know the blessing of God's presence with them. There will also be blessing for those outside of Israel, in accordance with God's promise – Rahab and her family exemplify this.

Listening to the text

Context and structure

These two chapters, as with the whole book, cannot be isolated from their relationship to the Pentateuch. This is the moment in the Bible's story when a temporal fulfilment of God's centuries-old promise is about to happen. As that fulfilment begins to unfold, Joshua and Israel hear and see God confirm His promise to them. Each scene in the narrative is marked by a speech or statement, which uncovers the significance of the event.

The scenes and the respective speeches unfold like this:

Confirming the Promise (1–2)

- God to Joshua 1:1-9
- Joshua to the leaders 1:10-11
- Joshua to the two-and-a-half tribes 1:12-18
- Joshua to the spies 2:1
- Rahab to the King of Jericho 2:2-7
- Rahab to the spies 2:8-14
- Spies to Rahab 2:15-21
- Spies to Joshua 2:22-24

When we examine the content of each of these episodes, they all have a connection to the idea of 'promise'.

This can be outlined as follows:

- 1:1-9   Continuity and the Promise (God to Joshua)
- 1:10-11   Preparation for the Promise (Joshua to the leaders)
- 1:12-18   Remember *your* promise (Joshua to the two-and-a-half-tribes)
- 2:1-7   Promise in jeopardy (Rahab to the King of Jericho)
- 2:8-14   Recognising the Promise (Rahab to the spies)
- 2:15-21   Making their own promise (Spies to Rahab)
- 2:22-24   Confidence in the Promise (Spies to Joshua)

Working through the text

Continuity and the Promise (1:1-9)
As the book of Deuteronomy closes, we find the people of God, led by Moses, gathered together and about to move into their inheritance – the Promised Land. The great moment has arrived, but the book ends ... with a funeral.

The book of Joshua opens with the people still in the same place, the plains of Moab, but without their great leader. But he is not forgotten! Moses' name is used three times in the opening verses, eleven times in the first chapter and forty-eight times in the whole book. Moses, of course, is rightly honoured by the people of Israel.

He is the one who:

- brought the Word of God to a whole generation
- was instrumental in displaying the signs and wonders of God
- was the mediator for the people when, because of their sin, they were in danger of being wiped out
- led them through the wilderness
- brought them to the edge of the Promised Land.

All of this simply highlights the fact that, while Moses is important to the flow of biblical history, he is not indispensible. It is now time for the new leader to step up and take command. But even the new leader, Joshua, is not the key to the life and continuance of the nation. The essential element of both Moses' and Joshua's leadership is contained in just three words, 'and God said' (1:1). They are leaders under the command, the promise, the Word of God.

Confirming the Promise (1–2)

The steady repetition of Moses' name signals the continuity of the promise. What God called Moses to do in terms of that promise, now Joshua is called to accomplish. A simple comparison of God's words to Joshua (1:3-5) and to Moses (Deut. 11:24-25) makes this clear. So, God speaks to Joshua in the opening verses of the chapter, and fundamental to all He says is His promise of old. The threefold theme we identified from creation, through the promise to Abraham and reaffirmed to Moses, now appears afresh in God's words to Joshua. Very clearly, the promise of *a place to live* is reaffirmed (1:2-4). It is a land of defined boundaries and, as Joshua and the people have already learned from Moses, it will be a land of complete contrast to their desert experience the last forty years (see 5:6). There is also an implicit progression in their acquisition of the land built into God's words.

> I will give you every place where you set your feet, as I promised Moses. Your territory will extend from the desert to Lebanon, and from the great river, the Euphrates – all the Hittite country – to the Mediterranean Sea in the West (1:2-4).

This 'now and not yet' tension exists throughout the book as the land is subdued, but there remains work to be done (cf. 11:16 and 13:1 and comments on them). The other major element of the words about the land is that it comes as 'gift' not 'reward'. The tenses used in vv. 2 and 3 are significant, 'I am about to give to them' and 'I have given to you' (v. 3 ESV, not as NIV, 'I will give you'). This use of language underlines the certainty of the promise and the process by which it is fulfilled.[1] In this opening section of the book,

---

1. D. Howard *Joshua* NAC (Nashville, USA: Broadman & Holman, 1998) p. 86.

the land as both gift (vv. 2-3) and inheritance (v. 6) is clearly affirmed.[2]

The second of the overarching themes we traced earlier is clearly present in these opening verses as well. There is *a people to live there*. God speaks to Joshua in a way that makes it clear that His intentions are for a people, a family, not simply for individuals. The nation of Israel is not going into the land simply to claim a piece of real estate for themselves, either as individuals or as small family groups. God confirms this aspect of His promise as He says: 'Now then, you and all this people [not 'these people' as NIV], get ready to cross the River Jordan into the land I am about to give them' (v. 2). The promise is to the nation as a whole – a new family drawn together by God, constituted as His people and led to His rest-land. Further the *you* and *your* of verses 3 and 4 are plurals – this is not addressed to Joshua alone, but to the whole nation. Once more, verse 6 stresses the corporate nature of the nation – Joshua will lead *this* people to inherit the land (again not 'these people' as NIV). We will see later that the dialogue between Joshua and the East Bank tribes is a further indicator of the corporate, unified nature of the nation.

The tone of God's speech changes in verses 5-9. Here God addresses Joshua directly. This, of course, is not because His words are applicable to only Joshua; he is the appointed leader of the people and stands as the representative of them all.[3] Rather, as the leader of the people of God he must take the lead! Joshua's courage and authority come from his trust in God and His purposes and in being a man

---

2. See p. 36-37 above.

3. We see more of this function in Joshua 7.

Confirming the Promise (1–2)

under the Word of God. The promise that Joshua and the people he leads will have a *blessing, a relationship, to enjoy*, is stated here in the form of God's presence with them – 'for the LORD your God will be with you wherever you go'(v. 9). How is this blessing to be enjoyed? The answer is given in verses 7 and 8. Relationship with God, knowing Him and the blessing of walking with Him are available through His Word and obedience to it. Without His Word, His self-revelation, He cannot be known. Without His Word, it is impossible to know what pleases Him and what He requires of His people. The promise of God can only come through the spoken Word of God. So, Joshua is told to 'obey it', 'not turn from it' and 'meditate on it day and night' (vv. 7 and 8).

Once more, the continuity with all God has said and promised to Moses is clear. The foundation of Israel's knowledge of God is that He has spoken to them. Moses made this clear to the people as he reflected on their meeting with Him at Sinai (see Deut. 4). Linked to the promise of the land is the blessing of the presence of God with this people.

As Moses asks them:

> What other nation is so great as to have their gods near them the way the LORD our God is near us whenever we pray to him? (Deut. 4:7)

Moses goes on to stress that God's words were at the centre of their experience at Sinai (see Deut. 4:10-14). Moses was the mouthpiece of God but he was not going to be there forever. In Deuteronomy 31 he commits the teaching (*torah*) from God to writing. The people now have a book and are called to meditate on it as they prepare to move into the Promised Land (Josh. 1:7-8).

There is both the continuity *of* the Promise, God is faithful to His Word and purpose; and there is also continuity *in* the Promise – whoever its leaders, they are people under authority, not autocrats.

Preparations for the Promise (1:10-11)

In this next brief episode, Joshua turns to those with responsibility for the people. These are the officers or, perhaps better, the officials to whom the administration of the tribes is committed. They are not military commanders. Not only is their role in the nation significant, but also the commands they are to pass on. It is not directly connected with warfare; it is more about suitable provisions to survive until they enter the land – 'Get your provisions ready' (1:11). These apparently mundane preparations mark a confidence in God's great provision – the land is theirs by gift not by force of arms.

The time period specified – 'three days from now' (v 11) – has caused some debate among commentators, especially as it appears again in 2:22 and 3:2. The most likely explanation is that 2:22 concerns the days to prepare supplies and 3:2 the days of preparing to move following the ark of the covenant. This would also involve some spiritual preparations as Joshua told the people to consecrate themselves (3:5). It would be during this whole period that the spies were away as their three days were not necessarily three complete 24 hour periods. Calvin expresses no concerns about the chronological order of these events.

He suggests that:

> It was only after their [the spies] report furnished him [Joshua] with the knowledge he required, that he resolved to move camp ... Nor is there anything novel in neglecting the order of time, and afterwards interweaving what has been omitted.[4]

However the timetable is resolved, encouraged and convinced by the Word from God, Joshua turns to active obedience, preparing the people to receive the promise. And unlike the Exodus, where the preparations are done in haste, here there is sufficient time, because the land is given to them in advance by the Lord. One event is a rescue; the other is their entry into their inheritance.

To set the preparations in motion, the officers are to 'go through' the camp. The same word is used later in the verse when they are told 'you will cross the Jordan' – literally they will 'go/pass through' the river. This command not only triggers their preparation, it signals continuity within the promise of God. The same verb is used in 1:2 (and over 30 times more in the book). It also picks up the vocabulary of Exodus and Deuteronomy (12 times more in Exodus; over 40 times in Deuteronomy mainly with reference to entering the Promised Land). Even the language used in such an apparently 'mundane' situation speaks of 'promise'.

Remember your promise (1:12-18)

Mention has already been made of the two-and-a-half tribes whose inheritance is to be the East Bank territories. The story of their request for the land and Moses' response is recorded in Numbers 32. There Moses was obviously suspicious of their request – he saw it as a possible cause

---

4. John Calvin, *Joshua, Calvin's Commentaries* (Grand Rapids, USA: Baker 2003) vol 4 p. 36.

of disunity for the people of God. To maintain the unity, Moses demanded a commitment from the tribes of Reuben, Gad and the half tribe of Manasseh. Joshua now calls upon them to honour the promise they made, to be frontline troops in the invasion of Canaan. This honouring of their promise was at considerable cost to the East Bank tribes. They already had an established base – cities taken and fortified, pens for their flocks, an established home for their wives and children (see Num. 32). But they were prepared to send their fighting men in as part of 'all Israel', knowing that the whole nation must receive their inheritance of land together. David Firth sums it up in a way that has continuing significance: 'The unity of the people in the purposes of God was thus vital to the full enjoyment of God's gifts.'[5]

Joshua does not simply issue instructions on his own authority. His words to the East Bank tribes clearly echo the words of Moses (cf 1:13-15 and Deut. 3:18-20). He is already applying the principle of 'not turning to the right or to the left from the Law of Moses' (see 1:7). And, in fact the tribes' response (1:16-18) recognises this fact. It is also clear from Joshua's speech to these tribes that the possibility of 'rest' (a settled and secure life) will only become a reality as the whole nation achieves rest (see 1:13 and 15).

It is unnecessary, I think, to make the reply in verses 16-18 the response of all the tribes, as one or two commentators do (on the basis of the plural 'they' in v. 16). The immediate context seems to demand that this is the ready response of the East Bank tribes. Their willingness to be on the 'front-

---

5. David Firth, *The Message of Joshua* (Nottingham, UK: IVP 2015) p. 40.

Confirming the Promise (1–2) 105

line' is evidenced later when they take the lead in crossing the Jordan (see 4:12).

Robert Hubbard Jr captures the implication of their agreement:

> Though speaking of themselves literally they articulate the loyalty expected of all the tribes from here on. A subtle argument undergirds their words: If the Transjordanian tribes with no personal interest in West Bank lands affirm what follows, how much more so the others.[6]

To remember and honour the promise their tribes have made in the past, they now put themselves completely under the command of Joshua (1:16). They recognise him as the true and only successor to Moses (1:17), and their desire is for Joshua to experience the Lord's presence with him in the same way that Moses had. Indeed, they reinforce that commitment by saying that any rebellion against Joshua would be considered as rebellion against God – hence the death penalty (see further notes on chapter 7).

Promise in Jeopardy (2:1-7)

This section begins with a brief and simple command from Joshua – 'Go, look over the land ... especially Jericho' (2:1). There has been a great deal of conjecture on the part of commentators and preachers as to why Joshua should do this, hard on the heels of God's assurance to him about being given the land. The text provides us no evidence for suggesting a loss of nerve or faith on Joshua's part. Indeed, in the light of God's promise and the support of God's people, Joshua makes the next obvious military move at the

---

6. Robert Hubbard, Jr, *Joshua NIVAC* (Grand Rapids, USA: Zondervan 2009) pp. 86-7.

beginning of the conquest; he secretly sent two spies from Shittim (2:1). There are, without doubt, some ambiguities in the text both regarding the spies' actions and the nature of their relationship with Rahab. Despite some attempts to treat this ambiguity of language in a way that suggests sexual motivation by the spies, this is difficult to maintain.[7] Probably, the most we can read out of the text is the ineptitude of the spies – they were sent 'secretly', but were apparently discovered immediately!

The main element of the narrative, at this point, leaves Joshua behind and is concerned with the dialogue between the King of Jericho (through his messengers) and Rahab. The spies have gone to the town's brothel presuming, perhaps, that in the comings and goings there, they wouldn't be noticed. Rahab's house was also located in a strategic position, it 'was part of the city wall' (2:15). Some estimate of the town's fortifications could be made; and an escape route was available. Whatever their intentions, immediately a report gets back to the King that there are Israelites in Jericho (2:2). Naturally, the King wants to deal with the situation (2:3); even if he overestimates the spies' capabilities. In response Rahab seeks to appear helpful – misleading the King and preserving the spies (2:4-6). Her subterfuge works, 'the men set out in pursuit of the spies on the road that leads to the fords of the Jordan' (2:7).

Although, for a moment, the promise seems to be in jeopardy – there is no way of telling if or how the King of Jericho might have profited from capturing the spies – the means by which the problem is averted is open to question. I used the term 'subterfuge' above to describe Rahab's

---

7. See Hubbard, pp. 113-116.

action, but that really only softens somewhat the fact that it was a lie.

Whatever else may be said, Rahab's strategy worked – 'the men set out in pursuit of the spies … and as soon as the pursuers had gone out the gate was shut' (2:7). The rapid closing of the gates probably testifies to the real fear that existed in Jericho because of the approach of Israel. The next dialogue puts that fear into words.

> # Further thoughts on … Rahab's lie
>
> It is worth pausing to consider not only the lie itself, but the way the narrator handles it. Consider first the outcome of the lie:
>
> + it saved the lives of the two spies
> + it brought them time to escape
> + it began to reveal where Rahab's growing loyalty was to be found.
>
> None of this is to suggest that the end justifies the means. The context in which the lie is spoken, however, needs to be considered:
>
> + there is the possibility that Rahab's house may have been the object of 'police' scrutiny, so this was a moment of extreme tension.
> + an immediate answer was required; as Adolf Harstad wryly remarks: 'Rahab must respond

> "on the spot" without the benefit of a seminar on ethics'.[1]

- even if her action was an imperfect step, it was a step in the right direction – as we will see in the next section, she has a growing understanding and allegiance to the God of Israel.

Once more it is important to remember that the text in front of us is a narrative. It simply describes the action and makes no moral judgement on Rahab's words. The NT remains silent concerning the lie, rather it commends the faith of Rahab that prompted her to act on the spies' behalf (see Heb. 11:31 and James 2:25, and comments on them in the next section).

As David Jackman says about Rahab's lie:

> Probably it came quite naturally to her since, like us, she was a fallen human being living in a fallen world, as we need to remember before we are too eager to point the finger.[2]

Further, might not the extreme tension and anxiety of the moment, while not necessarily justifying the lie, at least have a mitigating effect? Rhett Dodson asks some very pertinent questions:

> ... is it possible to see Rahab's actions as part-and-parcel of war's necessary subterfuge? Were Rahab's deeds any different from Corrie ten Boom's family hiding Jews from

---

1. Adolph Harstad, *Joshua Concordia Commentary* (St Louis USA: Concordia Publishing House, 2004) p. 116.

2. David Jackman, *Joshua, People of God's purpose* (Wheaton USA: Crossway, 2014) p. 35.

> Nazi Stormtroopers during World WarII? If members of Al Quaeda came to your door and demanded to know the whereabouts of your family, would it be a sin to say 'They are not here'?[3]
>
> Christians will have different answers, as Dodson points out, but the text is silent on the issue. Here is a woman moving from total paganism to belief in the one true God, who 'is God in heaven above and on earth below' (2:11) – we should not expect a high level of sanctification from her at this point!
>
> ---
> 3. Rhett Dodson, *Every Promise of Your Word* (Edinburgh, UK: Banner of Truth, 2016) p. 45.

Recognising the Promise 2:8-14
The grammar of verse 8 (indeed of vv. 6-8) is, according to some commentators, rather disjointed. The reason offered for this is that the writer is moving quickly over the ground to get to the confession of Rahab. This confession is the content of verses 9-11, with verse 11 as the final grand statement of her faith. But it is wise not to move too quickly to that statement in verse 11, we must not miss how the narrator takes us there. The emphasis in verses 9 and 10 is on what has been heard. This is important for at least three reasons:

1. The testimony to God's mighty acts in history is sufficient evidence for who He is and what He does. Despite the fact that Rahab had neither seen not experienced any of these events – they were, they are, historical realities.

2. Rahab's reaction to them, therefore, becomes a classic case of 'faith, comes by hearing' (see Rom. 10:14). The testimony she heard was both sad news and good news. For Rahab it was good news because it led her to a proper understanding of God and trust in Him.

3. This testimony was openly available. If Rahab has heard it, it is reasonable to think it was common knowledge in Jericho. Surely, the same response was also open to her fellow citizens? The news only becomes 'bad-news' when the claims of God are ignored or rejected.

The testimony to the mighty acts of God in history does not, then or now, allow anyone to sit on the fence. Only two courses of action are open – rejection or submission.

And what is this testimony about God and His actions? It concerns:

> ... how the LORD dried up the water of the Red Sea for you when you came out of Egypt, and what you did to Sihon and Og, the two kings of the Amorites east of Jordan, whom you completely destroyed (2:10).

This brief description of the LORD's action for and through Israel is no fantasy – it produced real fear in the hearts and minds of the people (v. 9 'great fear', 'melting in fear'; v. 11: 'hearts sank', 'courage failed'). To what extent Rahab realised it, we cannot be sure, but it is clear from the context that this testimony is to God keeping His promise to Israel.

All of this leads her to a straightforward declaration that:

> ... the LORD your God is God in heaven above and on the earth below. (2:11)

We should not be sidetracked into thinking that this is simply an observation or comment on the God of Israel, or of these spies. When Rahab says 'the Lord *your* God', she is certainly not distancing herself from the Lord. Rather she is distancing herself from the gods, many and various, of Jericho and the Canaanites. She is saying *this* God, and this God alone, is the only true God, Sovereign over all. And that confession is one that should be made by a true Israelite. In both accounts of the Ten Commandments (Exod. 20:4 and Deut. 5:8) the exclusivity of God in 'heaven above' and on 'the earth below' is maintained. This is at the heart of Israel's belief: they are called to:

> Acknowledge and take to heart this day that the Lord is God in heaven above and on the earth below. There is no other (Deut. 4:39).

And this is precisely what Rahab confesses. She recognises, in what she has heard, that the one true God is at work – and, as she will learn, this work is in fulfilment of His promise.

Recognising all of this, she acts on it by allying herself and her family with Israel. She seeks a guarantee from the spies that her confidence is not misplaced and that safety is assured. So, she asks for a 'sure sign' (2:12) that they will be saved from death (2:13). In doing this, she has burnt the bridges to her past life and allegiances and can now only trust the Lord and His two representatives who stand before her. The very terms she uses to make her request and the repetition of them in the spies' reply are significant. The 'kindness' of verse 12 is the Hebrew word for grace (*hesed*); and the 'sure sign' (lit. 'a sign of faithfulness') is the Hebrew word for truth (*'emet*). The same two words are repeated back to Rahab by the spies when they make their promise to her:

> 'Our lives for your lives!' the men assured her. 'If you don't tell what we are doing, we will treat you kindly and faithfully when the LORD gives us the land' (2:14).

The two words are closely connected on at least fifteen occasions through the Old Testament. They speak often of the character of God (Gen. 32:10, Exod. 34:6, Ps. 25:10, etc.) and carry overtones of the covenant relationship. Rahab is here moving into a new situation, that brings her and her family within the covenant. When the spies reply 'Our lives for your lives', they are not offering a commercial deal – an exchange of benefits – they are putting themselves under a solemn oath (see 2:7), one that is approved later by Joshua (6:22).

Calvin comments:

> They imprecate death upon themselves, if they do not faithfully make it their business to save Rahab ... their intention was simply to bind themselves before God. They constitute themselves, therefore, a kind of expiatory victims, if any evil befalls Rahab through their negligence.[8]

As the LORD is kind (gracious) and faithful to His people Israel through His promise, so now His people must exhibit that grace and faithfulness as well.

An alternative interpretation has been offered by a few commentators on this story of Rahab. She is seen as a 'smooth operator' who gets a good deal in her negotiations with the spies.[9] Obviously Rahab is not devoid of insight

---

8. Calvin, *Joshua*, p. 53.

9. See Hubbard, pp. 124-125, and L. Daniel Hawk, *Joshua, Berit Olam* (Collegeville USA: Liturgical Press, 2000) pp. 48-49.

or a certain amount of cunning – she would not have survived long otherwise in her particular profession! Yet to simply read this out of her speech here is both to ignore the depth of her statements and the testimony of the wider canon. She is listed in the genealogy of Jesus (Matt. 1:5) and the writer to the Hebrews says, 'By faith the prostitute Rahab because she welcomed the spies, was not killed with those who were disobedient' (Heb. 11:31). Indeed, what she did that day in Jericho meant that she was 'considered righteous' (James 2:25). This story is not one of a smart woman who pulled off a clever deal – rather it is a classic case of an outsider who became an insider. It shows the depth and reach of God's mercy and the awesome scope of God's promise to bring blessing to all nations.

Making their own promise 2:15-21
Having assured Rahab of her safety, the next significant action has to be the securing of the spies' safety. To highlight how this is achieved the narrator moves on swiftly to their escape:

> So she [Rahab] let them down by a rope through the window, for the house she lived in was part of the city wall (2:15).

This element of the story poses a problem for some commentators, as what follows seems to be a conversation between Rahab and the spies while they are either dangling on the rope or at the foot of the wall. Wherever they are, they are opening themselves to being discovered. There is no need, however, to read verses 16-21 in this way. It is probably just another example of the way that the Bible writer is more focussed on the significant elements of the story, rather than producing a simple linear history. We mentioned earlier the way Bible history is not written in a simple chronological way and gave 'telescoping' as an example of this. Here we have proleptic summary of the outcome of this story – 'the placing of an event in the narrative before its actual point in time.'[10]

To do this:

> ... is natural when, in the writer's view, completing a topic or theme takes precedence over a strictly chronological narration... the author mentions it first to fill out the description of the action in the episode.[11]

As Richard Hess points out, the NIV (1984) seeks to show the logic of this by translating the opening of verse 16 as 'she had said to them'.[12]

If the conversation was, in fact, conducted at the end of a rope it is, according to David Firth, evidence of the 'clear lack of competence demonstrated by the spies'!

Further, he says:

> If so, not only were they unable to arrive secretly, but also they appear to do their best to attract attention to themselves while leaving.[13]

We will assume that the dialogue that follows took place before they were let down the city wall.

Once Rahab had the assurance of the spies' oath (2:14), she takes the initiative to solve the problems that they still

---

10. Harstad, *Joshua* p. 142.

11. Ibid.

12. Richard Hess, *Joshua* TOTC (Leicester UK: IVP, 1996) p. 93 and other comments there.

13. Firth, *Joshua* p. 51.

Confirming the Promise (1–2)

face. Having evaded arrest by the King of Jericho's men, they still have two major hurdles to overcome. These are, as Richard Hess states it: 'the shut gate and the agents guarding the river'.[14] The fact that Rahab's house is 'part of the city wall' (2:15) solves the first of their problems. Her advice to go west instead of east and throw their would-be pursuers off the scent solves the second problem (2:16 cf. 2:22-23). Whether or not the men were conscious of the remarkable providence behind their rescue, they were willing to act on Rahab's advice. But they also had to make certain of both their safety and that of her and her family.

In vv. 17-21 they make their own promise again – 'their blood will be on our head if a hand is laid on them' (2:19). It comes with further stipulations this time; they repeat the need for silence, for secrecy (2:20 cf. 2:14). And they add two further qualifications:

- the scarlet cord to be tied at the window
- the need for the whole family to be in one place

The second of these is certainly based on pragmatism; in the mayhem of battle, they could not conceive of protecting random members of Rahab's household who might be out in the streets.

The first of these qualifications – the scarlet cord – has been the subject of much debate among generations of expositors. An oft-repeated interpretation sees the colour of Rahab's cord as a type of the blood of Christ.

A number of things work against this, just two examples will have to suffice:

---

14. Hess, *Joshua* p. 93.

1. the New Testament nowhere picks this idea up and makes this connection
2. the word 'scarlet' is never used to describe the colour of blood; a completely different word ('red') is used.

It is better to see this action against the broader backdrop of salvation history.

As Graeme Goldsworthy explains it:

> That Rahab found safety from this judgement and was saved through the instruction to display a sign of identification, has many real parallels to the Passover in Egypt. In that sense the tying of an easily seen coloured cord to the window had saving significance for Rahab, and the fact that she became incorporated into the people of God (Joshua 6:25) is a type of salvation.[15]

Once again, it is worth pointing out that this incorporation of Rahab and her family brings about a fulfilment of God's promise to Abraham, albeit in a small way. But, in saying that, we must not minimise the wonder of grace that transformed an outsider into an insider. This section of dialogue concludes with Rahab's statement, 'Agreed ... let it be as you say'; and with her action: 'So she sent them away, and they departed. And she tied the scarlet cord in the window' (2:21).

Again, this comment about her action should probably be seen as a proleptic summary. She was told to tie the scarlet cord in the window 'when we enter the land' (2:18). The writer includes this action here to complete this part of the story.

---

15. Graeme Goldsworthy, *Gospel and Kingdom* (Exeter UK: Paternoster press, 1981) p. 107-8; see also Jackman & Howard ad loc.

Confidence in the promise 2:22-24

In this final brief section the details of three or more days are passed over quickly. Just the most basic things are included:

- the men acted on Rahab's advice and hid in the hills for three days
- the pursuers searched thoroughly – but were looking in the wrong place
- they returned to Jericho empty handed
- the spies made their safe return to Joshua.

Back in the safety of the Israelite camp they reported on 'everything that had happened to them' (2:23). But this is all preamble to their final, significant statement:

> The LORD has surely given this whole land into our hands;
> all the people are melting in fear because of us (2:24).

Their report is not so much a detailed account of their reconnaissance than a repetition of Rahab's testimony (cf. 2:24 and 2:9). The confidence portrayed in it stands in direct contrast to the spies who reported back so negatively to Moses (see Num. 13). Joshua, along with Caleb, had returned to Moses with a much more positive report but only now is he about to see a completion of the conquest. Did he remember the prophetic words of Moses?

In his great song, Moses sang:

> The chiefs of Edom will be terrified,
> the leaders of Moab will be seized with trembling
> the people of Canaan will melt away (Exod. 15:15).

Whatever the shortcomings of the two spies, the outcome of their venture was sure to give Joshua confidence in the promise of God.

From text to message

There are a number of dangers that face us as preachers when we approach narrative texts like Joshua. We may read it as a self-contained story, isolating it from the wider biblical narrative and, especially, the flow of the story of salvation. Individual stories may have a particular appeal, but their context is vitally important – it helps determine the real meaning and significance of the story. There is also the danger of determining the idea or theme we want to preach on and finding a story that enables us to do that. The first two chapters of Joshua suggest a variety of themes that could be preached – leadership, obedience or reversals, for example – but these themes arise from the main thrust of the story. As helpful as it can be, concentration on the ancillary elements will blunt the key idea.

Although these first two chapters of the book can be divided into a number of sections – the most obvious are: 1:1-9, 10-18; 2:1-24 – there is an advantage in first seeing them whole. They set up the context for the occupation of Canaan, linking what is to come with what had gone before in the overall story.

Getting the message clear: the theme

What has brought Joshua and the people of Israel to this point and what will enable them to take possession of the land is the gracious and faithful promise of God.

The terms in which the gaining of the land is expressed are clearly in line with the Lord's foundational promise to

Abraham (Gen. 12:1-3) and reach back to creation itself. The focus on the Rahab story in chapter 2 is a forceful reminder that God's intention is to bring blessing, not just to Israel exclusively but to all people on earth (Gen. 12:3).

Getting the message clear: the aim

It is not that uncommon, that despite preachers and teachers insisting that God has no 'plan B'; the way many of our hearers approach the Old Testament shows that they actually think He does. We need to show, therefore, the consistency of God's Word of promise with its outworking in history. So, we need to help people grasp the 'shape' of that promise and how it leads to Christ. 'For no matter how many promises God has made, they are "Yes" in Christ' (2 Cor 1:20).[16]

A way in

Have you ever been in the situation where everybody is constantly talking about your predecessor? How did you react? Joshua certainly had this experience. There are so many references to Moses in just the first chapter (11 times) as well as the rest of the book (a further 37 times). But then Moses was an extremely important character in the life of Israel, as much of the Bible narrative testifies. It should be no surprise he was held in great honour. Why?

- He brought the Word of God to a whole generation and all subsequent generations.

- He acted as mediator for the people when, because of sin, they were in danger of being wiped out.

- He led them through the wilderness.

---

16. See *In the big picture* pp. 28-31.

- He brought them to the very edge of the Promised Land.

Despite all he has done, the book of Deuteronomy ends with Moses' funeral; and the book of Joshua opens with the reminder: 'After the death of Moses ... the LORD said to Joshua ... Moses my servant is dead' (Josh. 1:1-2) It cannot be clearer than that, can it?

This emphasis simply stands as a reminder that the people of God, in every age, are not dependent on a human leader. While Moses was important, the key to the life of the people of God is God Himself. They must depend wholly on the God who makes and keeps promises.

Ideas for application

- God's grace is the origin and driving force of His people's life. There is nothing we have by right – everything comes as gift from God.

- In grace God commits Himself to us by His promise – the right way to relate to God is to trust His promise. Jesus is the embodiment of all God's promises.

- We only know *that* God promises and *what* God promises because of His Word. Without His self-revelation there would be no knowledge of Him or relationship with Him.

- To walk with the LORD we need both to hear His Word and respond in obedience to it.

- The presence of God is mediated to us though His Word; God comes in person to us and speaks.

- As He speaks it equips us for the present 'be strong and very courageous'; and prepares us for the future – gaining our inheritance.
- All of this grace comes to us, not just as individuals but as a people. Unity among the people of God is a necessary part of the life of faith
- God's grace is surprising – we should set no limits as to who is or is not likely to be an object of His grace.

Suggestion for preaching

Sermon 1
Preaching on these two chapters together will naturally require some selectivity to keep the sermon in a manageable and digestible form. The story of Rahab and the spies can be briefly retold with a focus on the key statements made within it. The advantage in dealing with the two chapters as a whole is that it gives an opportunity to show people the marvellous scope of God's promise. The introduction could highlight the continuity of God's promise and presence (as suggested above). Then the main elements of that promise developed as follows:

The promise re-affirmed 1:1-9
The basic elements of the ancient promise to Abraham are present in God's commission to Joshua:

- a place to live
- a people to live there
- a relationship to enjoy – God's presence

Obligations under the promise 1:10-18
The promise has to be trusted and acted upon; this is particularly seen in the response of the East Bank tribes.

The scope of the promise 2:1-24
At the very beginning of the book, it is made clear that God's promise has a wider significance than just the nation of Israel. Even a pagan prostitute can be counted among the people of God by faith.

Each of these elements can be developed to show that Christ is the fulfilment of the promise God has made. They also point us to the final outworking of God's purposes in Christ's return to usher in the everlasting inheritance of God's people, in His presence forever.

This large section (chapters 1-2) will readily break down into the three parts as outlined above, allowing three sermons to be preached from it.

Sermon 2 (1:1-9)
The text needs to be read in the context of God's promise, the significance of what God says arises from that foundation. It also makes sense of the narrative flow of the book. So, this first section highlights the main aspects of the promise.

God is giving them a place to live
In verses 2-4 this idea is firmly stated in the vocabulary used – 'land', 'where you set your foot', 'territory'. The emphasis is also in the place as God's gift.

God has created a people to live there
In verses 2-4 plural pronouns are used to signify the people as a whole. It is a people who have been redeemed (through

Confirming the Promise (1–2)

the Exodus), disciplined (in the wilderness) and now stand on the borders of their inheritance (1:6).

This people are assured of the presence of God.
The greatest blessing the people of God have is their relationship with Him. His presence is their guarantee for both the present and future (1:5) And that presence is mediated to them through the Word of God (1:7-9).

Once again, the outworking for this promise in and though the person and work of Christ offers us a fruitful line of application for today.

Sermon 3 (1:10-18)
The role and authority of the new leader must now be put into practice.

It is time to move (1:10-11)
The command to the officers, and the preparations they tell the people to make, mark the first step in receiving their inheritance.[17] It is not a call to arms because the land is being *given* to them.

It is time to remember (1:12-15)
The East Bank tribes have received their promised inheritance – now it is time to make good on their promise to Moses. Promise involves responsibility and fulfilling those responsibilities is vital to the unity of the whole people.

It is time for commitment (1:16-18)
The pledge of the two-and-a-half tribes is clear and firm – but it is not just to Joshua. They recognise the greater

---

17. See pp. 102-103 for note on this passage.

authority that stands behind him (v. 17). Their leader does not lead by force of personality but by God's direction.

The promise of God demands a response, especially in the light of the fulfilment of it that has already been received and the knowledge of what is still to come. There are similar commitments called for from the believer today in the light of Christ's fulfilment of God's promises.

Sermon 4 (2:1-24)

The narrator has provided a good fast-paced story; we must avoid defusing it by turning it into a set of simple propositions. Some basic movements and moments in the story can be picked up in a sequence like this:

Another look (2:1-7)

This is the spies' commission, to look at the land afresh. It is a simple piece of strategy by Joshua as they approach the land from a different direction. The spies hoped that the people of Jericho would not give them another look as they went into Rahab's house. But that wasn't the case – they needed to be protected, perhaps from themselves!

No other God (2:8-14)

The surprise of finding faith in Jericho – Rahab's confession and her request for safety. It is an amazing move from paganism to true belief.

No other way (2:15-24)

A deal is struck with the spies. Rahab's house is marked out just as once the houses of Israel were marked to avoid the coming judgement on the land. No 'Plan B' is offered.

The spies are not the only ones that need saving (especially from themselves) – all need a way of escaping judgement.

Faith in the one true God and His gracious provision is the only way – no 'Plan B'! The grace and truth of God is most clearly shown in Jesus (John 1:14), but is it shown in His people?

Suggestions for teaching

Questions to help understand the passage

1. How does the opening statement of the book look back to what has gone before? Read Numbers 27:18-23; Deuteronomy 31:7-8, 32:44-47.

2. Review the promise God first gave to Abraham (Gen. 12:3). How do Exodus 3:7-12; 6:2-8 and Deuteronomy 7:1-10 develop that promise?

3. Which boundaries in 1:4 are consistent with the earlier promise of God? (See Gen. 15:18 and Num. 34:1-12)

4. In what ways are the unity of God's people and Joshua's solidarity with them emphasized in 1:2-6?

5. How does the text describe the importance of God's Word (the Book of the Law)? What role does it play for the people of God?

6. 'Be strong and very courageous' is spoken three times to Joshua. By whom are these words spoken and for what purpose?

7. Do you think the East Bank tribes' response (1:17) represents an advance over the previous generation's attitude?

8. How does the text portray the spies and Rahab? What are the surprises concerning all three of them?

9. What is the significance of Rahab's attitude to the evidence she has heard about Israel's God?

10. What do you think the main function of the scarlet cord is; and is it connected to any other OT idea?

Questions to help apply the text

1. Are we dependent on a succession of God's servants/ministers or on the God they serve?

2. Is my life shaped by my inheritance, or am I living for this world?

3. What place does the Word of God have in my life? Are there changes I need to make to give it its rightful place?

4. Joshua is commanded to be 'strong and very courageous' three times on the first chapter. Why do you think this is? What lessons are there for us in this?

5. How do we work for the unity of God's people? Are there any particular lessons from chapter 1 we can learn for our own situation?

6. What do you consider to be the most important quality of a leader? How does Joshua 1:12-18 help us in deciding this?

7. In what way does the story of the two spies help us when we seem to mess things up?

8. How does Rahab's faith challenge us not to write any individual off with regard to coming to faith?

9. Are there lessons to learn from chapter 2 about God's sovereignty and our responsibility? Why didn't the spies just say, 'Trust God and all will be well'?

2

Witnessing to the Promise (3–4)

Introduction

Some while ago, I read four books that covered the same period of history – 1935-1995. Two of these books were personal reminiscences of people who played a considerable part in the affairs of the Christian Church in that time. The other two were biographies written from a much more detached view, the authors being younger people who had not experienced a substantial portion of that period. I did not question the factual accuracy of any of these books. What struck me, however, was the way their different perspectives contributed to the wider picture. Each author had to select (or omit) certain elements that others reckoned as vitally important. This raised the question in my mind, how do you write history?

We have touched on the way the Bible writes history, when we considered the question, 'Is Joshua among the prophets?'[1] But, it is worth reminding ourselves that

---

1. See the section *Joshua In the OT* above pp. 23-28.

Bible history, like all history, is selective and structured to make a point. The Hebrew Bible classifies this book as prophecy because it stresses the perspective highlighting God's activity – how He is at work and what He says. It is also important that we remember that the original writers of OT books like Joshua wrote, in the first place, for an audience who would *hear* the book, rather than read it. So, a variety of literary devices were used to make it more memorable. And this is true of the chapters before us. As the narrator recounts this story of the crossing of the Jordan, he does not hide or falsify facts – but he does tell them in a way that will lodge in people's minds and help them draw lessons from them.

Two brief examples may be given:

- The frequent mention of the Ark – ten times in chapter 3, a further seven in chapter 4. As Ralph Davis says:

    > Thus the Ark – sign of Yahweh's presence among his people – meets us at every turn, reminding us that it is Yahweh himself who leads his people into Canaan, who cuts off flooding waters and holds them back as it were by his hand. The whole affair is Yahweh's feat and the Israelites, though active, are still primarily spectators.[2]

- The pile(s) of stones. The focus on this element of the story occupies a central position in this section of the narrative. It tends to slow the flow of the story to make

---

2. Ralph Davis, *Joshua – No Falling Words* (Fearn, UK: Christian Focus, 2000) p. 33. Statistics from D. Howard, *Joshua NAC* (Nashville, USA: Broadman & Holman, 1998) p. 120 n177.

an important point. It also highlights the reason in the narrative.

More will be said on these and other literary devices as we work through the text.

Listening to the text

Context and structure

Joshua has now received encouragement from God and the people for the task ahead. He has also received evidence from the spies, chiefly through Rahab's testimony, that the time is right for action. So, he prepares the people for that action – the 'crossing over' the Jordan and into the Promised Land. On God's command the movement begins.

These two chapters are something of a puzzle for some commentators. There seems to be disruption of the chronological sequence and other 'logical digressions' to produce a convoluted story.

According to Richard Nelson:

> The convolutions of chapters 3 & 4 result from the concentration of a large number of themes into the narrow nexus of Jordan crossing. Too many topics have been crammed into too constricted a narrative space so that the thematic threads have tangled and knotted.

He puts this down to 'a complicated history of composition and redaction' and suggests there is no generally accepted solution to the problem.[3]

---

3. R. Nelson, *Joshua* OTL (Louisville USA, Westminster John Knox Press, 1997) p. 5.

These difficulties, I would suggest, are not as apparent as Nelson suggests. The narrative unfolds in a straightforward sequence:

- an introduction that prepares the people for what is going to happen (3:1-6)
- the crossing of the Jordan by the people (3:7-17)
- the memorial made of stones from the Jordan (4:1-14)
- all Israel in the Promised Land and the return of the waters of the Jordan (4:15-24)

Each of these main sections, after the introduction, have some common features. They are more than just a bare recital of 'what happened next'. They all follow the same sequence:

- God speaks to Moses
- Moses passes on God's command to the people
- The Word from God is obeyed and the action completed[4]

The repetition serves to make the story more memorable and to emphasize God's rule as the initiator and chief actor in the event.

The structure can be outlined in the following way:

3:1-6	get ready to be amazed
3:7-17	crossing on dry ground
4:1-14	witnessing to the promise

---

4. C. F. Keil, *Joshua* (Grand Rapids USA, Eerdmans reprint 1960) p. 39. See Adolph Harstad, 'Joshua', *Concordia Commentary* (St Louis USA: Concordia Publishing House, 2004) p. 153 for a similar analysis.

4:15-18	safely in the land
4:19-24	that all may know

All four of these sections underline the fact that God is at work for His people, and on the basis of His promise.

Working through the text

Get ready to be amazed (3:1-6)
Joshua and the people need now to prepare for the crossing into Canaan. The first thing they do is to move nearer the river (v. 1). They have been at Shittim for some time, their arrival (and problems) there are recorded in Numbers 22 and 25. This journey is approximately 8 to 10 miles, according to where scholars identify the site of Shittim to have been. After three days they are instructed by their officers to prepare to move once more. These preparations are of a different order to the ones in 1:10-11. Now, their

> # Further thoughts on …
> # the Ark
> It is worth pausing at this point to think briefly about the significance of the Ark. Here we must let our thinking be controlled by Scripture rather than Indiana Jones! The Ark is *the* symbol of God's presence with His people. When the people were in the camp it was placed at the heart of the Tabernacle. The book of Exodus devotes a considerable amount of space to the planning and construction of the Tabernacle. Central to the Tabernacle was the Holy of Holies and it was there that you found the Ark of the Covenant.

> In it were the two stone tablets on which were written the Law of God. This Law is a reflection of the divine nature – God's Law bears His image. So, God's people know who dwells among them:
>
> - the one and only God
> - the one to be honoured above all other
> - the God of relationship and faithfulness
> - the God of truth and love[1]
>
> If this is the God who is present with His people, it is no surprise that the call will go out, 'Consecrate yourselves' (3:5).
>
> ---
> 1. I owe this approach to the Ark to lectures by Alec Motyer.

attention is focussed on the Ark and its movements. This begins the long series of references (mentioned above) that keep the Ark at the centre of the narrative.

To return to the command that the people are given concerning the Ark:

> When you see the Ark of the Covenant of the LORD your God, and the Levitical priests carrying it, you are to move out from your position and follow it. (3:3)

The fact that it is the 'Levitical Priests' who carry the Ark serves to underline the need for everything to be done in proper order. As the Ark moves off first, the people can see that the LORD is the real leader of Israel. A further instruction means that Israel must keep a certain distance (probably about half a mile) behind the Ark. The reason given in the text is not clear in the NIV as it reverses the order of v. 4.

The NASB follows the order of the Hebrew more closely:

> However there shall be between you and it a distance of about 2,000 cubits by measure. Do not come near it, that you may know the way by which you should go, for you have not passed this way before.

In the first instance, it is clear that the LORD, symbolised by the Ark, will lead them into this unknown territory (at least for them). The distance will also mean that a majority of the people will witness the amazing things ('wonders' NASB) that 'the Lord will do… among you' (3:5). As their forebears witnessed the parting of the waters at the Red Sea, so now, they will see the drying up of the Jordan. Although another implicit reason for this distance is because of the holiness of the Ark, the extent of the gap between people and the Ark suggests the first two reasons are the principle ones. This was a special occasion demanding special measures – ordinarily the Tabernacle and its contents travelled in the middle of the people (see Num. 2:17).

Joshua, having told the people that tomorrow would be a day of wonders, then tells them to prepare for it.

> Joshua told the people, 'Consecrate yourselves, for tomorrow the LORD will do amazing things among you' (3:5).

Exactly how the people are to consecrate themselves is not stated. Martin Woudstra suggests that Exodus 19:10, 14-17; Numbers 11:18 explain what is entailed. But, the emphasis is not on what the people do, rather it is a preparation for what God is going to do. Woudstra sums this up as, 'Outward rites were meant to further inward openness towards God and his acts.'[5] And the next day they would all witness the promise being fulfilled (in part) as they entered the land. The preparation is also necessary, for in following the Ark of the Covenant they are following the Covenant LORD.

Once again we find that the command in verse 6 and the response to it is an anticipation of the next major episode in the story.

Crossing on dry ground (3:7-17)
When God speaks to Joshua, He first gives Joshua a personal word of encouragement and assurance before He gives him the command concerning the Ark. This word of encouragement, 'Today, I will begin to exalt you in the eyes of all Israel' (3:7), will demonstrate to the people that Joshua is truly God's chosen leader. More than this, they will also know that the work that He began through Moses, He is continuing through Joshua. We may presume that the command from God to Joshua in verse 8 is a summary statement of what now needs to happen. Joshua relays a more detailed set of instructions to the people in verses 9-13. As the narrator does elsewhere in the book, information is included in stages helping both to build the tension in the story and jog the memory of the first readers. Joshua gathers the people and addresses them, but the authority comes from God – 'listen to the words of the LORD your God' (3:9). And the emphasis continues to be placed on God as the chief actor in the drama that is unfolding before them. What they are about to experience, and to know,

---

5. M. Woudstra, *Joshua* NICOT (Grand Rapids USA: Eerdmans, 1981) p. 81.

is that the 'living God is among you' (3:10). Israel knows already of the gods of other nations. Their whole history has shown the distractions and dangers that are involved in living in a world where 'there are many "gods" and many "lords"' (1 Cor. 8:5). But, of all the gods, there is only one 'living God' and He is about to demonstrate that fact. The demonstration the LORD is about to give has a purpose – it is to assure Israel that God 'will certainly drive out before you' the seven nations who occupy the land at the moment (3:10).

Rhett Dodson comments:

> This assurance would provide them with the spiritual strength they need for the battles that lay ahead ... They could face Jericho, Ai, Hazor or any of the other Canaanite cities by looking back at what God had already done.[6]

This is, of course, a principle that holds true not only for OT believers but also for NT believers.

Within these two chapters there are many echoes of the Exodus. Already in the opening verses a stress is placed on what Israel will 'know' (see 3:4, 7, 10). This picks up a dominant theme in the book of Exodus, which is particularly concerned with people knowing the LORD as the only, true God. There are other echoes as well; the opening words of verse 10 are exactly the same as those of Numbers 16:28. In both cases God is authenticating the leadership of Moses and then of Joshua. Here again the continuity of God's promise and purpose can be seen.[7] It is

---

6. R. Dodson, *Every Promise of Your Word* (Edinburgh, UK: Banner of Truth, 2016) p. 66.

7. I owe this reference to Howard, *Joshua* p. 125.

also worth remembering that the verb 'to know' in Hebrew is seldom used in a purely intellectual sense. There is usually a sense of the knower being involved in what is known – whether by action or relationship or in some other form.[8]

So for example:

- for Israel to know God is to know His salvation (Exod. 6:7)
- for Egypt to know God is to know His judgement (Exod. 14:4)
- to know the way to go is to walk in it (Josh. 3:4)
- to know God is with Joshua as He was with Moses is to follow Joshua as God's appointed leader (Josh. 3:7)
- to know what God is about to do at the River Jordan is to trust Him for the battles to come (Josh. 3:10)

What Israel are about to see and experience will help them know in a practical way that the conquest of the land will be achieved.

As Joshua lists the nations the people are about to face (3:10), he is not giving a comprehensive list of every people group they will encounter. The national names are linked with geographical regions; they give an overall impression of the extent of the land and the kind of people they will encounter (cf. Deut. 7:1 for a similar list). However difficult the task may seem, once more there is reassurance:

> See, the ark of the covenant of the Lord of all the earth will go into the Jordan ahead of you. (3:11)

---

8. See T. Fretheim, art. 'Know' in *New International Dictionary of Old Testament Theology and Exegesis vol 2* (Grand Rapids USA: Zondervan, 1997) pp. 409-414 (hereafter *NIDOTTE*).

Almost every single word of Joshua's statement carries theological weight.

So, for example:

- 'ark of the covenant' – the presence of God, who is committed to His people
- 'of the LORD of all the earth' – however many nations (and their gods) Israel face, there is only one true sovereign
- 'will go ... ahead of you' – the initiative and the power to accomplish both crossing and conquest are God's.

He also now tells them something of how the crossing is to be accomplished by 'the LORD of all the earth' – the water of the Jordan will cease to flow (3:13). A further indicator of the fact that something significant is about to happen is signalled by the choosing of twelve men (3:12), who will act as representatives of the whole people. It is another example of an anticipation of what is yet to unfold in the story.

Joshua had received his instructions from the Lord, passed them on to the people and now (3:14-17) that action is completed. The people are packed up and ready to go but the priests with the Ark go ahead of them (3:14). But, before continuing to describe the crossing, the narrator inserts a seemingly innocent comment – 'Now the Jordan is in flood all during harvest' (3:15). The Jordan Valley, which Israel is entering, is between 3 and 14 miles wide as it runs north to south, from Galilee to the Dead Sea. The flood plain in the valley extends from 200 yards to 1 mile wide. Covering this flood plain is dense undergrowth and the only way through it is via the roads to the fords. The average drop in the level of the river bed is 40ft. in every mile, which determines the speed of flow of the water.

> This means that that river Israel faced ... was no placid stream but a raging torrent probably a mile wide covering a mass of tangled brush and jungle growth.[9]

And when does this happen? Normally about now! This was the time and the conditions under which the Israelites were to make their crossing. The impossibility of the people negotiating this crossing was obvious (at least to them!). Yet, they had heard from Joshua what was going to happen (note the progression of 3:8, 13, 16), and as the priests' feet touched the water, the promise became a reality (3:15 &16). And the narrator underlines the extent and completeness of the miracle in the four verbs that are used: The water *stopped* flowing, it *piled* up, it was *completed/finished* (NIV 'completely') and it was *cut off*. David Howard wryly remarks: 'The vocabulary "piles up" in a manner that reminds us of the waters themselves piling up!'[10]

The God of creation is not hard-pressed to sort out a problem like crossing the River Jordan in full flood. As He had made a path through the Red Sea, now He does so with the River Jordan. Exactly how He achieved this, we do not know. Much speculation exists about the possibility of a landslip further upstream – notable examples of this happened in 1276 and 1921 with many other instances often quoted. In many ways, this speculation misses the point. What we do know is that it perfectly suited the need, and the timing was impeccable. God was in control

---

9. Davis, *Joshua* p. 38. Info from *ibid* and R. Boling & G. E. Wright, *Joshua Anchor Bible* (Garden City USA, Doubleday 1982) p. 178.

10. Howard, *Joshua* p. 131.

– 'The priests who carried the ark of the covenant of the LORD stopped in the middle of the Jordan and stood on dry ground' (3:17). As the people crossed the river bed, they were in no doubt as to who had accomplished this. Again the narrator points out that it is 'all Israel' who passed by the Ark and adds that 'the whole nation' completed the crossing. According to Richard Nelson: 'The people are now identified as a "nation" … perhaps indicating that crossing the Jordan to become a landed people has meant a change in national status.'[11]

They each have their own experience of this great event in the history of salvation, but they are also part of the 'one body'. This section of the narrative closes with the simple yet amazing fact that they all crossed 'on dry ground' (3:17) an echo of their past and a stimulus to their faith as they face a new situation in the land.

Witnessing to the promise (4:1-14)
One of the great enemies of any relationship is forgetfulness.[12] When one party in the relationship forgets the acts or character of the other party, problems begin to arise. If this is true of human relationships, it is also true of our relationship with God. Forgetfulness is the enemy of faith. Moses, by the inspiration of the Holy Spirit, certainly understood this and was moved to instruct the people of God about it. Looking forward to the day when Israel would live a settled life he warned them:

> You may say to yourselves, 'My power and the strength of my hands have produced this wealth for me.' But remember the LORD your God, for it is he who gives

---

11. R. Nelson, *Joshua* p. 62.
12. I owe this line of thinking to Ralph Davis, see *Joshua* pp. 29-40.

you the ability to produce wealth, and so confirms his
covenant, which he swore to your ancestors, as it is today.
(Deut. 8:17-18)

There would always be, for the people of God, a strong temptation to forget all that God had done and to trust in themselves or, worse still, to trust in other gods (see Deut. 8:19). This kind of forgetfulness would, in the end, prove fatal; as Moses went on to say:

Like the nations the LORD destroyed before you, so you
will be destroyed for not obeying the LORD your God.
(Deut. 8:20).

It is to guard against this lapse of memory that Joshua acts as soon as they arrive in the land. The anticipatory choosing of a man for each of the twelve tribes (3:12) now comes into play.

This section follows the pattern we have seen so far:

- the Lord issues instructions to Joshua concerning the twelve and their task
- Joshua relays the command to the twelve explaining the purpose behind it
- the accomplishment of the task and crossing is recorded.

The stones that are taken from the Jordan witness to the promise of God and its fulfilment. They guard against the enemy of the faith – 'they are there to this day' (4:9).

The narrator presumably records an excerpt of God's command to Joshua (4:1-3); we hear a fuller version as Joshua instructs the twelve men. Doubtless the twelve relayed the nature of their mission to their own tribe, and

Witnessing to the Promise (3–4)

the whole nation would be witness to their subsequent action. It is important to note what they witnessed:

- a representative from each tribe was involved
- the stones came from the dried-up river – only the miracle had made them accessible
- they are taken from 'where the priests are standing' (4:3) with the Ark – God's presence making the whole venture possible
- they are carried to the people's first resting place in the land of rest.

From this point on the stones are not just a simple memorial, rather they are a constant reminder of who the people are and how God acts on their behalf.

This is all amplified and clarified in Joshua's words to the twelve men. The representative nature of their action is stressed in 4:5; and the purpose spelled out more fully in 4:6-7. And the purpose is more than simply passing on a piece of information to the next generation when they ask, 'What do these stones mean?' (4:6). The question the children are to ask carries a sense of the personal significance of the memorial. The Hebrew text allows the following possibilities:

- 'what are these stones **for you?**'
- 'what do these stones represent **for you?**'[13]

This pile of stones becomes part of the witness, the testimony of every Israelite to what the promise of God

---

13. Harstad, *Joshua* p. 192 & T. Butler, *Joshua* WBC (Grand Rapids USA: Zondervan, 2014) vol 1 p. 271.

has done for them. The question and answer are part of a God-instituted method of transmitting the faith from one generation to another. It is a process that encompasses the whole sweep of God's saving activity (see the question to be asked of the Passover Exod. 12:24-27) and His ongoing relationship with His people (see Deut. 6:20-25). They are not a momentary expedient, but a permanent reminder. Marten Woudstra helpfully summarises the Hebrew concept of remembering:

> The notion of remembering in Hebrew is more than calling to mind. It involves a remembering with concern; it also implies loving reflection and, where called for, a corresponding degree of action.[14]

Old Testament illustrations of this concept can be found in Deuteronomy 26:5-9 where the movement from third to first person pronouns signal personal involvement in what is remembered; and in 1 Samuel 1:12-20, when God 'remembered Hannah', He acted in answer to her prayer. Each generation were to pass on this witness – 'These stones are to be a memorial to the people of Israel for ever' (4:7).

The instructions from the Lord, conveyed through Joshua, are now obeyed. The twelve men, having carried the stones out of the Jordan, deposit them at the campsite (the verb used does not necessarily imply any kind of construction in this action). With these stones, it is Joshua who will construct the memorial (assuming 4:9a is an anticipation of 4:20a, where the same verb is used). A problem for some commentators is deciding just how

---

14. Woudstra, *Joshua* p. 92.

many piles of stones there are in these verses. The dilemma can be seen in different translations of verse 9:

- 'Joshua set up the twelve stones that had been in the middle of the Jordan' (NIV)
- 'Then Joshua set up twelve stones in the middle of the Jordan' (NASB, similarly ESV and note NIV margin).

Richard Hess has offered four grammatical and stylistic reasons why a translation like that of the NIV is to be preferred. The evidence he offers cannot be considered conclusive, and other arguments offered by scholars suggesting emendations to the text have no real foundation either.[15] Although there are some unresolved questions, such as, 'Was Joshua commanded to do this?' and "If not, what was his purpose?'; one thing is certain, if there were two piles of stones, they are clearly linked in the narrative as we have it. One marks the position of the Ark during the crossing and the other marks the accomplishment of the crossing. The one in the river may disappear at the time of flood, but its reappearance season by season would be a graphic reminder of all that God has done for them. Once more there are echoes of the Exodus in the text.

As David Jackman points out;

> The language is similar to that used about the Passover in Exodus 12:26.27, which is to be an annual sign, reminder, or memorial of the miraculous deliverance of God's people from their slavery in Egypt and the execution of God's

---

15. Richard Hess, *Joshua* TOTC (Leicester UK: IVP 1996) p. 109. See also P. Pitkanen, *Joshua* Apollos OT Commentary (Nottingham UK: Apollos, 2010) p. 138 who says: 'Admittedly there is however no actual textual evidence in support of the differing reading.'

wrath. Future generations need to know these things happened… but also they testify about the character and promises of God.[16]

The next few verses (4:10-13) are a summary statement concerning the crossing. They look both backwards and forward in the narrative as they add to the story and its significance. Yet again, the emphasis falls on the role of the Ark in making the crossing possible. It remained 'in the middle of the Jordan until everything the LORD had commanded Joshua was done' (4:10). The line of command is also stressed once more – from the Lord to Joshua. This time though, the role of Moses is included in that line. A further reference to Moses in verse 12 prepares for the concluding statement of this section (4:14). The actual crossing is expressed in an extremely economic way, 'The people hurried over' (4:10). Their haste does not imply fear of the water's return, rather it is a sign of their willingness to enter the land. It also may imply that no obstacle stood in their way.

Once the people have all crossed, the priests move from the centre of the river-bed; this, again, may be an anticipatory statement, amplified in 4:15-18. The whole nation has the opportunity to witness this action: it is a further means of stressing God's control of the whole event. To complete the picture, the narrator records that the East Bank tribes, faithful to their promise, were the spearhead of the advance into Canaan. As we saw in 1:12-15, they are honouring the original promise they made to Moses. They go ahead 'armed for battle', prepared 'for war' (4:13). Questions are

---

16. David Jackman, *Joshua, People of God's purpose* (Wheaton USA: Crossway, 2014) p. 52. See further Dodson, *Every Promise* pp. 80-82.

sometimes raised concerning the statistics given in Exodus, Numbers and Joshua. There are two things in this debate which are relevant to our text here:

- if we take the figures given in the census of Numbers 26, the number of armed men in the East Bank tribes is in excess of 110,000. A proportion of them, therefore, are allocated to be the vanguard of Israel's army. Presumably the rest remain at home to keep secure both property and families.

- the number, 40,000, is used elsewhere in the OT as 'a round number meaning "huge army" (Judg. 5:8; 2 Sam. 10:18; 1 Kings 4:26; 1 Chron. 12:36).'[17]

- the word used for 'thousand' can be used for smaller social groups or for military units, or sometimes as hyperbole (see Josh. 23:10).[18]

It is difficult to determine definitively which is the appropriate meaning. When preaching I always use the numbers as the text records them.

This section of the narrative concludes with a statement about Joshua and his relationship with Israel. It brings full circle the promise God had made at the beginning of the account of the crossing – that the Lord would exalt Joshua 'in the eyes of all Israel' (3:7). The people have now seen that God was with Joshua, just as He had been with Moses. This meant that they would follow him as their God-appointed leader 'all the days of his life' (4:14). Indeed, 'they stood in awe of him ... just as they had stood in awe of Moses' (4:14).

---

17. R. Hubbard Jr, *Joshua NIVAC* (Grand Rapids, USA: Zondervan, 2009) p. 159.

18. P. Jenson, *NIDOTTE* vol 1 pp. 416-418.

Safely in the land (4:15-18)

In a briefer account, almost staccato in form, the same pattern is repeated for the last time in these chapters:

- God commands Joshua concerning the priests
- Joshua commands the priests to come out of the river
- The priests come out and the river's flow returns

As the crossing was initiated by the priests carrying the Ark stepping into the river, so now the crossing is brought to completion as the Ark comes up out of the river. From beginning to end, the entry of the People of God into the Promised Land is a work of the Lord alone. Two elements of vocabulary in this section deserve particular mention:

> 'the ark of the covenant law' (v. 16) is literally 'the ark of the testimony'. This is the most common description used in the book of Exodus, but it is used only here in Joshua. David Howard comments helpfully: 'The written words of the Law [contained in the Ark] constitute the Testimony and the use of this term here is appropriate in the context of command or promise and fulfilment that we have seen in chaps 3-4. God's word was to form the basis of everything Joshua and Israel did (cf. 1:7-8).'[19]

> 'Command the priests… to *come up* out of the Jordan'. From this point on in the narrative the emphasis is more on 'coming up out' of the river – the perspective is not so much of entering the land, but of being in the land, God's promise having been accomplished. Further, as Hubbard suggests the use of this verb 'probably intends to evoke

---

19. Howard, *Joshua* p. 140.

Witnessing to the Promise (3–4)

memories of the Exodus ... It says, "Israel came up out of the Jordan, just as they came up out of Egypt."'[20]

So, on Joshua's command, the priests with the Ark arrive on the West Bank, and:

No sooner had they set their feet on the dry ground than the waters of the Jordan returned to their place and ran in flood as before (4:18).

To describe the waters to be 'in flood as before' closes off the crossing episode, underlining its completely miraculous nature. The very river itself acts as testimony to the power of God; as Calvin says:

Thus the river, though dumb, was the best of heralds, proclaiming with a loud voice that heaven and earth are subject to the God of Israel.[21]

That all may know (4:19-24)

What may appear to be an almost incidental piece of information is not, of course. The 'tenth day of the first month' is loaded with significance. It was on that day, forty years earlier, that the Israelites began their preparations for the Passover, the escape from Egypt. On that day they selected the lamb for the Passover meal, ready for that awesome night when the Lord passed through the land in judgement (see Exodus 12:3). The timing of the event links what is happening into God's wider plan of salvation. Although the place where they camp on that first day in the

---

20. Hubbard, *Joshua* p. 160.

21. J. Calvin, *Calvin's Commentaries Vol IV Joshua*, (Grand Rapids USA: Baker Books, 2003), p. 73.

land is named, Gilgal, the significance of that name has to wait for its explanation (5:9).

Joshua's first action once they have made camp is to set up the memorial with the twelve stones from the Jordan. In recording this as the first action, the narrator is returning the focus to what has been witnessed. The purpose of the stones is to witness to the promise of God – fulfilled by His miraculous intervention, bringing the people into the land. To confirm this central idea of witness further, Joshua issues some instructions concerning the way the memory of what God has done should be kept alive. Although His instructions are similar to those spoken to the twelve men in 4:5-7, there are some differences:

- they are spoken to all the Israelites
- they look further ahead than the next generation – 'In the future your descendants ask ... '
- the explanation is fuller, it encompasses the whole of God's rescue from Egypt to the Promised Land.

With regard to this last point we have seen on a number of occasions how what is happening in the story carries echoes of the Exodus. Now, Joshua makes that connection explicit:

> The LORD your God did to the Jordan what he had done to the Red Sea when he dried it up before us until we had crossed over (4:23).

In this way Joshua points out the continuous thread of salvation history, of the grace of God that runs through Israel's own history.

The section comes to a conclusion with Joshua declaring the great purpose of God. It is 'that all the peoples of the earth might know that the hand of the LORD is powerful' (4:24). This statement, in one sense, brings the narrative full circle. It began with an emphasis on what Israel will 'know' as a result of this event (see above on 3:7-17). Now, however, 'all the peoples of the earth' will know of God, who He is and what He does. There are, however, implications for Israel too – they are, 'that you might always fear the LORD your God' (4:24). This 'fear' is an expression of faith in the Old Testament; it speaks of reverence, awe and obedience before God. To put it another way: 'The surrounding pagans may be struck with wonder, but the Lord's people should worship.'[22] In the light of all that unfolded in the narrative so far, we may ask, 'And who are the Lord's people?' The answer must be those who truly recognise and trust the Lord. And these may be outside the nation of Israel. The words of 4:23 echo the words of Rahab – 'we have heard how the LORD dried up the water of the Red Sea' (2:10). This news caused her to confess in her own way 'that the hand of the LORD is powerful' (4:24); that He is God and there is no other. It is clearly one thing to 'know' and another to 'fear'. Marten Woudstra comments: 'In Rahab's case this recognition led to her rescue; in the case of her fellow Canaanites this same recognition led to their doom.'[23]

In many ways, through these two chapters and their story of the crossing the Jordan, the Ark has been centrestage. As the sign of the presence of God with them, it has enabled

---

22. Dodson, *Every Promise* p. 87.

23. Woundstra, *Joshua* p. 97.

them to cross over into the Promised Land. Another major thread that runs through the narrative is that all Israel at various moments and from different perspectives have been able to witness the Lord working on their behalf. And what they witnessed is to be remembered, preserved and passed on to future generations. Having witnessed this fulfilment of God's promise, they need to continue witnessing to the promise, generation after generation.

From text to message

For some commentators the narrative of chapters 3 and 4 do not have a coherent structure. As we noted at the beginning of this chapter, some consider 'too many topics have been crammed into too restricted a narrative space.' This has resulted in these themes becoming 'tangled and knotted'.[24] We have tried to show, as we have worked through the text, that this kind of judgement cannot be the last word. The narrative we have been looking at shows a clear development. It moves the people of Israel (literally) from one bank of the flooded River Jordan to the other. The story may be told with each episode at a different pace, with glances both forward and backward – but these are all part of the story teller's art. If, as we may rightly presume, the book of Joshua was written to be heard in the first place, many of these features are to be expected, rather than to be considered problematic. In any storytelling a brief hint of what is to come, for example, raises both interest and expectation, encouraging the listener to stay engaged with the story. When we preach these narratives we need to use, as far as we are able, similar strategies.

---

24. See full quotation from Nelson, *Joshua* above p. 131.

When it comes to the issue of 'too many topics' being 'crammed into too restrictive a narrative space', the problem may well be one of majoring on minors – elevating narrative ploys to the level of major themes. Recognising both the chief actor in the story and the whole book context will help us identify the main ideas of this section.

Getting the message clear: the theme
The majority of the references to the Ark of the Covenant have been noted in our 'listening to the text'. And the significance of the Ark's role in indicating the presence of God with His people has also been highlighted. But it is clear from the narrative that God's presence is for a purpose; and the major purpose is to bring the people into the Land of Canaan. This is being done in fulfilment of His promise which stretches all the way back to Abraham and has its root in God's creational purposes.

Above all, the events of this whole narrative are witnessing to this promise and the God who stands behind it. As Israel sees and witnesses each part of this story they learn more of their God. So, the story begins and ends:

- 'This is how you will know the living God is among you' (3:10)
- '…all the peoples of the earth might know the hand of the LORD is powerful' (4:24)

Getting the message clear: the aim
The story of these chapters records 'amazing things' (3:5), and we must not minimize or sideline that in our efforts to teach some practical lessons for today. On the other hand we should not spend too much time in our preaching and teaching elevating the exciting at the expense of the

explanation. At least two clear themes from the passage will help us communicate the message of this section to others:

+ the impossibility of people reaching the goal of God's rest without His direct, personal intervention

+ the need not only to experience that intervention for ourselves but also to witness to it

A way in

Rhett Dodson suggests a helpful way in to the story:

> If I said to you, 'Let us meet for coffee on December 24th', what is one of the first things that would likely pop into your mind? 'Why, that is Christmas Eve!'[25]

A very similar reaction would be provoked in the minds of the first readers of the book of Joshua. They would immediately see the connection to the Passover – the date being the day on which preparations began forty years ago. What is happening now is intimately connected with what happened then. God's promise, His plan of salvation, is continuing to be worked out. Another way to approach the events of these chapters is to liken it to a military operation. Although no battles are fought in this section of the book, there is a clear and distinct 'chain of command'.

The sequence in that chain is something like this:

+ the plan and its necessary orders are issued by the 'High Command'

+ the general responsible for the operation gives the orders to the divisions and companies involved

---

25. Dodson, *Every Promise* p. 84.

Witnessing to the Promise (3–4)

+ the plan is carried out by the troops on the ground

As has been indicated earlier this pattern is repeated through these chapters.

Ideas for application

+ God reveals His plan in advance on many occasions in the Old Testament – sometimes with reference to the very near future, sometimes to the long-term future. His Word is shown to be reliable (see Isa. 44:24-26). He kept His Word when He sent Jesus and will keep His Word about Jesus' return.

+ Although God's people had to keep their distance from the Ark, they are able to witness the fact that God was with them, 'up close'. Peter Bolt says:

> The cross is at a distance. It is an event that occurred long ago in a world and culture that, in many ways, seems so foreign to our own. But if we understand this cross correctly, we discover that it is there in that distant cross, that we see God up close.[26]

+ From the very beginning of this part of the narrative the emphasis is on God's activity on behalf of His people. This is what they witness and witness to, and God's people in **every** age bear the same witness to the work of God on their behalf.

+ Joshua's authority is not simply found in the qualities he undoubtedly possessed. It is found, first and foremost, in the fact that he brings to the people an

---

26. P. Bolt, *The Cross from a Distance* (Nottingham, UK Apollos 2004) p. 17.

authoritative word from God. This is the fundamental quality required in all leaders.

- As we have 'listened to the text' above, there have been numerous echoes of the Exodus in these chapters. They provide a further opportunity to stress the consistency and continuity of God's purpose and promise. Numerous lines into the New Testament can be followed. Examples are:
    - Matthew's use of 'this took place to fulfil what the Lord had said though the prophet...' (Matt. 1:22)
    - Mark's 'as it is written' (Mark 1:2)
    - Luke's 'the things that have been fulfilled among us' (Luke 1:1)

  These and many more can be used to encourage people to have confidence in the Word of God, especially for the future.

- The strong emphasis on the Ark of the Covenant is these chapters, focuses attention on the presence of God who is acting on behalf of His people. This focus moves to Jesus, God with us, in the New Testament; and His continuing presence through the Holy Spirit.

- The information concerning the timing of the crossing, pointing to the impossibility of the people moving into the land because of the Jordan in flood, has great significance. What people cannot do for themselves, God does by His saving acts – this is true in both Old Testament and New Testament.

- 'Forgetfulness is the enemy of faith'. The need to be constantly reminded of God's action on His people's behalf is evident in this story. The fact that salvation

Witnessing to the Promise (3–4)

is rooted in history is vital for believers in every age. In our preaching and teaching, in the Lord's Supper, and in many other ways, the links to our historical foundations need to be confirmed.

- The responsibility that every generation to pass on the truths of God's work to His people is clear. Encouragement and strategies to do this need to be given for this communication to happen.

- As this section of the story closes, one of the purposes of God's action is 'that all the people on earth might know' of God's rule and power (4:24). Christ has achieved a far greater rescue; what are we doing to continue the testimony of this world-changing event?

Suggestions for preaching

Sermon 1
A sermon covering the whole of this section can give no more than an overview of the story. Each major episode of that story can be used to teach ideas that are both theological and practical.

The living God is with you (3:1-13)
The people are told in advance what God will do, the significance of it and the fact that He alone performs these 'amazing things.' Key moments are:

- the opportunity to witness God at work (3:1-5)
- knowing 'the living God is among you' (3:10)
- assuring them of a future victory (3:10)

- God is the sole actor in the drama – making the water 'stand up in a heap' (3:13)

Remember all he has done for you (3:14–4:14)
The whole event must be not only a part of their collective memory but also a living faith passed on from generation to generation.

- what they saw and experienced (3:14-17)
- the need to remember and pass on the truth of this event (4:1-9)
- remembering cannot be separated from obedience (4:10-14)

Honour God as the 'Lord of all the earth' (4:15-24)
After one more demonstration of God's control over all things, a fuller explanation of the event is given, linking it back to the Exodus. Finally the purpose behind the event is explained. Key points are:

- the return of the waters (4:18)
- the date of Israel's arrival in Canaan (4:19)
- the fuller explanation of the stones (4:21-23)
- the contrasting reactions – 'know' and 'fear' (4:24)

As Christians, we have the living God with us through Christ and His death for us and by His Spirit indwelling us. The right response is to honour Him as Lord in both word and deed.

Sermon 2 (3:1-17)
One of the difficulties in preaching from narrative is to involve our hearers in the story while teaching the

Witnessing to the Promise (3–4)

underlying truths. A suggested way of working with the flow (no pun intended!) of the story is:

The right way to begin (3:1-5)
This part of the story can be re-told with an emphasis and explanation on three key phrases:

- 'keep a distance' (3:4)
- 'consecrate yourselves' (3:5)
- 'the Lord will do amazing things' (3:5)

The wrong time of the year (3:6-15a)
The chain of command is followed through – from the Lord to Joshua, from Joshua to the priests and the Israelites. The instructions prepare for the crossing, but in our division of the chapter it ends with a very significant comment (3:15a). Some important markers in the text are:

- the crossing will act as a guarantee for the conquest – because 'the living God is among you' (3:10)
- the waters will 'stand up in a heap'; only 'the Lord of all the earth 'can do this' (3:13)
- even though this might seem impossible because the river is in flood – it is the wrong time of the year (3:15a)

The only way in (3:15b-17)
Entry into the Promised Land is only possible through the work of God. Note again the focus on the Ark:

- the water stops as it reaches the edge of the river
- its presence guarantees safe crossing
- 'all Israel' cross on dry land, no one and nothing is lost.

What the Ark symbolises, Christ fulfils; as 'God with us' He has done the 'amazing thing' – given Himself for us – that there can be no barriers to prevent us entering our 'Promised Land'.

Sermon 3 (4:1-14)

The line of command is once more on view, but this time it includes references to Moses. This helps the people to see that Joshua is the true, God-appointed leader. It also confirms that the instructions concerning the memorial are not simply a personal whim of Joshua.

Stones that speak (4:1-9)

The purpose of the stones is to remind and teach the whole nation, generation after generation, concerning the marvellous deeds of God. This is seen particularly in:

- a man from each tribe (4:1-5a)
- a means of education (4:5b-7)
- a permanent sign to the people (4:8-9, see also 4:7)

Feet that obey (4:10-14)

The value of instructions is in the doing of them not just in the knowing of them. It is one thing to know the way – another to walk in it.

- 'the priests remained standing… in the Jordan' (4:10). God's presence is both providing and protecting the way
- 'the people hurried over' (4:10c) and note the comment on this above
- the two-and-a-half tribes played their part

- the chain of command is complete – Joshua's leadership is confirmed (4:14)

There is now only one God-appointed leader for us as the people of God. Remembering Him, communicating the truth about Him and walking in His ways is our calling as the people of God.

Sermon 4 (4:15-24)
A final series of commands and responses closes this section of the book. As before, nothing has happened without a word from the Lord; and through His power the outcome has been achieved. This last episode brings closure to the first stage of Israel's possession of the land. The sequence of events and dialogues unfolds in this way:

The final act (4:15-18)
The 'amazing things' (3:5) are concluded with the water returning in full flood. Once again, no explanation is offered of how it happened, but the timing is perfect and the river 'seals' the people inside the land.

The plot explained (4:19-23)
A fuller explanation is given as to what 'these stones mean' (4:20). Note particularly:

- the 'thread' of dry ground that runs through these verses
- the link to the Exodus

The purpose made clear (4:24)
As noted above (p. 151), the contrast between the nations knowing the power of God and the people of God fearing the Lord.

The final point concerning fearing God can be developed in New Testament terms – faith is more than simple assent to information about the person and work of Christ.

Suggestions for teaching

Questions to help understand the passage

1. How does the way the Ark is portrayed in Joshua, and the names that are used for it, indicate that it is more than a 'lucky charm'?

2. Do you think 'keep a distance' from the Ark and 'consecrate yourselves' have different functions and purposes? Why or why not?

3. Why do you think God promised to 'exalt' Joshua (3:7)? (See also 4:14.)

4. In what sense will witnessing what God does at the River Jordan prepare the people for the conquest of the Land (see 3:9-13)?

5. Note the different names used of the Ark. What does each one add to your understanding of it?

6. What indicators are there in the text that the writer is concerned to emphasise the unity of the people of God?

7. Why do you think the emphasis on remembering is so important in this part of the narrative?

8. In the summary of the crossing (4:10-13) what are the main features and why are they important?

9. How does the story draw to a close and why are these details included?

Witnessing to the Promise (3–4)

10. What is the significance of the way the story ends (4:24)?

Questions to help apply the text

1. The Israelites are instructed by Joshua to keep their focus on God's presence among them. How can we keep our minds, will and hearts focussed on the Lord?

2. What lies at the root of Joshua's authority? What does that mean for us as God's people today?

3. What would you say are the chief qualities the priests need in the task God has given them? What lessons can we learn from this?

4. How has being forgetful hurt your relationships with other people? How does forgetfulness undermine our faith and trust in God?

5. Without building a memorial, how can Christians remind themselves and show the world that God is among us?

6. What provision do we need to make to be able to pass on the faith to future generations?

7. In what ways do the actions of the men from the East Bank tribes challenge and encourage us?

8. The writer has marked out the actual day the crossing was completed. It had great significance for the people. Why is history so important for us as individuals and especially as Christians?

9. Can others really see whom I belong to and whom I serve?

10. In what ways can I show that I believe in God's absolute power and holiness?

3

Realising the Promise (5–6)

Introduction

A promise that is never fulfilled or a hope that is never realized is of little value. Our hearts and minds long to see some realization of the hope that is held out to us. Sometimes it may only be a token of what is to come, a down payment guaranteeing the complete fulfilment. While not trying to second-guess the psychology of the ancient Israelites' minds, the chapters before us certainly offer that sense of realization. The waters of the Jordan have closed behind them bringing them into the Promised Land. The next step is to begin possession of it. Except, before that can happen, there are some necessary preliminary activities that have to be completed. There is no sense in the narrative before us that the people of God are at liberty either to do what they like with God's gift, or to assume that they now can manage without Him. As we explore this story we will see that both the people of God's present, as well as their future, is inextricably linked with their past. We will also see that the promise cannot be realized without the continuing presence of God – the God who fights on behalf of His people.

Listening to the text

Context and structure

Joshua and the people of Israel have had God's promise re-affirmed and have witnessed the dramatic prelude to the gift in the land. At the heart of all they have seen has been the Ark, reminding them it is by God's power and action that their inheritance will come to them. Now, as they move to the next phase of the story, their standing as God's own people has to be recognised and they need to remember continually that they are a rescued people, with a God who fights for them.

The next stage in the drama can be outlined in the following episodes:

5:1-9	a problem solved
5:10-12	the promise celebrated
5:13-15	allegiance or obedience?
6:1-5	how to achieve the impossible
6:6-14	the silent threat
6:15-21	God's battle
6:22-27	a welcome and a warning

Working through the text

A problem solved (5:1-9)

A number of commentators see 5:1 as the conclusion of the previous story – and it does give a summary of the reaction to the events of chapters 3 and 4. But the verse also acts as a hinge on which the story turns, so I have chosen to include

Realising the Promise (5–6)

it in this section. It acts as a prologue to what is about to happen among the people of Israel. It records the response of the Amorite and Canaanite kings:

> **Now** when all the Amorite kings along the coast heard how the Lord had dried up the Jordan before the Israelites until they had crossed over, their hearts melted in fear and they no longer had the courage to face the Israelites. (5:1 emphasis mine)

The word translated 'courage' here is the Hebrew word for 'spirit' or 'breath'; so the NET Bible translates this as 'they could not even breathe for fear of the Israelites'. If we ask, 'Why are they so unnerved and dispirited?' Adolf Harstad suggests the answer is:

> They are forced to ask, 'If not even the surging river can block the Lord from leading his people to their promised inheritance, what can?'[1]

With this information, we are prepared for what comes next in the story. The people of Canaan are immobilized before the command is given that will temporarily immobilize the people of Israel. The Lord provides the condition that will allow His people to obey His command. And they certainly need that provision – otherwise, what they are about to do represents a catastrophic failure in strategic thinking. Because:

> At that time the Lord said to Joshua, 'Make flint knives and circumcise the Israelites again' (5:2).

It might seem that this command puts the whole enterprise at risk. The fighting men will be disabled for some days.

---

1. Adolph Harstad, *Joshua Concordia Commentary* (St Louis USA: Concordia Publishing House, 2004) p. 221.

But this is only a problem if you lose sight of the promise of God and His sovereign assurance of it. Obedient to God's command, this is exactly what Joshua did (5:3). Before we can even raise the question, 'Why do this?' and 'Why do it now?', the narrator provides the answer. In the first place, the army that God would use in the conquest was made up of uncircumcised men. Secondly, this was a completely new generation, the old having died in the wilderness (5:4-6a). Our perception of the rite and importance of circumcision is often coloured by our reading of the New Testament. Paul, in particular, engages in controversy over its use and value. We need to consider it in its Old Testament context. Since the days of Abraham (Gen. 17) circumcision had been the distinguishing mark of the people of God. Here, in the book of Joshua, it is commanded afresh of the people. There has been little mention of the rite between Genesis 17 and our chapter – the incident with Moses being an exception in Exodus 4. The emphasis on the need for circumcision at this point in the narrative is to mark a new era for the people of God. They are being reconstituted as God's people as, under this sign, they take their place within the promises of God.

The progression through verse 5-7 makes this new start clear:

> All the people that came out had been circumcised, but all the people born in the wilderness during the journey from Egypt had not (5:5).

A distinction is being drawn between the two generations; and a dark shadow hung over the older generation, they:

> ... moved about in the wilderness for forty years until all the men who were of military age when they left Egypt had died, since they had not obeyed the LORD (5:6).

The demise of this generation in the wilderness was not just some unfortunate fact of history, it was God's judgement on them.

> The LORD had sworn to them that they would not see the land that he had solemnly promised their ancestors to give us, a land flowing with milk and honey (5:6).

This, however, is not the end of the story, the promise persists and is now applied to the next generation:

> So he [God] raised up their sons in their place, and these were the ones Joshua circumcised. They were still uncircumcised because they had not been circumcised on the way (5:7).

If the people of old had failed, the promise of God had not – He raised up a new people for Himself. And this new people are marked once more with the covenant sign of circumcision.

The most obvious incident in the story of Israel, which might be in the background of 5:6, is Numbers 14. There the disobedience of the people, the forty years of wilderness wandering, the death of the current generation, according to God's oath to their ancestors, are all clearly recorded. At the heart of the former generation's attitude to God was a refusal to obey the Word of God – 'they had not obeyed the LORD' (5:6). Their disobedience was particularly evidenced by their grumbling and complaining about God and His provision for them, both the land and the leaders. Despite all they had experienced, their rebellion meant that 'their bodies were scattered in the wilderness' (1 Cor. 10:5; the whole section 1 Cor. 10:1-13 sheds light on this part of their history and applies it to New Testament believers).

The new generation, however, submitted to the command of God. The narrator gives no hint of dissension in the camp, despite the precarious situation (humanly speaking) in which the people found themselves. In undergoing this rite a major problem is solved for the people. David Firth offers this explanation of the problem:

> Since male circumcision was meant to be the sign of the covenant that existed between Yahweh and Israel, those who were not circumcised were effectively excluded from the divine promises, and that included the land.[2]

The narrator has already hinted at a further aspect of the problem for Israel in 4:19 with his reference to the tenth day of the first month – the day preparations must start for the Passover. Any uncircumcised male should automatically be excluded from the feast according to Exodus 12:48. Again, a problem is solved for the people. Although it has not yet been announced, they are appropriately prepared for the Passover (5:10-12).

This whole section has a pair of matching bookends:

- 5:2 a word of command from the Lord
- 5:3 a report of the completed action.

This is balanced by:

- 5:8 a report of the completed action
- 5:9 a word from the Lord.

The writer begins and ends the section with a focus on God and His Word. In doing this he underlines the fact that the

---

2. David Firth, *The Message of Joshua* (Nottingham, UK IVP 2015), p. 68.

initiative for the act of circumcision comes from the Lord and not from the people. It is not a work offered **to** God, but an act of grace *from* God.

The closing 'bookend' offers both a demonstration of God's sovereign control and an explanation of His command. The demonstration of His control is seen in the fact that:

> ... after the whole nation had been circumcised, they remained where they were in camp until they were healed (5:8).

And they had the peace and security they needed for their recovery because the surrounding nations were paralyzed with fear (5:1). The explanation for this act of covenant renewal comes in 5:9:

> Then the LORD said to Joshua, 'Today I have rolled away the reproach of Egypt from you'. So the place has been called Gilgal to this day.

A variety of views is offered by commentators as to what the 'reproach of Egypt' is. Some point back to the time of slavery in Egypt, but this is not mentioned directly in the text. It is more likely a reference to the time of wilderness wandering, which is in focus in the text (5:4-7). This period would have given opportunity for the Egyptians to mock the wandering nation concerning the inadequacy of Israel's God to bring them to their final destination. But chiefly it points to the disobedience and punishment of the generation that left Egypt.

Robert Hubbard Jr encapsulated both aspects when he says:

Through circumcision (and in Canaan, too!), this generation confirms its obedient spirit and gives Yahweh warrant to declare the past humiliation dead and buried, never to be thrown accusingly at Israel again.[3]

As the name 'Gilgal' and verb 'roll away' come from the same Hebrew root, the place stands as a picture, a reminder of God's great declaration. With this renewal of the covenant relationship, a new day can dawn.

The promise celebrated (5:10-12)

Once more the narrator adds an important time-marker. Our attention is turned to 'the fourteenth day of the [first] month' (5:10). The link with the Exodus is made clear by the mention of this date. Forty years on from the original Passover, they celebrate it again – and in the Promised Land! An indication of the certainty that the journey was over for Israel is the threefold repetition of the fact that they could now eat the produce of the land, rather than the manna that had sustained them through the wilderness:

- the day after the Passover they ate some of the produce of the land (5:11)
- the manna stopped the day after they ate this food from the land (5:12a)
- that year they ate the produce of Canaan (5:12b)

This does not imply any lessening of God's care for His people – where once He supplied their needs by 'supernatural' means, He now does so by 'natural' means. The people of God do not need a constant series of

---

3. Robert Hubbard, Jr, *Joshua NIVAC* (Grand Rapids, USA: Zondervan 2009), p. 182.

extraordinary events to see the faithfulness of God – that can be seen in the events of everyday life. In mentioning the time-marker of 5:10 above, we did not highlight how specific it is; it tells us that it was 'on the evening of the fourteenth day'. The new generation are acting in obedience to the Law (see Exod. 12:6 and Deut. 16:6) and this is not just an ordinary celebration of the Passover. There are three elements connecting this brief account that mark it as being of great significance.

They are:

- the textual link to the Exodus from Egypt. In Exodus 12:3 and Joshua 4:19 the day of preparation is recorded. This does not appear in any other account of the Passover.

- the description of Canaan as 'a land flowing with milk and honey' is only mentioned in the context of both the original Exodus Passover and in Joshua (see Exod. 13:5 and Josh. 5:6).[4]

- In Exodus the Passover anticipates the move to the Promised Land, and in Joshua that move is accomplished.

This Passover celebrates what we might call the finished work of God – the redemption from Egypt and the beginning of new life in God's land. So, in this somewhat cryptic account, we see the promise of God celebrated. The Passover looks back to what that promise has accomplished; it strengthens and assures the people of what is still to come.

---

4. See David Howard, Jr, *Joshua NAC* (Nashville, USA: Broadman & Holman 1998), p. 153 for details.

Further thoughts on …
the Passover

Despite its importance in the life of Israel, the Passover is not given a high profile in the majority of the Old Testament; while the Exodus is frequently referenced and alluded to in many places. The main passages that contain a record of the Passover being celebrated are:

- Exodus 12 – it is part of the initial act of redemption from slavery and the prelude to new life in Canaan.

- Numbers 9 – a year after their rescue the people of God are called to celebrate it again 'at the appointed time' (Num. 9:2).

- Joshua 5 – celebrating the end of the 'reproach' and the beginning of the new life in the Promised Land.

- 2 Chronicles 30 – in the days of Hezekiah it was celebrated a month later than prescribed in the Law. It was to mark a national turning back to God and representatives from all Israel were present.

- 2 Kings 22–23 – in the reign of Josiah, after the dark days of Manasseh, the Passover represented the beginning of reform and temporary relief from Assyrian oppression.

- Ezra 6 – c. 515 B.C., this Passover marked the return (albeit partial) from exile and the restoration of the Temple in Jerusalem.

Each of these celebrations recorded in the Old Testament mark great turning points for the people of

> God. They mark the leaving behind of a dark period in their past and the beginning of new hope and life. They reflect on the grace of God demonstrated in salvation and mercy towards those who respond to Him. Both singly and together they point towards the great, final Exodus to be accomplished in Christ, our Passover Lamb (see Luke 9:31 marginal reading & 1 Cor. 5:7).

Allegiance or obedience? (5:13-15)

For a brief while the focus of attention is turned on Joshua alone. The people have been prepared for the conquest to come, they are now in the right relationship with God through those two great signs of the covenant – circumcision and Passover. It would seem from these verses that there is one final, and decisive, preparation to be made. The focus is on Joshua as the leader of the people and it makes a statement about the basis on which he will lead and how the battles ahead will be won.

Why Joshua is where he is, is not explained. The emphasis in the story is on whom he meets.

> Now when Joshua was near Jericho, he looked up and saw a man standing in front of him with a drawn sword in his hand (5:13).

The narrator records the incident from Joshua's perspective, he is suddenly surprised to see an armed man in front of him. Our English translators do not have an appropriate way of expressing the surprise contained in the Hebrew text. Two attempts to convey that sense are:

+ Joshua 'raised his eyes and looked – and look – a man.'

- 'He looked, and what do you know! A man standing opposite him.'[5]

Apparently, as if from nowhere, this threatening figure with a drawn sword comes on to the scene. It is no surprise that Joshua immediately asks, 'Are you for us or for our enemies?' He needs to know if this is a friend or foe. It is his immediate priority to find out about this man's allegiance.

The enigmatic answer given by the man to Joshua is variously translated by our English versions. The NIV by translating the opening word as 'neither' can imply that the man was not on Joshua's side or his enemy's. The context clearly shows this is not the case. A simple and more accurate translation is given by the ESV, 'No!'. The rest of his reply clarifies his negative answer:

> ... as the commander of the LORD's army I have now come (5:14).

This immediately changes the terms of Joshua's confrontation with this man. It is no longer a question of where the man's allegiance lies, but rather where Joshua's will. Will he be obedient to God's commander? Will he recognise that it is the army of the LORD that ensures victory? To reinforce the idea that it will be God's victory, the Commander says, 'I have come now'. Calvin asks in what sense can the Commander and the army of the LORD be said to come 'now'. There is every evidence that God has been with them so far. Calvin goes on to say (quaintly but accurately):

> ...according to the common usage of scripture, God is said to come to us when we are actually made sensible of

---

5. Hubbard suggests this translation in *Joshua NIVAC* p. 185. See also Howard, *Joshua NAC* p. 156.

his assistance, which seems remote when not manifested by experience. It is therefore just as if he were offering his assistance in the combats which were about to be waged, and promising by his arrival that the war would have happy issue.[6]

Joshua immediately recognises that he is in the presence of someone who is enormously superior to him, and he acts accordingly. He 'fell face down to the ground in reverence,' thereby showing his submission to the man's authority. This is immediately followed by Joshua's question, 'What message does my Lord have for his servant?' The relationship between the two is clearly expressed in the words 'Lord' and 'servant'. To underline the heavenly nature of this appearance and intervention, the Commander says:

> 'Take off your sandals, for the place where you are standing is holy.' And Joshua did so (5:15).

Now we may be tempted to ask, 'What kind of preparation for battle is this?' And the answer is, 'The most perfect and complete kind of preparation'. Joshua had been promised that 'the LORD your God will be with you wherever you go' (Josh 1:9) and as he lies prostrate on the ground, he knows that to be true.

Marten Woudstra puts it beautifully:

> Joshua has been made aware of the presence of the One greater than man whose drawn sword clearly speaks of combat readiness and whose army is nothing less than that of the Lord himself. What more is there to know before the Conquest is to begin in earnest?[7]

---

6. J. Calvin, *Calvin's Commentaries Vol IV Joshua*, (Grand Rapids USA: Baker Books, 2003) p. 88 see also Harstad, *Joshua* p. 217.

7. Woudstra p. 106.

The issue is no longer one of allegiance – 'Whose side are you on?' – but of obedience.

> ## Further thoughts on ... the Commander of the Lord's army
>
> Viewing this passage from the perspective of the first readers, two earlier incidents would probably have come to mind.
>
> They are:
>
> - Numbers 22:23-31 – when 'the angel of the LORD with a drawn sword in his hand' blocked the path of Balaam. This story was undoubtedly known to Joshua and yet for some reason, he did not immediately make the connection.
>
> - Exodus 3:1-10 – when Moses was confronted by the burning bush and 'the angel of the LORD appeared to him in flames of fire from within the bush.' When God spoke to Moses He used almost identical words to those spoken to Joshua – 'Take off your sandals, for the place where you are standing is holy ground.'
>
> In both of these incidents there is a movement from the angel to God Himself:
>
> - Numbers 22:35 – 'The angel of the LORD said ... speak only what I tell you'.
>
> - Numbers 22:38 – 'Balaam replied ... I must speak only what God puts in my mouth.'
>
> - Exodus 3:2 – 'the angel of the Lord appeared to him'.

- Exodus 3:4 – 'God called to him from within the bush'.

With this basic data in mind, we can turn to the three most common ways of understanding this particular appearance – the Commander of the Lord's army.[1]

- The Commander is an angel who is sent with a particular purpose or message to prepare Joshua for what lies ahead.

- This is an appearance of God Himself as the divine warrior to reassure Joshua before the battle and to demonstrate His control of the situation.

- It is sometimes suggested that this is a Christophany – an appearance of the pre-existent Christ – the one portrayed in the book of Revelation as the great Victor (see Rev. 19:11-16).

As the story unfolds in the book of Joshua, there is a movement similar to the one noted above in the passages from Numbers and Exodus. Chapter 5 ends with the words of the Commander and chapter 6 continues with the words of the Lord (see below for the role of 6:1 as a 'hinge' in the story). This would suggest that in terms of the Old Testament narrative there is a considerable overlap between the first ways of understanding who the Commander is. But, do we have any evidence for making the final step and understanding him to be the

---

1. Howard, *Joshua NAC* p. 159f; Harstad, *Joshua* pp. 253f and see Andrew Malone, *Knowing Jesus in the Old Testament* (Nottingham, UK: IVP 2015) chapter 6.

pre-existent Christ, I am not sure we can definitively make this claim. As David Howard points out, the New Testament readily identifies Christ with the Old Testament characters of King, Messiah and Priest, but it never makes the identification of Christ as the Angel of the Lord.[2] Bruce Waltke offers evidence that a common feature of Old Testament times was that 'an earthly royal messenger ... was fully equated with his sender ... and is to be treated with all the respect and deference expected to be accorded to the king himself'. His conclusion is worth quoting in full:

> Also, bear in mind that the New Testament writers equate Jesus Christ with *YHWH*; they never dishonour him by demoting him to the status of a mere angel. In sum, the angel of *I AM* is best regarded as a special heavenly messenger that is so closely related to God's presence that he is equated with God's self-manifestation.[3]

---

2. Howard, *Joshua* NAC p. 160.

3. Bruce Waltke, *An Old Testament Theology* (Grand Rapids, USA: Zondervan, 2007), p. 602 n34.

How to achieve the impossible (6:1-5)
There is some debate as to how 6:1 fits into the narrative. It is thought by some to round off the previous section, by others, to introduce a new section. These functions are not exclusive and it is better to see the verse as a hinge on which the story turns. The verse looks back to the narrative before, showing what effect the various episodes have had on the inhabitants of Jericho. It also looks forward to how such an impossible situation will be dealt with by extraordinary means. Whether the city of Jericho was 'shut up inside and

out because of the people of Israel' (6:1 ESV) or because they had barricaded themselves in, or the Israelites had laid siege to the city is not clear. Previous comments about the fear the Canaanites felt because of Israel and her God probably indicate the former.

As in earlier parts of the story, the chain of command is maintained – God speaks to Joshua (6:2-5) and Joshua passes on the order to the people (6:6-7). In God's words to Joshua we begin to see how the impossible will be achieved. Once again, it will all be accomplished by God:

> Then the LORD said to Joshua, 'See I have delivered Jericho into your hands, along with its king and its fighting men' (6:2).

God tells Joshua of the guaranteed outcome before He tells him how it is to be accomplished. As we know by now, this is a constant theme through the early part of the book – the land is a gift from God. If the fighting men have been delivered into Joshua's hand there is really only one other barrier to overcome – the walls. God's instructions now turn to this issue (6:3-5). The armed men are to march round the city once each day for six days. On the seventh day they are to march round seven times. Then, on a signal they are to shout, the walls will collapse and the city will be taken. An obvious question at this point is, why wait for seven days? It would certainly be possible for the Lord to bring the walls of Jericho down in an instant, but that is not the plan. Knowing that plan, the Israelites must trust God to fulfil it. The taking of Jericho is the first major conquest in the land and it sets the pattern for all future battles. The people must believe in and rely on the Lord's provision and timing, this is the only route to victory.

This need for faith is crucial according to the writer of Hebrews:

> By faith the walls of Jericho fell, after the army had marched round them for seven days. (Heb. 11:30)

It was not by force of arms that Jericho was defeated but by the sovereign act of God. The non-military nature of the defeat is emphasised by other elements in the text:

- The priests seem to have the primary role in the instructions given by the Lord. Although the fighting men are part of the procession the role of the priests with their trumpets – heralding the progress of the Ark – is centrestage.

- The Ark, symbolising the presence of God, is again in evidence. God with His people is the guarantee of victory; the fighting men have a 'supporting role' in the drama.

- The repetition of the number 'seven' is surely significant as well: seven priests, seven trumpets, seven days of circling the city and seven circuits on the seventh day. In the Old Testament the number 'seven' is often associated with the idea of completeness and fulfilment. Philip Jenson adds: 'The association of seven with completeness, totality and perfection makes an association with divinity and holiness a natural one. Ritual actions occur seven times and correspond to the invocation of God's power, as in the fall of a city (Josh. 6), the raising of the dead (2 Kings 4:35), or the "performative" pronouncements of blessing and curses' (Gen. 4:24; Deut. 28).[8]

---

8. Philip Jenson, art. Seven, *New International Dictionary of Old Testa-*

These emphases show that Israel are not 'merely acting out some superstitious ritual,' they are following the command of God to whom the city is dedicated in judgement.[9] Facing a city that is 'securely barred' against them (6:1), the Israelites are singularly unprepared by their desert experience to engage in siege warfare. But, the instructions from the Lord prepare them to achieve the (apparently) impossible.

The silent threat (6:6-14)

The command that Joshua had received is now relayed to the priests (6:6) and then to the people (6:8). As on previous occasions some extra information is given. The priests' role is yet again subservient to the Ark – they are the heralds and bearers of it (see comment on 6:11 below). It is possible that they were heralds of something else of great significance. In 6:4 they are instructed to use 'trumpets of rams' horns;' and the addition of the qualifier 'rams' horns' may have a deliberate echo of the Jubilee as prescribed in Leviticus. Of the twenty-seven occurrences of this word in the Old Testament, twenty of them are in Leviticus with a direct relationship to the year of Jubilee. The trumpets of *rams' horns* that announced the start of the festival gave their name to it. A chief focus of the festival was the transfer of land and property. In 6:6-8, the NIV omits the qualifier 'rams' horns' and just speaks of trumpets (cf. ESV). The first readers would have heard a distinct echo of the Jubilee and that at a time when land was about to be transferred into their possession.

---

    ment Theology and Exegesis (Grand Rapids USA: Zondervan, 1997), vol 4 p. 35.

9. Harstad, *Joshua* p. 277; we will deal more with the idea of dedication below.

Daniel Hawk comments that:

> By evoking the Jubilee, the narrator also deflects any notion that possession constitutes ownership. The land is YHWH's to give, and Israel will possess the land only because YHWH has promised it will be so.[10]

Another significant choice of vocabulary by the narrator in these verses is the verb that he uses to speak of the progress of the procession. The verbs highlighted in the verses below are all the same in Hebrew:

> And he ordered the army, '**Advance**! March round the city, with an armed guard **going ahead** of the ark of the Lord'. When Joshua had spoken to the people, the seven priests carrying the seven trumpets before the Lord **went forwards** blowing their trumpets … (6:7-8).

In each of these cases, the verb is the one used approximately 28 times in the narrative to this point – it is most frequently translated 'cross over' and is a key word of the conquest. What Israel is now doing at Jericho is part of the greater plan and promise of God.

The march round Jericho is orderly and consistent. The column takes up the same positions day by day – fighting men, priests, the Ark and the rear-guard (cf. 6:6-7 & 8-9). Central to the procession is the Ark and the one it represents. At one point the narrator does not feel the necessity of mentioning the Ark and simply says, 'the priests carrying the trumpets before the Lord went forward' (6:8). The only noise while the people circled the city was that of the trumpets. The army were to keep perfectly silent – 'Do

---

10. L. Daniel Hawk, *Joshua, Berit Olam* (Collegeville USA: Liturgical Press, 2000), p. 95.

not give a war cry, do not raise your voice, do not say a word' (6:10). Rather than insult or seek to unnerve the people of Jericho, rather than sing, chant or joke to boost their own spirits, they present a silent threat day after day. The day would come when they would shout. Day one ends by the narrator noting the most important element of it, Joshua 'had the ark of the LORD carried round the city' (6:11).

Day two begins bright and early. As when they prepared to cross the Jordan, the early start to the day is an indicator of willingness, of prompt obedience (see 3:1). The column goes out in the same order and in silence apart from the trumpets. The narrator records this in an almost pedantic way underlining the consistency of the event. And he adds, 'They did this for six days' (6:14). It is, to a degree, fruitless to try to analyse the psychology of those on either side in this situation. The writer does not give us any material on which to speculate. For Israel, all we can say is that they had to continue to act by faith, trusting that God knew what He was doing. Concerning the people of Jericho, they had at least six days of grace to respond as one of their fellow-citizens had – Rahab. Meanwhile the silent threat continued; the nature of that threat was yet to be revealed.

God's battle (6:15-21)

The story now moves quickly to its conclusion. Where it had been Joshua who 'got up early' on the first day (6:12), on the seventh day the whole nation 'got up at daybreak' (6:15). There is already a sense of anticipation in the air. And the focus now seems to be more on the people than on the progress of the Ark. This is the day that the people have their part to play in the defeat of Jericho. First, however, they will need the intervention of the Lord to deal with the walls. That intervention will happen on this, the seventh day. Above all else, the seventh day signals the day of completion, the climax of the week.[11]

So:

> On the seventh day they rose early, at the dawn of the day, and marched around the city in the same manner seven times. It was **only** on **that** day that they marched around the city seven times. (6:15 ESV emphasis added)

After six days of silent marching and six silent circuits on the seventh day, finally a new order comes:

> The seventh time round, when the priests sounded the trumpet blast, Joshua commanded the army, 'Shout! For the LORD has given you the city.' (6:16).

Although the army is finally to go into action, the victory is already sure – delivered to them by the Lord.

Following this rousing command and word of encouragement, we would expect to plunge straight into the story of Jericho's fall. Yet again, the narrator changes the pace to deal with another issue first. He now records Joshua's words concerning what should happen to Jericho and its inhabitants.

First:

> The city and all that is in it are to be devoted to the LORD (6:17a).

This command makes concrete the earlier Word of God through Moses concerning the destruction of the cities and

---

11. See Gordon McConville & Stephen Williams, *Joshua, Two Horizons Commentary* (Grand Rapids, USA: Eerdmans 2010), p. 34 for a suggested link to creation story.

inhabitants of Canaan (see Deut. 7:1-5 & 20:16-18). It is part of God waging war through Israel on pagan nations. The term used for this 'devoting to the LORD' is the Hebrew *herem* sometimes translated as 'the ban'.

Robert Hubbard says:

> In a context of Yahweh's war, *herem* takes on a specific religious meaning. It requires the devotion to Yahweh of anything classed as *herem* either through special custody provision (e.g. Josh. 6:19) or through total destruction.

He observes that this means that nothing can be taken as plunder by the conquerors. Also, it should not be seen as a sacrifice offered to God in any way. He adds:

> ... it simply constitutes the way Yahweh requires Israel to implement his exclusive ownership. Thus, Joshua's declaration of Jericho as *herem* affirms that Yahweh owns it exclusively and seals the fate of everything in it.[12]

The implications of the ban for Israel are made perfectly clear by Joshua as he goes on to say:

> But keep away from the devoted things, so that you will not bring about your own destruction by taking any of them. Otherwise you will make the camp of Israel liable to destruction and bring trouble on it (6:18).

This, as we shall see, is a warning that is not heeded by everyone in Israel, with tragic consequences. The 'special custody provisions' mentioned by Hubbard are also made clear. Any articles of silver, gold, bronze and iron are to go into the Lord's treasury (6:19).

---

12. Hubbard, *Joshua NIVAC* pp. 191-192 see also *Further thoughts* below.

The second element of Joshua's speech concerns Rahab and the promise made to her by the spies.

> Only Rahab the prostitute and all who are with her in her house shall be spared, because she hid the spies we sent (6:17b).

Although the saving of Rahab (and her family) may seem to be in contradiction of God's earlier commands (Deut. 7:1-5 & 20:16-18), it is, in fact, further evidence of the implications of Rahab's confession of faith (especially in 2:11). This confession has removed her from the sphere of God's judgement and included her within the people of God (see 6:25).

Finally the blow falls on Jericho – 'the trumpets sounded ... the army shouted ... the walls collapsed' (6:20). The narrative style here gives the lie to the accusation by Richard Dawkins, quoted earlier, that Joshua is 'a text remarkable for the bloodthirsty massacres it records and xenophobic relish with which it does so.'[13] In fact, it is a brief, almost staccato account of the fall of Jericho. When compared to the episode of crossing the Jordan (3:14-17) it contains minimal information.

Having noted this feature of the story David Howard goes on to say:

> ... this fits the general outlook of the book, that military matters belonged to God and that he would effortlessly fight Israel's battles. Protracted attention to battle details would undermine this sense of the effortless taking of the land of Canaan.[14]

---

13. See above p. 17.

14. Howard, *Joshua* NAC p. 174.

The walls' collapse is described literally as 'the wall fell in its place' or 'the wall fell under itself', it was not as the result of any action by the Israelites. As the army took the city, we are left in no doubt that this is God's battle.

> ## Further thoughts on ... the ban (herem)
>
> At the risk of repeating some of the things I have already said in the section *Battles and bloodshed*, the final verse of the section we have been considering raises some uncomfortable issues for Christians:
>
> > They devoted the city to the LORD and destroyed with the sword every living thing in it – men and women, young and old, cattle, sheep and donkeys (6:21).
>
> Some preliminary comments are in order before we turn to the text again and look briefly as some of the implications. First, we must not let the shadow of Marcion fall across our approach to this story. We can do this in a number of ways, including:
>
> + ignoring this part of the story as either too difficult or too disturbing to communicate
>
> + devaluing the Old Testament narrative by treating the New Testament, and especially Christ's commands as a better way
>
> + imposing our own moral intuitions on it, rather than reading it in the context of the wider scriptural story.

Concerning the last of these approaches, Kevin Vanhoozer says:

> I find it interesting that [some] treat their own moral intuitions about what a perfect being *must* do as more reliable (dare I say inerrant?) than the biblical text. As Christians, they should know that the wisdom of the world is the foolishness of God.[1]

Secondly, we must remind ourselves that this is not the 'rules of engagement' for war generally in the Old Testament. This was a specific time-related event as part of the Conquest. We described it above as 'A war like no other.'

The verses before us speak of 'the ban' in at least three ways: it concerns *devotion* to the Lord, it warns of the *danger* involved and it results in *destruction*.[2] Each of these adds to the full picture of the nature of the 'the ban'.

Devotion: The NIV footnote explains 'devoted' in 6:7 as follows: 'The Hebrew term refers to the irrevocable giving over of things or persons to the Lord, often by totally destroying them.' The initiative for the action does not arise from among the Israelites; it comes to them as a command from God. This devoting of people and goods to the Lord has a particular theological significance. The events recorded in Joshua 5 make

---

1. Kevin Vanhoozer, *Five views on Biblical Inerrancy* (Grand Rapids, USA: Zondervan 2013), p. 232.

2. Based on the ESV rendering of these verses, Rhett Dodson sees a similar pattern in *Every Promise of Your Word* (Edinburgh, UK: Banner of Truth, 2016) p. 135.

this clear. Israel could not come to this battle without appropriate spiritual preparations.

Tremper Longman says:

> As odd as it may seem to modern sensibilities, battle is portrayed as an act of worship in the Hebrew Bible ... since at the heart of holy war is God's presence with the army ... Israel had to be as spiritually prepared as they could be to approach the sanctuary.[3]

Although 'holy war' may not be the best way to describe these battles, it underlines the importance of recognising the presence of the holy God, fighting for His people.

Danger: One of the major dangers of 'the ban', that is the removal of people and things from the normal sphere into God's sphere, is expressed in Josh 6:18.

> But keep away from the devoted things, so that you will not bring about your own destruction by taking any of them.

To do this, places the person who takes the devoted things into the same situation as the Canaanites. The seriousness and danger of this will be made clear in the Achan story (Josh. 7).

Destruction: The outcome of the ban is that 'every living thing' in the city is destroyed (6:21), and this is done in line with the commands given to Moses and subsequently to Joshua. This destruction is not a wanton

---

3. Tremper Longman III & Daniel Reid, *God is a Warrior* (Grand Rapids, USA: Zondervan, 1995) p. 35.

act of violence against innocent or harmless people. It is, as previously argued, a judicial act – imposing God's judgement on an evil people. Also, it is not an act that is a knee-jerk response or a mindless act of violence. It comes at the end of a few centuries of patience (see Gen. 15:6) and an ever-increasing tally of sinful acts. Further, it is not just the due punishment enacted – although it certainly is that – it is also preservative in nature. We suggested earlier that it is appropriate to see the ban as a disinfecting of the land. This is to prevent the contagion of Canaanite sin spreading into the people of God. The next story, concerning Achan, shows just how necessary that is.

The stipulation that 'every living thing' should be destroyed needs further comment. Among the many evil practices recorded, a variety of sexual (mal-) practices stands at the heart of Canaanite society.

We will note just two among many. Adultery was seen as a religious duty. As Clay Jones comments:

> The Canaanites even remake the God of the Bible, El, after their own image and portray him ceremonially having sex with two women (or goddesses). The ceremony ends with the direction, 'To be repeated five times by the company and the singers of the assembly.'[4]

Another feature of Canaanite life was bestiality. It was praised in their religious literature and dreaming of sex

---

4. Clay Jones, 'Killing the Canaanites: A Response to the New Atheism's "Divine Genocide"' www.equip.org/articles/killing-the-canaanites downloaded 16/01/2018

with an animal was seen as a good omen. Again, Jones comments,

> This explains why, in certain cities, Yahweh sentenced to death everything that breathes ... no one would want animals around who were used to having sex with human beings.[5]

The whole of a wicked and perverse society had to come under the total judgement of God – and that included the children. Surrounded by a culture of this kind, the habits and actions of one generation would be passed on to the next. Indeed, those actions, taken as the norm, might well be seen as just the starting point for further 'experimentation'.

So, as Tremper Longman says:

> In conclusion we must point out that the Bible does not understand the destruction of the men, women and children of these cities as slaughter of the innocents. They are all part of an inherently wicked culture that, if allowed to live would morally and theologically pollute the people of Israel.[6]

The fall of Jericho and the ban it was placed under reminds us that there are only two places to stand in this world – in the Canaanite camp or in the Israelite camp. They represent, at their simplest, those who are rebels against God and those who are in relationship with God. But there is a way to move from one camp

---

5. Ibid.
6. Tremper Longman III, *Show Them No Mercy* (Grand Rapids, USA: Zondervan, 2003), pp. 173-174.

to the other – and it comes into focus at the cross. It is there that our sin-bearing substitute took the ban on Himself so that, by faith in Him, we, like Rahab, can move from one camp to the other.

Robert Hubbard rightly says:

> I would argue that the book of Joshua reflects two aspects of God's nature, his righteous anger against opponents and his mercy and compassion towards those who turn to him. In my view, Christians come to experience both aspects of God's character through their relationship with Jesus Christ.[7]

---

7. Hubbard, *Joshua NIVAC* p. 202.

A welcome and a warning (6:22-27)
Now the time comes for Rahab, and her household, to physically move from one camp to the other. Joshua instructs the two spies who went to her house to bring her out 'in accordance with your oath to her' (6:22). It is not the oath that saved her, but her prior act of faith, acknowledging God in her 'Israelite' confession of faith (see 2:11). The spies, now identified as 'young men', act on Joshua's command and bring her and her family out. The task is surely assigned to them as they would recognise the house and people in all the confusion – they also have to take responsibility for their promise. It is worth noting what proportion of the story given to its different elements – 'bloodshed' and 'xenophobic relish' – are notably absent. Richard Hess points out that in the Hebrew text eighty-six words deal with the rescue of Rahab and one hundred and two deal with the defeat of the city. He concludes that 'The salvation of Rahab was as important as the destruction

Realising the Promise (5–6)

of Jericho.'[15] To identify Rahab as 'the prostitute' does not necessarily suggest that she continued to pursue her 'profession'. It forms a link with the earlier story, bringing it to a conclusion as she joins the people of God.[16]

We may well ask, 'But what kind of welcome does she receive?' The text says:

> They brought out her entire family and put them in a place outside of the camp of Israel (6:23).

The reason for this initial placement of Rahab is, most probably, that the whole nation had consecrated themselves for the task ahead – they were ritually clean. This would not have been possible for Rahab, so, she was 'outside the camp'. This expression is commonly found, especially in Leviticus (e.g. Lev. 10:5; 13:46 & 14:2, 8); it carries the implication of ritual uncleanness. But it is an uncleanness that can be rectified by the appropriate rituals. So, it was a welcome that showed proper regard for their safety and wellbeing. Whatever was done for Rahab and her family is passed over in silence by the narrator. He does record, however, that they were included in the camp of Israel after the destruction of Jericho because, 'she had lived in the midst of Israel to this day' (6:25 NASB).

The first city in the Promised Land has been taken, and taken in a truly remarkable way. Joshua's final act towards

---

15. Richard Hess, *Joshua* TOTC (Leicester UK: IVP, 1996), p. 134.
16. Harstad, *Joshua* p. 292, adds an interesting observation: 'By continuing to call her "the prostitute" the author does not imply that she still acts as one ... We speak in the same way when we recall the penitent "thief" on the cross, whose time of thievery was in the past when he spoke the confession of faith for which he is remembered' (Matt. 27:38; Luke 23:39-43).

the city is to pronounce a curse on anyone who tries to rebuild it. Most commentators understand this to be directed at re-fortifying the city, rather than living in it – a clan from the tribe Benjamin had the city assigned to them in the later allotment of the land (see Josh. 18:21). There is a clear fulfilment of the curse later in the Old Testament. When Joshua says:

> At the cost of his firstborn son
> he will lay its foundation;
> at the cost of his youngest
> he will set up its gates.

That is exactly what happened to Hiel of Bethel as he sought to rebuild Jericho (see 1 Kings 16:34). The curse is not a final vindictive act on the part of Joshua. The penalty pronounced had its origins in Deuteronomy. There, the penalty is to fall on any Israelite town where people say, 'Let us go and worship other gods' (Deut. 13:13, the whole section 13:12-18 should be read). From the outset of the conquest, any compromise with Canaanite religion is shown to be off-limits. It is a stark warning.

As this chapter closes, the focus is back on Joshua – 'his fame spread throughout the land' (6:27b). But, his fame is not purely on account of his own ability or prowess; it is because 'the LORD was with Joshua' (6:27a). There has been a progression in the 'fame' of Joshua:

- it begins with obedience to the Word of God and will lead to him prospering and being successful (see 1:8)
- as he leads Israel in the way of obedience, just as Moses did, God will exalt him in the 'eyes of all Israel' confirming his leadership (3:7)

Realising the Promise (5–6)

- now 'his fame spread throughout the land' – he is the servant of the Lord with whom the nations of Canaan will have to deal.

The fame of Joshua and his actions to date as the agent of God and the leader of God's people stand as a warning to the people of the land. But, as we will see, fame does not equal infallibility.

From text to message

Dramatic presentations of some of the action in this section, particularly the circling of Jericho and the shouts of the army, can lead us to miss the vital theological emphasis of these two chapters. We do not want to flatten the narrative out into cold abstract theses but the progression of the story needs to be seen with its theological significance. It is for this reason, among others, that the story of Jericho needs to be seen in the light of the preparations that precede it. The people of God cannot expect the action and intervention of God unless they are in a right relationship with Him. The other side of this coin, is the peril of not being in that right relationship, is clearly to be seen as well. As Israel experience the realisation of God's promise, God is also bringing to realisation, making real His promise concerning the Canaanites (Gen. 15:16). Salvation and judgement are inextricably bound together in Scripture.

Getting the message clear: the theme

It is not illegitimate to speak of Israel as a renewed people in this section. With the circumcision of all the males in the nation, a new chapter in their history opens and the 'reproach of Egypt' is removed. They are now in a position to celebrate afresh God's grace in the Passover. Joshua's encounter with the commander of the Lord's army epitomises the nature of the authentic response required of this renewed people – reverence for God and obedience to His Word. The realisation of God's promise – the reality of a land of their own – comes as a gift of grace. But, it demands a response – a total reliance on Him and complete obedience to His Word. These are the marks of a renewed people at every stage of the scriptural story.

Getting the message clear: the aim

There is often a danger in contemporary Christianity to assume (by implication at least) that God is in the business of serving our particular desires and needs. This section of the book of Joshua helps to correct that assumption. At the heart of it is Joshua's encounter with the commander of the Lord's army. The important issue in that meeting is not 'Is God on our side?' Rather, it is a question of 'Are we on His side?' That is, are we in a right relationship with Him and obedient to Him. This section helps us to focus on those questions and enables us to point to Jesus through whom all God's promises are realised; and who makes that relationship possible.

A way in

Have you ever been in a situation where you have found yourself saying 'Well, I wouldn't have done it that way'? It is not uncommon and you might be able to provide a graphic example of such a situation. There is a sense in which God's command to circumcise the men of Israel seems quite illogical seeing the context in which it is given. God, however, does not ask the impossible without providing the means to achieve it. This holds true for many aspects of the narrative before us.

The fact that food and drink play a large part in our lives may offer an alternative way in. Many of us have experienced meals that go far beyond the function of just keeping us alive. Meals have important relational aspects as well.

For example:

- celebration – weddings, anniversaries, personal triumphs
- creating relationships – first dates, new ventures, group bonding
- ceremonial functions – state banquets, honouring an individual, clinching a deal

Each of these involves preparation, participation and a significant purpose. The Passover has all these implications and more.

Alternatively, you may want to approach this section from the perspective of the promise. Promises are fine, but they do not feed a family or pay the bills. They need to be fulfilled. It is no good the Bank of England promising to 'pay the bearer on demand the sum of £20' or whatever, if there is no reality backing up that promise. The reality for Israel is that they are now standing in the Promised Land. God delivers on His promises.

Ideas for application

- Our section opens with a great illustration of the fact that God's grace always goes before us. The people of Israel seem to be in a difficult situation, their military advantage taken away by the command about circumcision. But God acts first – by disabling the enemy (5:1). We can trust God to go before us in our

Christian lives – He did so at the beginning of them (see Rom. 5:8) and will continue to do so (see Heb. 4:16).

- A disobedient generation does not mean the end of God's promise, although it meant rejection for that particular generation. Paul encourages Christians to use this as an example to keep us 'standing firm' (see 1 Cor. 10:1-13).

- The Passover is a sign to God's people that says: 'God is your God and Deliverer, and you are His people.' As Joshua celebrated the first Passover in the land, so Christ celebrated the last Passover – He Himself becoming 'our Passover' (1 Cor. 5:7).

- Both circumcision and Passover are signs *from* God, given to His people to assure them of His grace. This should condition our attitude to Baptism and the Lord's Supper. They are not our acts *towards* God.

- Joshua's meeting with the Lord's commander reminded him of the need to submit to the sovereign Lord, rather than assess where God's allegiance lay or what His detailed plans were. Ralph Davis quotes H. L. Ellison as saying:

    > We can easily become more interested in special guidance than in a right relationship with the Guide.[17]

- As we have noted above, one of the primary aspects of the Jericho story is its focus on the presence of God (the Ark). Nothing is achieved without His presence. We must be wary, however, of allegorizing 'Jericho'.

---

17. Davis, *Joshua* p. 53.

Realising the Promise (5–6)

Some suggest that Jericho can picture for us the 'citadel' of greed, lust etc in our hearts, or of sin and disunity in our churches – and only God's presence can give victory. This can quickly become an exercise in imagination rather than an attentiveness to revelation. The walls are real walls and their collapse is historical fact. There is greater spiritual benefit in emphasising the action of God in history on behalf of His people than there is in allegorizing elements of the story.

- The people of God are not entirely passive in all the events of this story. The important point is that what they had to do, they had to do in God's way. Both the means and the end are important in God's eyes.

- The rescue of Rahab reminds us afresh that there is mercy for any, whoever they are, if they will turn to God. How we welcome people into our fellowships and how we reach out to others must not be conditioned by our preferences or presuppositions.

Suggestions for preaching

Sermon 1
A summary sermon covering the whole of this section is difficult, but not impossible. The suggested outline below makes the assumption that there is a good degree of familiarity with the Jericho episode and, therefore, it can be dealt with in a few broad brush-strokes.

Signed (5:1-9)

- the renewing of the nation's relationship with God
- the importance of the God-given sign

Sealed (5:10-12)

- the Exodus 'revisited'
- confirmed in the relationship with God

Delivered (5:13-6:20)

- God in command
- Jericho delivered to Israel
- Rahab delivered from Jericho

The battle is God's battle and He does all that needs to be done. The only response is (like Rahab) to acknowledge Him as the only God. In the same way, Christ is the victor over sin and death – our response is to trust Him.

Sermon 2 (5:1-12)
Only within a renewed relationship with God can the promise be realised.

God steps in (5:1)

- the testimony the enemy heard
- the effect it had

A step of faith (5:2-9)

- the people must now trust God for protection
- they must obey His Word

In step with God (5:10-12)

- remembering God's deliverance (then and now)
- celebrating His grace

Seeking any kind of 'Promised Land' or relationship with God in our own strength is futile. We must trust in His provision.

Sermon 3 (5:13-15)

It is easy to think that God will fit in with our plans. The real question is, 'Will we fit in with His?'

Asking the right question (5:13)

- the situation Joshua is in
- the surprise he receives
- the reason for the question he asks

Understanding the answer (5:14)

- the puzzling 'No!'
- the important clarification – commander of the Lord's army
- getting the message – an appropriate response and question

Clarifying the situation (5:15)

- the continuity of God's purpose
- the only response – obedience

Just as Moses met by God at the 'burning bush', so now Joshua has an encounter with the Lord's commander. The similarity of words and actions shows that Joshua stands, as Moses did, within the purposes of God. There is no 'Plan B' from eternity to eternity.

Sermon 4 (6:1-27)

It is helpful to contrast the scene portrayed in this text with a contemporary book or film's depiction of a war. The TV series *Band of Brothers* was a milestone in special effects, not glamorising, but showing the horror of war. Joshua 6 is almost mundane in its repetitiveness and lack of emotive detail. The reason for this is its chief focus lies elsewhere.

The presence of the Lord (6:1-14)

- the Ark dominates these early verses
- it is the Lord who will defeat Jericho
- Israel had a part to play – but under God's command

The rescue of Rahab (6:15-27)

- Rahab's prominence in the account
- the spies' responsibility
- Rahab's inclusion in God's people

The end of Jericho (6:15-27)

- the miracle of the walls
- the judgement of defeat and curse

The pattern of salvation and judgement is a consistent biblical pattern – it needs to be recognised and made known.

Realising the Promise (5–6)

Suggestions for teaching

Questions to help understand the passage

1. How has the crossing of the Jordan made an impact on both Israel and the surrounding nations? Why is this significant?

2. God commands the Israelites to be circumcised – but why here and why now?

3. Why do you think the writer is so specific about the dates, which he includes?

4. What is the significance of the Passover for Israel at this moment in their history?

5. Compare Joshua's confrontation with the 'commander of the Lord's army' (5:13-15) with Moses' meeting God in Exodus 3:1-10. What are the similarities and why do you think they are important?

6. How does the comment about the city of Jericho in 6:1 help the flow of the story?

7. Circling the city in the way God has instructed Israel cannot simply be an empty gesture. Suggest some reasons why not.

8. Why do you think the writer breaks off his account of the assault on Jericho to recount Joshua's further instructions about the people and goods of the city?

9. Why is it important that Israel should follow these instructions to the letter?

10. What are the chief things we are told about Rahab and why are they important?

Questions to help apply the text

1. How does God's concern for a right relationship between the people and Himself overrule any other consideration? How is this true for His people today?

2. Why is history so important? What do we lose if we don't take seriously the historical facts of our faith?

3. The emphasis on the unity of the people of God is in evidence throughout these early chapters of Joshua. In what ways can we work for unity among God's people today?

4. The Passover was the major celebration in Israel of God's saving acts on their behalf. Does such a celebration feature in our local fellowships?

5. How can we become 'more interested in special guidance than in a right relationship with the Guide'? How does Joshua help us here? (See 5:13-15.)

6. When we find ourselves facing what seem like impossible situations, how can the lessons of the battles for Jericho help us?

7. Israel is forbidden to take anything 'devoted to God', are there things that are under 'the ban' for us? (See e.g. Eph. 5:3-7.)

8. What practical lessons are there for us to learn concerning Rahab's acceptance by God and incorporation into His people?

4

Responses to the Promise (7–8)

Introduction

The first city to fall in the Promised Land is taken with relative ease and in virtually a ceremonial way. So, Israel can continue on its triumphant progress through the land ... or can it? Progress is not solely dependent on military strategy and prowess. The need for holiness, for dedication to the Lord, has been made clear to the people as a vital factor in possessing the land. Rhett Dodson helpfully puts it like this:

> With the implementation of the ban at Jericho God answered the question 'Can the paganism, the immorality, the iniquity and idolatry of Canaan coexist peacefully with the Israel of God?' God made a comprehensive claim to Jericho and its inhabitants in order to judge them and to protect Israel. God's holiness demands the punishment of sin and provides the protection of his people.[1]

---

1. Rhett Dodson, *Every Promise of Your Word* (Edinburgh, UK:

The reality of the demands of God's holiness becomes very clear in the chapters before us. There is no possibility of even Israel 'coexisting peacefully' with God when 'Canaan' comes into the heart of the camp.

Jericho is defeated, but now it is Israel's turn. This defeat happens because the people bring themselves under the wrath of God. Until the offending action is dealt with, the Israelites are in no better situation than the Canaanites. The narrative of chapters 7 and 8 deals with this problem - both its causes and its cure.

Listening to the text

Context and structure

God has brought His people into the land, which is His gift and inheritance for them. At His initiative they have been reconstituted as His people, signalled by both circumcision and the Passover. The first step in the conquest has been completed in the destruction of Jericho. A major issue in that part of the narrative was the saving of Rahab and her household. Success is not inevitable, however, as the opening episode of chapter 7 demonstrates. If the first readers (and we in our turn) have been lulled into a false sense of security by the emphasis on 'all Israel' we are now to be sharply reminded of who really is part of that 'all Israel'. F A Spina points out concerning chapter 7 that:

> It demonstrates that ethnicity, regardless of its purity, is no guarantee for remaining part of God's people. Just as Rahab's confession of faith got her and her family

---

Banner of Truth, 2016), p. 136.

included, Achan's violation of faith got him and his family excluded.[2]

These two chapters can be taken as individual episodes in the larger narrative, both of them opening and closing with matching ideas. Chapter 7 opens and closes with an emphasis on the wrath of God and hinges on God's Word on the problems it contains, especially how to deal with it. So:

- The LORD's anger burned against Israel (7:1).
- 'I the LORD will not be with you any more unless …' (7:12b).
- Then the LORD turned from his fierce anger (7:26b).

As chapter 8 tells the story of the defeat of Ai, it shows us the role of the Word of God for His people in bringing them victory; the key moments are:

- 'Then the LORD said to Joshua …' (8:1) God's encouragement to Joshua is in terms that are, by now very familiar (see e.g. 1:9 & 6:2).
- 'Then the LORD said to Joshua …' (8:18) A direct command for dealing the fatal blow to Ai and its forces.
- 'There was not a word of all that Moses had commanded that Joshua did not read to the whole assembly of Israel' (8:35). All are gathered as the people of God under the Word of God.

While this way of dealing with these two chapters has much to recommend it; there are two important threads

---

2. F. A. Spina, *The Faith of the Outsider* (Grand Rapids, USA: Eerdmans 2005), pp. 70-71.

that suggest they should be handled as one unit. The first is simply the demand of the narrative flow – the events at Ai constitute a major feature of both chapters. We hear both the story of defeat and its reason, then the story of victory and the way forward. The second thread is seen in the fate of those who reject God and His demands; also the reminders that are constructed to mark their folly – 'which remain to this day' (7:26 and 8:29). Taking them as a single unit we will explore the text looking at the episodes within it as follows:

7:1-5	the enemy within
7:6-9	praying in the dark
7:10-15	threat or promise?
7:16-23	all is revealed
7:24-26	rocks and reminders (i)
8:1-8	remembering the Word of God (i)
8:9-13	setting the trap
8:14-17	springing the trap
8:18-23	the fatal blow
8:24-29	rocks and reminders (ii)
8:30-35	remembering the Word of God (ii)

Working through the text

The enemy within (7:1-5)

After the resounding success of Jericho, the next episode in the conquest story opens on an ominous note:

> But the Israelites were unfaithful in regard to the devoted things; … Achan took some of them. So the LORD's anger burned against Israel (7: 1).

Indeed, even the next town they approach – Ai – has an ominous feel to it; the town's name literally means 'the ruin.'

The possibility of it being the ruin of Israel is a real and present danger. Having set the scene with this comment about Israel's rejection of God's Word in the person of Achan, the narrator goes on to explain how God's anger is demonstrated against Israel.

As part of his approach to the city of Ai, Joshua sends out spies, who seem to be somewhat more adept at the job than the spies sent to Jericho. They come back with a report that the whole nation need not go up against this city. Their assessment of the strength of Ai and its fighting forces leads them to suggest that 'about three thousand' fighting men were all that was necessary (7:3). This assessment proves to be false, because the men of Ai rout the detachment sent and there are thirty-six fatalities. The net result of the expedition is an even greater disaster – 'the hearts of the people melted in fear and became like water' (7:5).

Some possible reasons are:

- Over-confidence by the spies, reckoning on the appropriate military strength needed rather than on the Lord's strength.[3]

- over-confidence on the part of Joshua after the great victory at Jericho.

- A lack of prayer before going on the attack[4]

The problem with these approaches is that there is no clear justification for them in the text. The narrator has already spelled out the reason in 7:1, and that cannot be ignored.

---

3. Bruce Waltke, *An Old Testament Theology* (Grand Rapids, USA: Zondervan 2007), p. 244.

4. Observed but not recommended by Ralph Davis, *Joshua – No Falling Words* (Fearn, UK: Christian Focus, 2000).

Until the offence of Achan is dealt with, there will be no resolution to Israel's problem. Once it has been dealt with, the narrator tells us that the Lord turned from His fierce anger (7:26).

With the basic shape of the narrative in mind, we can begin to grasp the logic behind it. It can be expressed in four simple ways:

>   Achan = disaster
>   Achan = equals Israel
>   Israel = Canaanites
>   Israel = disaster

Achan = disaster Immediately after the statement about the Israelites' unfaithfulness is made, an individual is singled out. He is Achan who is also given the name Achor (1 Chron. 2:7) which means 'disaster'. There is a further play on this name in Josh 7:24-26, where the place of Achan's death is called the 'valley of trouble/disaster.'[5] Achan's act of unfaithfulness spells disaster for Israel.

Achan = Israel The question that immediately springs to mind is why does one person's crime cause punishment to come to the whole nation? In the first place the narrator locates Achan at the heart of Israel. The mini-genealogy takes us into the very centre of the nation – the tribe of Judah. Richard Hess observes that:

> No other figure has been introduced in the book of Joshua with such details about his family background. Four generations are listed. Achan's sin is part of the

---

5. Richard Hess, *Joshua* TOTC (Leicester UK: IVP, 1996), p. 144 n.1.

action of the 'sons of Israel' ['Israelites' NIV] who have acted unfaithfully.[6]

Israel = Canaanites The act of unfaithfulness, taking some of the things that were under the ban, means that the Israelites are reduced to the position of the Canaanites. They are under the wrath of God, and just like the Canaanites their hearts 'melted in fear' (see 2:11 & 5:1). But in fact, this situation is even worse because their hearts 'became like water' (7:5).

Israel = disaster if their true position was now the same as that of the Canaanites, the real disaster, to their minds, was that God had abandoned them and His promises to them. Surrounded by hostile nations who were emboldened by Israel's defeat, they were faced with a dark future. The narrator has let us in on a secret, yet to be revealed to the Israelites. That secret is of an enemy within. Defeated and perplexed, they were in a very dark place.

Praying in the dark (7:6-9)
Joshua's reaction here is not unexpected, he is thrown into confusion as shock, grief and questioning all arise at once. This confusion stems in part from his ignorance of the reason behind the defeat at Ai. At the news of the defeat, Joshua, followed by the elders of Israel show their grief:

> Then Joshua tore his clothes and fell face down on the ground before the ark of the Lord remaining there till evening. The elders of Israel did the same, and sprinkled dust on their heads (7:6).

---

6. Ibid p. 144. See *Further thoughts on ... Achan* below.

This action is a normal sign of grief throughout the OT (see e.g. Gen. 37:29; 1 Sam. 4:12; Job 2:12 etc). The campaign at Ai was a disaster; and Israel's leaders mourn not just for the loss of life, but also the loss of face before the Canaanites. Furthermore, the text seems to point to a loss of hope for Israel (7:7&8) and the loss of honour for God (7:9).

The shock felt by Joshua is conveyed in his cry to God, which opens with 'Alas' (7:6). This is a word often used to express a sense of hopelessness (see e.g. Judg. 11:35 ESV; 2 Kings 6:5 & 15 NASB). In the light of all that has happened so far in the conquest there is clearly confusion in Joshua's mind. Immediately the question arises, 'Why?'

There are two main approaches taken concerning Joshua's questioning of the Lord:

- His words are seen as echoes of Israel's complaints in the wilderness (e.g. Exod. 16:3, 17:3). Joshua questions God's purpose in bringing them so far, only, to let them die. His words, therefore, 'were bitter ones ...'; he appears to have forgotten God's promises.[7]

- As Joshua is still ignorant of the real issue behind the defeat, we may ask, 'Is it appropriate for him to bring his anguish to God?' The frequency with which the Psalmist asks the question 'Why?' gives warrant to Joshua (and to us) to do the same.[8]

Ralph Davis sums it up clearly:

---

7. David Howard, Jr, *Joshua* NAC (Nashville, USA: Broadman & Holman, 1998), p. 191.
8. See Trent Butler, *Joshua* WBC (Grand Rapids USA, Zondervan, 2014), vol 1 p. 410.

> These are words of despair, not unbelief. Joshua complains to God in prayer; complaining to God is not the same as complaining about God (Israel's wilderness practice).

I find this second approach more persuasive and more practical – as Ralph Davis goes on to say:

> There are periods in which confusion strikes and we haven't any idea what God is about. We have no recourse but Joshua's – anguished prayer to a mystifying God, pleading both our danger and his honor.[9]

It is also clear in this section that Joshua continues to approach the Lord with humility. In saying, 'Pardon your servant Lord' (7:8), he is using a standard OT form of address by an inferior to a superior. It is an acknowledgement often used in seeking permission to speak. This does not necessarily seem to be the attitude of a complainant. As Joshua is praying in the dark he is looking for a practical answer to Israel's present situation. Joshua is yet to see that there is a spiritual issue at stake.

Threat or promise (7:10-15)

Here we reach the heart of the problem and the pivot on which the whole story turns as God says to Joshua:

> I will not be with you any more unless you destroy whatever among you is devoted to destruction. (7:12b)

Joshua is getting what he wanted, a response from the Lord – but it is not exactly what he expected. The language used by God is stern. It would seem that there was no point in Joshua falling face down and lamenting, when there was sin in the camp that needed to be uncovered. The Lord

---

9. Davis, *Joshua* p. 61.

immediately goes on to make this plain – Israel has sinned (7:11a). How Israel has sinned is made clear in the string of five verbs that follow (7:11):

- they *have violated* my covenant
- they *have taken* some of the devoted things
- they *have stolen*
- they *have lied*
- they *have put* them with their own possessions

Each of these is linked by the word 'also' and this linkage is to 'indicate a progressive buildup of specificity and in the process, they describe the totality of what Achan did.'[10] There are two consequences of that action, according to the Lord. The first is that they cannot stand before the enemy, because they have become God's enemy themselves. They have to turn and run from the Canaanites, as they are now under the same ban as the Canaanites. This is not the worst aspect of their situation – the God who has brought them this far will no longer be with them, unless the ban is carried out on the things that have been stolen. This second consequence can only be removed in the way that God prescribes. That way is now made clear to Joshua. Achan's action has polluted the Israelite camp, so now the camp and the people must be cleansed. To remedy the situation the people must consecrate themselves for the solemn business of discovering where and with whom the fault lies (7:13). Until the devoted things are destroyed, Israel are told that they 'cannot stand against your enemies' (7:13). The process by which the offender will be discovered is explained – tribe

---

10. Howard, *Joshua* p. 194.

by tribe, clan by clan, family by family, man by man (7:14). Finally, God pronounces the judgement that must fall on the person who is found with the devoted things (7:15). The full weight of the Law's sanctions must fall on him.

It is clear from what the Lord says, how serious this offence is. It brings upon Israel the threat of God abandoning them. With the threat, there comes a note of promise – the situation can be remedied; the relationship can be restored.

All is revealed (7:16-23)

Joshua acts promptly. The expression 'early the next morning' (7:16) uses exactly the same Hebrew words as in 3:1. It implies there is an immediate response to God's command. There is no description of the actual process by which the tribe, clan and family were selected; this is not a matter of major significance for the writer. The vocabulary used **is** of importance as it emphasizes a theological truth. Where the NIV says that the tribe, clan, etc 'was chosen' (four times in 7:16-18) the word use there is literally 'was taken' (see NASB). David Firth points out that this verb is often used in the context of capturing something or someone in time of war.

> It is the same verb as will be used when Joshua does capture Ai, and in this context is thus another reminder that this is a story of Yahweh at war against sin among His people.[11]

Having sketched the outline of the process of 'taking' Achan, the narrator gives more weight to the words that

---

11. David Firth, *The Message of Joshua* (Nottingham, UK: IVP, 2015), p. 91.

are spoken. Joshua's 'my son' asserts his superiority and therefore his right to question a member of the Israelite camp. Joshua's question has a double edge:

> ... give glory to the LORD, the God of Israel, and honour him. Tell me what you have done, do not try to hide it from me. (7:19)

David Howard notes that 'the four actions commanded by Joshua are part and parcel of one event.'[12] The confession of sin is an act of glorifying God as opposed to self-assertion. With regard to this link between praise and confession, David Firth helpfully says:

> Although the public confession of sin might not seem much like praise, the reality is that it is because it reminds us that the essence of praise is authenticity before God. To declare God's greatness while consciously living contrary to what this means cannot be praise.[13]

In response to Joshua's demand, Achan confesses his sin using a common OT formula – 'I have sinned against the LORD' (7:20). His crime is not 'just' covetousness or theft but an offence against the Lord Himself. The expensive robe from Shinar (7:21), the silver and gold were too tempting, so they were taken and hidden in his tent. The description of the sequence of his action is noteworthy: he saw, coveted and took the things. Exactly the same sequence, with the same Hebrew words, were used by Eve in the garden of Eden.[14]

---

12. Howard, *Joshua* p. 196.

13. Firth, *Message of Joshua* p. 92.

14. See below *Further thoughts on ... Achan*.

Immediately messengers are sent to Achan's tent and the stolen goods recovered. All the people witness with Joshua what has been taken. All is now revealed – the crime, the culprit and the evidence. What God has seen all along is now seen by the nation.

Rocks and reminders (i) (7:24-26)

This part of the story now moves swiftly to a close. Once more there is no dwelling on the final moments of Achan and his family. The details are sparse, all that belongs to Achan – that has been contaminated by the devoted things – are gathered together and destroyed. At the centre of this final act the narrator records the words of Joshua:

> Why have you brought this trouble on us? The LORD will bring trouble on you today. (7:25)

His words echo his previous statement before the fall of Jericho, that no-one was to take any of the devoted things otherwise trouble would fall on Israel (6:18). The truth of these words is now evident; trouble has come on Israel and now on Achan. As Israel had been unfaithful (7:1) so now 'all Israel' exact God's punishment on Achan (7:25b). When the punishment has been delivered, 'the LORD turned from his fierce anger' (7:26). Now, the Valley of Achor' is the 'valley of trouble' but once sin is dealt with, there is always the possibility of hope (see Hosea 2:15). In that valley they erected a pile of rocks over Achan; they did not have the same significance as the earlier pile at Gilgal, but they both stood as reminders to the people. Gilgal reminded them of God's grace, Achor of the seriousness of sin.

Further thoughts on …
Achan

It may be useful to pause at this point and reflect on some of the issues raised by the text we have been considering. To read Joshua 7, in particular, apart from its OT context might well make us rush to unwise judgements concerning its value as Scripture. What the points set out below are designed to do, is to bring together some of the information already included in the introductory material, and some of the issues raised by the text.

1. The nature of the curse.

We saw in 6:17-21 the first mention of the 'devoted things' in the book of Joshua, sometimes called the 'things devoted to destruction' or 'devoted to God.' The technical term *herem* has separation, as its root idea. It is, in many ways, the negative side of sanctify in the OT and involves the removal of things from the ordinary sphere of human life. A further use of the word is as a word of judgement. It can be used of judicial sentences pronounced on things or persons, especially those who violently and steadfastly oppose the work of God.

As a concept it is used infrequently in the OT, mainly in the context of the conquest (Num. 21:2-3; Josh. 6:21, 8:26, 10:28, 11:11). These particular incidents are seen to be the wider judicial outworking of God's purpose. The key text here, concerning that purpose, is Genesis 15:13-16, where Abraham is told that his descendants would not inherit the land of Canaan for 400 years

– until the sin of the Amorites has 'reached its full measure' (Gen. 15:16). When, finally, the Israelites came into the land they were not only to take it from them but also to destroy the nations there. They were to do this, not as an act of ethnic cleansing, but because of the judicial sentence passed on by God.

We must note the patience of God in all of this; there are 400 years of mercy to allow for a change of life. Apparently, however, the Amorites (= Canaanites) are on a course of self-destruction – giving themselves over to that which is accursed by God. It is important to see that it is God who is judging, not Israel as Deuteronomy 9:5 makes clear. Israel had its own faults, so it could not be an act of self-righteousness on their part. Further, the nations of the land were destroyed to prevent the corruption within them from spreading into Israel and, indeed, the whole world (see Deut. 20:16-18).

As Leviticus makes plain, when a nation starts burning its own children as gifts to its gods and practices all kinds of loathsome vices, then, the days of God's mercy are running out and judgement is coming (see Lev. 18:21-29).

The God of Scripture is not a weak bystander reduced to watching the debased activities of nations and trying to make the best of them. God is consistently portrayed as acting in both salvation *and* judgement. If we as twenty-first century Christians find all this puzzling or embarrassing – it is because we do not understand the seriousness of sin. The NT does not have this problem. Paul in Acts 13:18ff speaks of the conquest, the overthrow of the nations in Canaan, as the work of God and not humans. When challenged, Jesus refused to moralise or philosophise on human violence or natural disasters. He saw them primarily as signs of the world ready to perish, a world under judgement and as a summons to repentance (see Luke 13:1-5).

When we come to the story of Achan, therefore, we need to see that it is no light thing that he is doing. He is associating himself with Canaan, is taking things that are under the curse/ban into the heart of the Israelite camp. He is putting himself and those around him outside of the covenant – he is rejecting the promise of God.

2. *The nature of the community*

A major issue raised by the Achan story is, 'Why does one man's action have such an effect on the whole people?' It is certainly an idea that is alien to the modern Western mind, saturated with an individualistic outlook. The text has shown us that there is a strong link between the individual and the nation:

- The Israelites were unfaithful – Achan took the devoted things (7:11)
- Israel has sinned (7:11) – I have sinned (7:20)
- Achan and all his family are eradicated (7:24)

This linkage is often referred to as 'corporate solidarity'; a set of relationships that makes individuals and their tribes inseparable. Such relationships still do exist in many non-Western societies.

In the OT this solidarity can be seen in a number of ways, for example in the importance given to genealogies. These serve to locate people, to give them an identity and to bind them together. While individuals are important, individualism is not. There was certainly no cult of 'the self'.

As Walter Kaiser has said:

> Individual responsibility, value, worth and importance is firmly grounded in the Old Testament doctrine of the image of God.[1]

In saying this Kaiser also argues that we cannot avoid the sense of corporate solidarity in the OT, but at the same time we must avoid 'mere collectivism.' We will follow his description of what is involved in the idea of corporate solidarity.[2]

There are three factors that define it:

a) **Unity** – the whole group is treated as a single unit. This has already been seen in Joshua 1 where the writer speaks of this people (ESV) not these people. A further example is in 1 Samuel 5:10-11 when the people of Ekron speak of themselves in the singular (the NIV disguises this by translating as a plural; it is literally, 'they have brought the ark of the God of Israel around to **me** to kill **me** and **my** people' [1 Sam. 5:10 NASB margin]).

b) **A representative figure** – often someone embodies the whole group such as the King or a priest. In Joshua the twelve men, one from each tribe, have that function when they take the stones out of the river

---

1. Walter Kaiser, *Toward Old Testament Ethics* (Grand Rapids, USA: Zondervan, 1983), p. 71.
2. Ibid pp. 69-70.

(Josh. 4). Isaiah's picture of the suffering servant plays a similar representative role.

c) **Oscillation** – there is a degree of movement between the two factors above – from representative to group or vice versa. So, an individual is seen as the embodiment of the group and the group can be focussed in an individual. Achan is a case of this movement. With these factors in mind, Walter Kaiser, concludes:

> Solidarity in the Old Testament is rather: (1) where the individual is able to implicate the whole group in blessing or reprobation or (2) where the whole group functions through one of its members who was designated as a representative of that group.[3]

The idea of corporate solidarity is not restricted to the OT; it can be seen in the NT as well. Some examples are:

- Acts 5: – the sins of a few affect the life and testimony of the church

- Romans 5:11-21 – Paul uses Adam and Christ as representative figures for the whole of humanity

- Revelation 2–3 – contains some stern warnings about individuals in the churches, their effect involves the removal of their lampstand (Rev. 2:5).

Joshua must be read, therefore, in the light of its own context not ours. By Achan's action the covenant was broken, the promise rejected and the curse that should have fallen on the enemy, now falls on Israel.

---

3. Ibid p. 69.

3. *The nature of the crime*

We have already, to some degree, seen the seriousness of Achan's sin; but we also need to consider the nature of his offence.

This can be approached in two ways: a) **the archetypal sin** – the text suggests a repetition of the sin of Eden. Achan took for his own use that which had been expressly forbidden by God, or reserved for Him. To take those things represents a complete failure to trust in God's Word, His promise and provision. It is to decide what God promises and provides is not good enough and that Achan knows better than God. In Achan's action we hear the immediate and strong echoes of Genesis 3:6.

There, the following account of Eve's actions is recorded:

> When the woman **saw** that the fruit of the tree was good for food and pleasing to the eye and also **desirable** for gaining wisdom, she **took** some and ate it.

The three words emphasized above are all verbs that are used in the same sequence by Achan in explanation of his action(Josh. 7:21). It is a frank admission that what God says and what He provides are not sufficient and that Achan has decided that he can do better. In this way, it echoes the archetypal sin.

b) **A rejection of God's promise** – it represents the breaking of the covenant. Recalling the same threefold theme we traced earlier, concerning the place, the people and the relationship with God and its blessing; Achan places them all in jeopardy. As 7:11 & 15 make clear, this breach of the covenant means that its curses will now apply. In relation to that threefold theme, this will mean that:

- The place – the people are in danger of being pushed out of the land.
- The people – they are in danger of being overrun and destroyed.
- The relationship and blessing – a rift has now opened up between God and the people; they themselves are under the ban.

The severity of the judgement on Achan is an indication of the enormity of his sin. Our failure to understand this incident may well be due to our lack of understanding of the seriousness of sin. If it is too drastic for us and we are tempted to dismiss it as 'too Old Testament,' then we need to hear afresh the words of Jesus:

> We should gouge out our eye or cut off our hand if they cause us to sin. That is better than our whole body going into hell (Matt. 5:29-30).

It is right to be afraid of the One who can destroy both body and soul in hell (Matt. 10:28).

Remembering the Word of God (i) (8:1-8)
Now the Achan incident has been dealt with there is both relief and irony in this opening section. The relief is that God's purpose and promise are unchanged. Now that the rift between God and Israel has been healed – the conquest

goes on. The irony of the situation is that the very thing that caused the risk, is now declared possible by the Lord. In Jericho Achan helped himself to goods that belonged to God; now the Israelites are permitted to take plunder. Achan brought trouble on himself and the people by his self-centeredness and unfaithful action.

The rift is healed, the Lord has turned 'from his fierce anger' (7:26), and now He speaks to Joshua again. As Joshua listens he is surely remembering the Word of God that had come to him earlier. What God had said to Moses (Deut. 1:21) Moses had also said to Joshua (Deut. 31:8): 'Do not be afraid, Do not be discouraged.' Joshua had heard these words at the outset of his leadership of Israel (Josh 1:9) and now he hears them afresh (8:1). As he remembers these words of God, as he hears them anew, he knows God and His purposes have not changed. It is clear that God's promise is consistent and true, for what Joshua heard before the defeat of Jericho, 'I have delivered Jericho into your hands' (6:2), is repeated as he turns to face Ai again (8:2). There is reassurance of total victory, permission to take plunder and a rather cryptic plan for this to be achieved: 'Set an ambush behind the city' (8:2). In line with the narrator's style, we have to wait to see the full plan spelled out later.

'So Joshua and the whole army moved out …' (8:3). The chain of command was functioning as it should, with God at the head. Whether or not the mission of the spies (7:2-3) had brought back accurate information, the key to success in these battles is the presence of God with His people. The nation now needs to witness that very fact to restore their courage and their confidence in God. They act now in the light of God's promise and Joshua will see the answer to his prayers, particularly, 'what then will you do for your own great name?' (7:9b). The instructions from the Lord for the taking of Ai are spelled out. It involves a degree of subterfuge as the main part of the army lures the forces of Ai out of the city by running from them. Meanwhile the troops hidden in ambush wait for Joshua's signal before they attack. It is a trap to catch the army of Ai between the two Israelite forces and defeat them. Although we have not been told how and when God communicated this plan to Joshua, the fact that He did is plain: 'do what the Lord has commanded' (8:8).

Setting the trap (8:9-13)

The plan is clear; all that is left to do is get everyone in position. The ambush party goes to its allotted place under cover of darkness, 'but Joshua spent that night with the people' (8:9). At daybreak the plan begins to be put into operation. Joshua and the main group of the people move camp to the north of the city (8:11). Their position, 'with the valley between them and the city' (8:11) was an open threat to Ai. It was also a means of guarding against a surprise attack. Commentators differ over how many days were involved in this manoeuvre, particularly because of the reference to the night in 8:9&13. Previously we noted the use of a proleptic summary in the Rahab story (2:15-21) where an event was included in the story out of chronological order. As this is part of the writer's literary technique, it does not seem out of place to see the same thing occurring here. There is also the possibility that it is a simple chronological observation; 8:13 may mean no more than Joshua (and presumably the troops) moved into the valley while it was still dark. A further question is often raised concerning the number of soldiers involved in this ambush – were there 30,000 or 5000?

Adolph Harstad reviews the possibilities and suggests:

a) 'Joshua may have appointed to ambush forces – 5000 close to the city, 30,000 camp farther away.' The larger group is sent out in 8:4-9 the smaller group in 8:10-11.

b) 'Joshua appoints one ambush force ... of 30,000 men' (8:3) out of these he selects 5000 to invade the city while the others would block any Canaanite retreat.

c) '... there is a scribal error in one of the two verses Keil says that 5000 is the correct figure.'[15]

The advantage of the first two options is that they do not require any emendation of the text. Whichever option is taken the main thrust of the story is clear; the trap is set, the ambush is in place and it is done under the Lord's direction.

Springing the trap (8:14-17)

The narrator tells the next part of the story at a brisk pace, the text is full of the vocabulary of haste and pursuit. Some of the details that we might want to know are kept from us. The main purpose is to show that the strategy worked perfectly; it was just as the Lord, through Joshua, had planned it.

The first move is made by Joshua to lure the men of Ai out of the city. The King of Ai and his troops, buoyed up by their previous victory, took the bait immediately. We are perhaps meant to smile or sigh, because we know as readers what he did not: 'an ambush had been set against

---

15. Adolph Harstad, *Joshua Concordia Commentary* (St Louis USA: Concordia Publishing House, 2004), p. 341.

him' (8:14). The King's plan wanted to do battle with Israel close to the Jordan Valley (Arabah) where there would be no way to escape. True to God's plan Joshua and his men retreated giving the impression they were defeated and on the run (8:15). To ensure victory over the Israelites 'all of the men of Ai were called to pursue them' (8:16); and so 'were lured away from the city' (8:16). The city was now wide open to the ambushers, all possible defenders had joined to the chase of Israel (8:17). There is a surprise in 8:17; from apparently nowhere, the city of Bethel makes an appearance – 'not a man remained in Ai or **Bethel**' (8:17). It is fairly certain that Bethel and Ai were approximately two miles apart and there was a degree of cooperation between them.

Richard Hess suggests that this cooperation involved 'the army of Bethel's participation in the pursuit of Israel,' indeed he claims it 'is necessary for the story.'

The reason he gives is that:

> If the army and Bethel had remained in its place, it would have observed the Israelite assault upon Ai ... and mounted a hasty attack against the Israelites. This would have prevented the Israelite ambush from destroying Ai and cutting off the retreat of the enemy.[16]

Bethel is, of course, not without significance in the OT narrative before its brief mention here. Abraham, having received the threefold promise of God in Genesis 12:1-3, moved through the land of Canaan. He received the promise of the land afresh (Gen. 12:7) while in the land and he went on towards the hills east of Bethel and pitched his tent with

---

16. Hess, *Joshua* p. 166.

Bethel on the west and Ai on the east. There he built an altar and called on the name of the Lord. (Gen. 12:8)

The people of Israel have now arrived at that place – the Lord being faithful to His promise.

The fatal blow (8:18-23)

When the city was defenceless, it was time for Israel to strike. But, the decision and command belonged to God, not Joshua. 'Then the Lord said to Joshua, hold out toward Ai the javelin that is **in your hand,** for **into your hand** I will deliver the city' (8:18).

The deliberate repetition of the words 'in(to) your hand' (emphasised above), makes it clear that the victory is from God. Joshua and Israel must not rely on the weapons they hold but on the Lord who will deliver the city to them. Joshua's outstretched arm may be more than just a signal to his troops. He held it out 'towards the city' (8:18). In doing so he also may be symbolizing God's judgement on that pagan city. There are many places in the OT where God stretching out His hand or arm is an act of judgement (e.g. Exod. 7:5; Isa. 9:12; Jer. 6:12 etc.). Human agents can represent God in doing this as well (e.g. Exod. 9:22, 14:16 etc.). Where once it was Moses who had this role, now it is Joshua. The word translated 'javelin' is an unusual word appearing only here in the hand of an Israelite. Robert Boling suggests that the weapon is a sicklesword (scimitar); this was in common use in the armies of the Ancient Near East.

He says that:

It was replaced by the straight sword at the end of the second millennium. By the time of its retirement from "active duty", the sicklesword had attained high importance, as a sign of sovereignty.[17]

If God's sovereignty over the battle is what is symbolized by Joshua raising this weapon, then it is no surprise that he did not withdraw the sign until victory was complete (8:26).

Once the weapon was raised the rout began. The ambushing troops broke cover and entered the city, setting it on fire. When the troops with Joshua saw the smoke from the city, they turned back to attack the men of Ai. The fatal blow had fallen and there was nowhere to run; the army of Ai were completely surrounded. Destruction was total; only the king of Ai was kept alive.

Rocks and reminders (ii) (8:24-29)
The trap has been sprung and the fatal blow delivered; the army of Ai have been encircled and destroyed. Israel now turns back to the city to complete the ban pronounced by God. We need to recognize that here again we are not simply seeing an act of violence resulting from the bloodlust of human beings, but an act of judgement by the Sovereign Lord of the universe. Every aspect of this part of the story shows Israel responding in obedience to the command of God.

Turning from defeating the army of Ai 'in the fields and in the wilderness' (8:24), they go back to the city and destroy both it and its inhabitants. They are following God's command to 'do to Ai and its king as you did to Jericho and its king' (8:2). The only difference between this battle and the earlier one of Jericho is that they are allowed to carry off

---

17. Robert Boling & G. E. Wright, *Joshua*, *The Anchor Bible* (Garden City, USA: Doubleday, 1983), p. 240.

Responses to the Promise (7–8)

some plunder, goods and livestock for themselves (8:2 cf. 8:27). All this is done at God's command and by His help. The narrator confirms this; the fact of Joshua's raised hand with its weapon suggests clearly that this was not merely a signal to start the attack. David Howard sees this act is echoing Exodus 17:8-16, when Moses lifted up his staff to symbolize God's presence in winning the victory over the Amalekites.

He concludes that:

> Undoubtedly this episode in Joshua was included in the book to show yet another way in which Joshua was the worthy successor of Moses.[18]

Once the destruction of Ai is completed, the Israelites take from the city all that God has permitted (the vocabulary of 8:27 matches that of 8:2). To answer the question as to why they were allowed to take plunder this time, Richard Hess suggests that when the ban was imposed on everything in Jericho it, perhaps, 'symbolized the dedication of all the land to God.' It can also be seen as a test of their obedience – which through Achan their representative they failed. He also suggests that permission to take the livestock was an acknowledgement of the precarious position in which Israel now finds itself.

As he goes on to explain:

> God no longer provided manna as he had done in the wilderness. Instead Israel had to find its own food. Even here God provided: he gave his people the livestock and so provided for their needs.[19]

---

18. Howard, *Joshua* p. 210.

19. Hess, *Joshua* p. 170.

The burning of the city is a further indicator that the city is under the ban. The word used in 8:28 is a different word to the 'setting on fire' of 8:8 & 19. The earlier word marks the fires set as a signal; the latter word is used of destruction by fire as in the Jericho account (6:24). It signals total devastation. Ai is now 'a permanent heap of ruins a desolate place' (8:28). Unlike Jericho there is no curse issued against rebuilding and this may also be an indicator of its complete destruction.

The rubble that once was Ai will remind Israel of what God has done for them as it remains to this day (8:29). It may also serve notice on other cities further into the land and warn of the coming danger. Joshua's final act is to deal with the king of Ai. He has been taken alive (8:23), but any relief he may feel will be short-lived! It is very doubtful that the king died by being impaled on a tree. So far in the story, Joshua and the Israelites have been completely obedient to the Word of God. Their action against the king would be no exception to this. The law of God mandates the following:

- Someone guilty of a capital offence is put to death.
- The body is exposed on pole.
- You must not leave the body hanging on the pole overnight.

These words from Deuteronomy 21:22-23 help us to understand Joshua's action concerning Ai's king. Peter Craigie explains what is happening here:

> The body was not accursed of God because it was hanging on a tree; It was hanging on a tree because it was accursed of God. And the body was not accursed of God simply

because it was dead (for all men die) but it was accursed because of the reason [a crime against God's law] for the death. [20]

The final act in this sequence of events is to throw the king's body down at the gates of Ai – where Israel was first defeated. A pile of stones was then raised over it. These rocks are another reminder of the foolishness of rejecting God. In Hebrew the reference to the pile of rocks at 7:26 is exactly the same as the clause here in 8:29. There are two stark reminders in the area of Ai, to all who care to take notice of them, and each one 'remains to this day' (8:29).

Remembering the Word of God (ii) (8:30-35)
At the end of the chapter 7 the problem of the curse in the camp of Israel has been dealt with; and in 8:1-29 the problem of the defeat at Ai has been reversed. Joshua was encouraged to rejoin the battle for the land (8: 1, 12-18) and the narrative makes clear that victory will come through the Lord's work on Israel's behalf. The covenant relationship between God and His people, having been breached by Achan's sin and restored when God's wrath has been satisfied, is now reconfirmed in a covenant ceremony. A number of commentators note the rather strange jump from Ai to a location 20 miles or so away; and from war to worship. As we have had cause to notice already, the book of Joshua does not necessarily follow a rigid chronological order. It often interleaves important statements or events into the narrative to make a point. The covenant renewal ceremony may be an example of this literary technique. Ralph Davis' judgement is that:

---

20. Quoted in Davis, *Joshua* p. 68.

> By placing the covenant renewal ceremony here, the writer is saying that Israel's success does not primarily consist of knocking off Canaanites but in everyone's total submission to the word of God. It is as if he is saying, 'Stop the war and listen to the word of God; this is the most urgent matter right now.'[21]

These verses also bring the initial campaign in Canaan to an end. There is a narrative arc from 5:2-12, which is all about covenant obedience, to our present passage reasserting covenant obedience.

The very act of going to Mount Ebal and building an altar there is a mark of obedience to the Word of God. This was what they had been commanded to do by Moses (see Deut. 27:4-5) and this is what Joshua and the people did (8:30-31). Two kinds of sacrifices were offered to the Lord on the altar, burnt offerings and fellowship offerings. Also 'Joshua wrote on stones a copy of the law of Moses' (8:32). Bruce Waltke sees these elements as part of a unified statement about the covenant renewal:

> The mandated altar symbolises God's claim to the land (cf Gen. 12:8; Exod. 20:24; Deut. 27:5), and the law written on the stones defines the character of his rule. The burnt offerings symbolise Israel's total consecration to God and serve to ransom them. The fellowship offerings celebrate their relationship with God.[22]

It is important to note that 'all the Israelites' are there (8:33); and who exactly they are is defined later in that verse. They are – 'Both foreigners living among them and the native born' (8:33). From the Exodus onwards, Israel

---

21. Davis, *Joshua* p. 72.
22. Waltke, *OT Theology* p. 520.

Responses to the Promise (7–8)

was an ethnically mixed nation. Douglas Stuart offers the following translation of Exodus 12:38 describing the people who left Egypt with Israel:

> A huge ethnically diverse group also went up with them, and very many cattle, both flocks and herds.[23]

The book of Joshua itself has already borne testimony to this mixed nature of the people. The great reversal of the inclusion of Rahab and the exclusion of Achan has been a major feature of these early chapters. We may ask, then, what is it that constitutes membership of the people of God? The text replies, 'it is those who hear and obey the word of God'. To underline the fact that this is the requirement for **all** the people, the section closes with a clear statement that:

> There was not a word of all that Moses had commanded that Joshua did not read to the whole assembly of Israel, including the women and children, and the foreigners who lived among them (8:35).

As with the mention of Bethel earlier in the narrative, so with the reference to Shechem in this section – the significance of the place would not escape the Israelites. It is strongly associated with the promise to Abraham (see Gen. 12: 1-8 esp. v. 6). In this covenant renewal ceremony, in this particular place, Israel are called afresh to remember the Word of God.

The responses to the promise of God shown in these two chapters are characteristic of the responses made by all humankind. Rejecting or remembering the promise

---

23. Douglas Stuart, *Exodus NAC* (Nashvile, USA: Broadman & Holman 2006), p. 303.

involved actions and lifestyles that result in condemnation and curse or relationship and blessing.

From text to message

The majority of commentators see these two chapters of Joshua as a narrative unit (although a few treat 8:30-35 as something of an appendix). We have attempted to show how the whole unit fits together and reflects on earlier elements both in the book and in the wider story of the Pentateuch. Having seen the success of Israel in the previous section, we now see its failure, the reason for it and the cure leading to continuing success. The breaking of the covenant and its renewal is part of the 'glue' which hold the whole narrative together. While it may be easy to focus on the many (and not unimportant) details, the essentials of the plot line will give coherence to our preaching of this portion of the book.

Getting the message clear: the theme

As with all narratives, the stories told in this section cannot be read or preached in isolation from their context. The immediate context in chapter 6, with its ban on the people and things of Jericho, is vital for a right understanding of the Achan story. The wider context makes clear that the ban is not simply some arbitrary imposition by God but part of His far-reaching decision to judge and punish sin. We are waiting in this wider narrative for the sins of the Amorites to reach their full measure (Gen. 15:16). Achan, by his action, identifies himself with those who reject God and thereby stand under judgement. Remembering the Word of God is the key to the renewal of the covenant and the restoration of the presence of God with His people. Key ideas in these chapters are then:

Responses to the Promise (7–8) 239

- God's hatred of and opposition to sin
- the need for sin to be dealt with before the covenant relationship with God can be restored

Getting the message clear: the aim
It would be foolish to attempt to minimise the difficulties of these stories in Joshua. They record some hard truths. But to say they are hard truths does not make them unnecessary. We will not help people by disguising the absolute antagonism of God to sin in His world. The fact of judgement is exactly that – a God-ordered fact. Our problem as preachers and teachers is to make that clear, but to do it in a way in which we are not judgemental ourselves. It is an often-repeated saying that we **must** preach judgement, but with tears in our eyes for those who will not listen or respond. We must not, however, neglect the other element of these stories – that there is a new beginning and hope for those who do listen and respond to the Word of God. Sin has to be dealt with, and it has been by the one who bore 'the punishment that brought us peace' (Isa. 53:5). So we need to help people:

- see the seriousness of sin
- the faithfulness of God to His promises
- the right response to make.

A way in
Picture this: the ship has gone down in a storm. Fortunately all of the crew has escaped in the lifeboat. Suddenly one man seizes a saw and begins to cut a hole in the bottom of the boat. When everyone else starts to protest, he says,

'What has it got to do with you? I'm only sawing under my own seat!'[24]

Despite our culture's obsession with the individual, our actions have implications, for good or ill, for others. The same is true in Israel – Achan is the man with the saw, but the whole nation are likely to sink with him.

Alternatively, Pauls' metaphor of the body provides a good illustration of what is going on at the beginning of this story. The people of God are seen in the Bible as a unit – a living body. If the foot stumbles, the whole body does. Achan is 'the foot' that wants to go its own way, and in so doing impacts the whole of the body.

Ideas for application

- To help express the seriousness of sin, Achan's act and its effect on all the people can be likened to cancer or gangrene (there will be some contexts where using this will be inappropriate!). Without the removal of such malignancy, there is only one outcome – death.

- A problem of this kind created by Achan is not 'just an Old Testament problem' – a similar story is that of Ananias and Saphira in Acts 5. Every aspect of that story does not exactly parallel the Achan incident. It does, however, shed light on the seriousness of sin within the people of God.

- There are times in the Christian life when we do not see or understand what God is doing. Our confusion, grief and even our questions must still be brought to God –

---

24. Netherlands Reformed Church, *The Bible Speaks Again* (London, UK: SCM Press 1969), p. 131.

there is nowhere else to go. (see the section *Praying in the dark* above).

- Vital to the life and health of God's people is His continuing presence with them. When a relationship with God is broken, it can be repaired – but only in God's way. Joshua could not invent a way to fix it and neither can we. Today there is the Gospel of Christ and Him alone. Only through Him will we know the presence of God.

- Frank Spina offers us a valuable lesson from this story:

  > The import of this text is that the community of faith must be constantly aware that outsiders are only a confession away from being included, while insiders are only a violation away (when it is a violation on Achan's magnitude) from being excluded ... Rahab should give all "outsiders" hope; Achan should make all "insiders" cautious and attentive to keeping the faith.[25]

- The renewed emphasis on the Word of God, especially the promise, may seem (to some) an unnecessary repetition. It is constantly foregrounded in Joshua because we, the readers, are often slow to believe it.

- The Lord gives both the victory at Ai and the necessary provisions (the plunder) for His people to continue their march into the Promised Land. This pattern can be seen elsewhere in the Old Testament and into the New Testament – God both saves and supplies His people in their service of Him.

---

25. Spina, *Faith of the Outsider* p. 71.

- 'In contrast to the King of Ai, the sinless King of the universe vicariously endured the curse of God for all people by hanging on the accursed tree'.[26] He, too, was taken down before nightfall, but His memorial is not a pile of rocks but an empty tomb.

- Joshua 8 ends with Israel on two hills – one where blessing is pronounced, the other where cursing is. The New Testament speaks of a single hill, Calvary, where wrath is poured out – the curse is applied. But, it is also the place of blessing – where sins are forgiven and relationship with God restored.

- How and when can we rejoice in the renewed covenant we share as God's people? Is there a special occasion in the life of our church where we can do this to remember and rededicate ourselves to be people of the Word?

Suggestions for preaching

Sermon 1

Any sermon that seeks to open up chapters 7 and 8 as a unit, will inevitably have to be very selective. The underlying themes in the narrative can help us give people a sense of the importance of what is going on in this story.

As an **introduction**, a very brief overview of the Achan story will set the scene. (6:17-21 & 7:1)

The nature of the curse

This will show why Achan's action demands such a drastic response. It is not just an offence against the Israelites' laws, but a direct offence against God.

---

26. Harstad, *Joshua* p. 353.

The nature of community (7:1, 11, 24)
Individuals do not act in isolation, there is always a wider web of relationships which are affected by our actions. Achan's theft brings Canaan into the heart of the camp – this has implications for the whole body.

The nature of the crime (7:20-21)
It is repetition of the sin of Eden – note the same expressions used in both. It is also a rejection of the promise and provision of God. This is also closely linked to humanity's fundamental rebellion. The crime demands the ultimate punishment.

The nature of the covenant (chapter 8 esp vv. 1-2 & 30-35)
When sin has been dealt with, God graciously speaks and restores His presence with them. They are once again His people under His Word.

Sermon 2 (7:1-26)
The Achan story is enclosed by references to God's anger (vv. 1, 26). A sermon might be structured around this fact.

The cause of God's anger (7:1-12)

- Achan's sin and its effect on Israel
- Joshua's cry
- God's response – losing the presence of God

Seeking the culprit (7:13-23)

- finding the man
- identifying the real problem – rejection /rebellion

The end of God's anger (7:24-26)

- penalty exacted

+ anger turned away

Sermon 3 (8:1-29)
Following the defeat of Ai and having remedied the problem behind it, the narrative focusses back on that city.

God sets the agenda (8:1-8)

+ the assurance of God's Word
+ the direction God gives
+ the necessity of obedience

God gives the victory (8:9-23)

+ His plan is perfect (8:9-17)
+ His power is effective (8:18-23)

God's justice and mercy (8:24-29)

+ the rebel king defeated
+ the people of God provided for
+ the reminder – 'to this day'.

Sermon 4 (8:30-35)
The short final section of chapter 8 offers the possibility of expounding the centrality of the Word of God for His people.

Gathered by the Word (8:30-31)

+ all is done 'according to what is written in the book of Moses' (8:31)
+ the sacrifices speak of a settled relationship with God

Responses to the Promise (7–8)

Centred on the Word (8:32-33)

- at the heart of the gathering is the Law of God (8:32)
- the Word is for the blessing of *all* the people

The necessity of the Word (8:34-35)

- it must be heard in its fullness – both blessing and cursing
- it must be heard and obeyed by all the people.

Suggestions for teaching

Questions to help understand the passage

1. Why is understanding the text of Achan's story vital to avoid wrong interpretations of what is involved?
2. Where else do we read of the sin of one person impacting the life of the whole community?
3. What are the important elements of Joshua's prayers?
4. Why is it right to describe the loss of God's presence as a threat to Israel?
5. How does Achan echo the words of Eve in the Garden of Eden? Why do you think this is important?
6. Why is God's 'fierce anger' turned away? What does this teach us about His attitude towards sin?
7. There are echoes of the earlier statements by God to Joshua at the beginning of chapter 8; what are they and why are they important?

8. Outline the steps needed to take the city of Ai. Is there any guarantee of their success this time? (cf. 8:1-2 and 8:8)

9. Memorials seem to be very important in the whole of the Joshua story. What is the significance of those mentioned in this part of the book?

10. What are the main features of the covenant renewal ceremony of 8:30-35?

Questions to help apply the text

1. What must Achan have originally agreed to do? What did he do, and why? How can we easily adopt a similar attitude?

2. Do I understand the seriousness of sin and do I live in the light of that understanding?

3. In what ways might my actions have repercussions for the church?

4. Is Joshua really putting the blame on God in 7:7? What is his chief concern and how should we express it today?

5. Why do you think God takes so long in pointing out the culprit? What can we learn from Joshua's attitude in 7:19?

6. The disease was serious and the cure drastic. What does that teach us about the things that prevent us serving God as we should?

7. What is the greatest evidence you have of the seriousness with which God takes sin? What are you doing with that knowledge?

Responses to the Promise (7–8)

8. Does God's Word strengthen and encourage you? What lessons can we learn from the chapters concerning the importance of listening carefully?

9. The memorials in these chapters are of great importance. Why do we so easily forget God and His Word? What can we do to stop this happening?

10. The story ends with a strong emphasis on the whole people of God (see 8:33, 35). Do we value being part of God's people and how can we help one another in doing this?

5

The Power of the Promise (9–12)

Introduction

The narrator wants to make it plain that God's promise is still fully operative as Israel moves out from the initial foothold that has been established – the territories controlled by Jericho and Ai. While the promise of God retains its power, Israel remains fallible; they fall for the trick played on them by the Gibeonites and find themselves locked into a treaty with them. Unable to destroy the Gibeonites, Israel presses them into service. The news of Israel's victories and of the treaty with the Gibeonites provokes a response from a coalition of other kings. Battle is joined and the first assault is on Israel's allies, the Gibeonites. Joshua and the people respond to the plea for help from Gibeon and march to their rescue. The narrative makes it clear, in a dramatic way, that it is the Lord who brings the victory.

The subduing of the land is dealt with in relatively brief compass. First the south is subdued, then the forces of

Israel turn to the north. At the centre of these campaigns is the reminder that 'the LORD, the God of Israel, fought for Israel' (10:42). In a variety of ways through this section the power of God's promise is evident. It is shown even in the lists of territories conquered. They demonstrate the scope of Israel's victories and the inheritance the people were given by the power of God.

Listening to the text

Context and structure

There has been both success and failure so far in the campaign to subdue Canaan. The need for a clear understanding of God's Word by all the people and obedience to it has been apparent as well. A significant amount of space has been given to make it plain that victory comes from the hand of God. This theme has its matching contrast in this story as it depicts God's people in need of constant reminders of this fact. Essentially, God's people are slow learners in God's school, as the next episode in the story (about the Gibeonites) will make plain.

The campaign for the central area of the Promised Land is completed in chapter 9 and then the battle moves both to the North (chap 10) and to the South (chap 11). A response to the earlier victories, or possibly Israel's failure at Ai, prompts an alliance of kings to join the battle with them (9:1-2) and their ally (10:1-5). Again, the descriptions of the fighting are relatively brief, especially when read in the light of 11:18: 'Joshua waged war against all these kings for a long time.' Finally, the story draws to a conclusion by reviewing the kings and territories conquered by Moses in the east and a list of kings Joshua conquered in the west.

The Power of the Promise (9–12)

Here again, the placing of Moses and Joshua side-by-side indicates the authority with which Joshua operated and the unity of the work of both men under God.

Some commentators treat chapters 9–11 as the main unit with chapter 12 as an appendix. The whole section, however (i.e. 9–12), is bounded by references to the kings of the land. It opens with the notice of an alliance of opposing kings being formed and closes with a list of defeated kings. The structure of the whole section builds on the growing dominance of Israel and the differing responses to it. Deception is the tactic adopted by the Gibeonites. Other cities and nations opt for direct confrontation. Commentators adopt a variety of structures based on literary features in the text; while these have not been ignored, they do not automatically lend themselves to preaching the text and its main ideas. The structure below follows the main elements of the story and we will seek to show the theological ideas that undergird them.

9:1-2	Opposition rising (i)
9:3-15	Success or failure?
9:16-27	Deceit unmasked
10:1-5	Opposition rising (ii)
10:6-15	A treaty honoured
10:16-27	A victory marked
10:28-43	The South subdued
11:1-5	Opposition rising (iii)
11:6-15	The North neutralised
11:16-23	The campaign completed
12:1-6	How the East was inherited
12:7-24	How the West was won

Working through the text

Opposition rising (i) (9:1-2)

The opening sentence of this section describes another reversal in the book. Many commentators point out the similarity between the words used here and in 5:1 – 'Now when all the kings west of the Jordan heard about these things… '(9:1). The response to the news is completely different in these two instances however. Instead of 'their hearts melted in fear' (5:1), now, 'they came together to wage war against Joshua and Israel' (9:1). What is it that provokes the response of these kings? It may have been the initial defeat of Ai, but that is, I think, unlikely. It is more likely to be the naked opposition to the people of God – even to God Himself. This may be an indication that the 'sins of the Amorites' are reaching their 'full measure' (see Gen. 15:16).

Marten Woudstra observes that:

> At this point, however, the Kings band together against God's people, and, as becomes clear from the testimony of the Gibeonites in 9:9, against Israel's God. Within the context of the theocratic viewpoint which imbues biblical historiography one may truly say that the spirit of Psalm 2 comes to expression here.[1]

The hostility between the world and the people of God is evident across the whole of biblical story.

A rapid geographical description by the narrator shows that this coalition occupies the central area of Canaan. Moving from the east to the west it includes:

---

1. M. Woudstra, *Joshua* NICOT (Grand Rapids, USA: Eerdmans, 1981), p. 53; see R. Hubbard, Jr, *Joshua NIVAC* (Grand Rapids, USA: Zondervan, 2009), p. 283 esp n5.

The Power of the Promise (9–12)

- the hill country – the more mountainous area where Jerusalem is located
- the western foothills – descending towards the Mediterranean Sea
- the entire coast – the region beside the sea

The six nations listed here are the same as the nations listed in 3:10 (minus the Girgashites). They represent an almost universal opposition to God's people who come 'together to wage war against Joshua and Israel' (9:2). In characteristic style just as we see the opposition rising and expect battle to be joined, the narrator breaks off to report another incident.

Success or failure? (9:3-15)

New actors appear on the scene – the people of Gibeon – they are the ones that set the agenda for the first part of this chapter. Their reason for approaching the Israelites is that they 'heard what Joshua had done to Jericho and Ai' (9:3); a piece of information they carefully omit when they speak to Joshua (see 9:9-10). Archaeological evidence suggests that the Gibeonites had a lot to lose – they had a carefully engineered water system, and artefacts found in tombs by the city suggest that it was a wealthy place (see also the description in 10:2). Rather than face confrontation with Israel, they resorted to a ruse (9:4); their aim was to persuade Israel to make a treaty with them (9:6). The ruse was elaborately constructed to make sure all the evidence they offered, that they had come great distance, was convincing. When all was prepared:

> ... the worn out sacks and old wineskins, cracked and mended. They put worn and patched sandals on their feet

and wore old clothes. All the bread of their food supply was dry and mouldy. They went to Joshua in the camp at Gilgal... (9:4-6)

The Israelites were rightly suspicious and they said to them, 'Perhaps you live near us, so how can we make a treaty with you?' (9:7). In saying this, they were making a right response in line with the law of God (see Deut. 20:10-18). The Gibeonites were obviously aware of this stipulation and were trying to take advantage of it by deception. Here in the narrative the Gibeonites are identified as 'Hivites' (9:7). The narrator uses the same designation later in the text when we hear of 'the Hivites living in Gibeon' (11:19). By introducing this name at precisely this moment the writer shows the real problem for both the Gibeonites and Israel. The Hivites are among those who are to be totally destroyed by Israel as they enter the land. They are included in the list of those to be driven out (3:10) according to the earlier Word from God (Exod. 34:11). The Gibeonites, those Hivites living in Gibeon, need to successfully deceive Israel to stay alive and hold on to their city.

When first questioned by the Israelites, the Gibeonites respond, 'we are your servants' (9:8a), indicating their willingness to be the lesser party in any treaty. Joshua's reply continues to show suspicion – 'who are you and where do you come from?' (9:8b). The implication of the Hebrew here is that Joshua thought that the Gibeonites were just passing by. Their reply – 'your servants have come from a very distant country' (9:9) implies that they have arrived at their destination.

David Howard comments:

> The Gibeonites' deception was working: their own (secret) destination was the Israelite camp, but Joshua believed they were on their way to somewhere else.[2]

Part of the effectiveness of the Gibeonite deception is that it sounds so spiritual; they have come because they have heard of:

> ... the fame of the LORD your God. For we have heard reports of him: all he did in Egypt and all he did to the two kings east of the Jordan – Sihon... and Og... (9:9-10).

Of great significance here is what they do *not* say, as much as what they do say. There is no mention of the crossing of the Jordan, or the defeat of Jericho and Ai.

As Ralph Davis says:

> After all, they are from 'a very distant land' (v. 9) and so couldn't possibly have heard of these latest developments! In a very distant land they could be expected to know the old, old story but hardly the latest news.[3]

The journey they have undertaken was at the instigation of the elders and all the people of their country (9:11) – all desiring a peaceful relationship with Israel. Further proof of the distance travelled is given – the bread, fresh from the oven when they left is now stale and mouldy (9:12). The rest of their equipment bears testimony to their long and arduous journey (9:13).

---

2. David Howard, Jr, *Joshua NAC* (Nashville, USA: Broadman & Holman, 1998), p. 225; see also Adolph Harstad, *Joshua Concordia Commentary* (St Louis, USA: Concordia Publishing House, 2004), p. 382.

3. Davis, *Joshua – No Falling Words* (Fearn, UK: Christian Focus) p. 77.

The deception is successful. After careful investigation of the evidence – sampling the provisions (9:14) – they get what they came for:

> Then Joshua made a treaty of peace with them to let them live, and the leaders of the assembly ratified it by oath (9:15).

Success for the Gibeonites, but failure for the Israelites – a wrong decision has been made, because they 'did not enquire of the LORD' (9:14). A literal translation of this part of verse 14 is: 'the mouth of Yahweh they did not enquire.' Where there was no clear provision in the Law to cover a particular situation, Joshua had been commanded to consult the Lord through the High Priest. This has been made clear when he was commissioned as Moses successor (Num. 27:12-23). Particularly, it was said to him that he must:

> ... stand before Eleazar the priest, who will obtain decisions for him by enquiring of the Urim before the LORD (Num. 27:21).

Human leadership is fallible and Joshua is no exception. The other leaders of the community implicate themselves in this failure, by ratifying the decision. They are walking by sight, not by faith.

Deceit unmasked (9:16-27)

It is not unusual that when deceit is unmasked problems ensue, especially in relationships. Accusations fly and trust breaks down. This is what happens in this episode. The next movement in the story happens after three days, in keeping with many of the major incidents in the book of Joshua (see e.g. 1:11, 2:16 & 22, 3:1). Knowing they have

The Power of the Promise (9–12)

been deceived, the Israelites march to the Gibeonites' cities. Once more the narrator builds the picture by spelling out the major cities they occupy. There can be no attack when the cities are reached, because of the treaty, an oath that has been sworn by the leaders of Israel (9:16-18). This produces discontent in the rank and file of Israel – 'The whole assembly grumbled against the leaders' (9:18). Grumbling by the Israelites is, of course, not a new thing; there were plenty of occasions in the wilderness when this happened. For once, the complaints against the leaders may, perhaps, be justified. Although, we must not give too much credit to the people. It is possible that they were set on destroying the Gibeonites despite the treaty. Towards the end of the episode, the narrator remarks that 'Joshua saved them [the Gibeonites] from the Israelites and they did not kill them' (9:26).

There has to be some resolution to the problem now that deception is out in the open. The leaders recognize this as they say, 'We cannot touch them now' (9:19). In essence the problem they face is:

- they have sworn an oath to the Gibeonites
- it is an oath 'by the Lord' (9:19)
- breaking the oath will bring God's wrath on Israel.

The resolution of the problem is found in letting the Gibeonites live, but pressing them into service as 'woodcutters and water carriers' (9:23).

Joshua pronounces this verdict on the Gibeonites, making it clear that it is the penalty for their deception. He also adds qualifications, which fill out the picture –

- it is service from which they will 'never be released' (9:23)
- it will be service 'for the house of my God' (9:23).

This action meant that the lives of the Gibeonites were saved (9:26); and they continued in service of 'the altar of the LORD' (9:27). 'And', the narrator concluded, 'that is what they are to this day' (9:27).

If we stand back from this episode for a moment and consider the bigger picture, some important elements can be seen:

- all decisions have consequences and not all those consequences can be removed.
- there is a glimmer of hope in this story. They are to serve at the sanctuary, which may lead to a surprising outworking of God's promise concerning all nations (Gen. 12:3).
- the Gibeonites were still linked with Israel in both Saul and David's reign (2 Sam. 21:1-6). Men from Gibeon were also involved in rebuilding the walls of Jerusalem in the return from exile (Neh. 3:7).
- it may also cast light on the nature of the ban as the Gibeonites/Hivites were doomed under it. Joshua is encouraged by them to do 'whatever seems good and right' (9:25). What was 'good and right' has to be including them, even as aliens, within the boundaries of Israel. The ban was not so absolute that it did not allow non-Israelites in by a variety of means.

Opposition rising (ii) (10:1-5)
Returning to the theme of the rising opposition to Israel, the writer focuses on a specific group of kings. This shows the battle now moves to an area more to the southwest of Jerusalem. Not only has the news of the defeat and destruction of Jericho and Ai reached King Adoni-Zedek in Jerusalem, so has the news of the treaty with Gibeon. A strategic city in the way of the Israelite advance had been lost; this was cause for alarm (10:2). The opposition were now facing a considerable foe – both Gibeon and Israel had crack units of 'mighty men' (the Hebrew for fighting men in 10:2 & 7). In response to this threat 'the five kings of the Amorites ... joined forces' (10:5). The name Amorite is used in a number of ways, sometimes as a broad term to include all Canaanites, sometimes to designate those who lived in the hill country. Although not all the five city states listed are in the hills, Adoni-Zedek's Jerusalem was taking the lead and, therefore, probably gave the name to the coalition. The threat to all of these kings is, of course, real. Israel is now driving into the very heart of the country threatening to split it in two, so weakening resistance further. Gordon McConville notes that Adoni-Zedek's name means 'the Lord is righteous' and that this story is part of a broader narrative in which the Lord's righteousness will be revealed in Jerusalem.

He notes that:

> Adonizedek, therefore, points to a goal of the story well beyond itself, while in the meantime he stands in defiant opposition to it. The irony points up well the nature of

the conflict: who has the right to claim the mantle of righteousness, and who really rules in the land?[4]

With opposition rising, a vital question for Joshua and Israel is, 'Is there still power in the promise of God?' This is an especially urgent question in the light of the silence of God since the second attack on Ai (8:18).

A treaty honoured (10:6-15)

The besieged city of Gibeon recognises their only hope is with their (now) allies – Israel. A question that may have been uppermost in the Gibeonites' minds is 'Is there any real power in Israel's promise?' We can presume that they thought there must be. Otherwise there was no real reason for them to call for Israel's help. It is possible that the same thought had crossed Adoni-Zedek's mind as well. If there was no real substance or power to the treaty Israel had made, the cities of Gibeon would be at the mercy of the coalition. Action by Israel would mean that there would be a major confrontation in which the coalition could settle the problem of Israel once and for all. So, the Gibeonites called for help (10:6), knowing their situation was desperate. If Gibeon was relying on the power of Israel's promise, Joshua's immediate reaction proves its power:

> So Joshua marched up from Gilgal with his entire army, including the best fighting men... After an all-night march from Gilgal, Joshua took them [the Amorites] by surprise (10:7 & 9).

---

4. Gordon McConville & Stephen Williams, *Joshua, Two Horizons Commentary* (Grand Rapids, USA: Eerdmans, 2010), pp. 51-52.

The Power of the Promise (9–12)

Joshua's response was both prompt and costly. He was very ready to meet his obligation to the Gibeonites; and the night march was around twenty miles over difficult terrain.

It is at this point in the story that the silence of God is broken:

> The LORD said to Joshua, 'Do not be afraid of them;
> I have given them into your hand. Not one of them will
> be able to withstand you.' (10:8)

Whatever doubts or misgivings there might have been about God's continuing relationship and concern for Israel; these are dispelled by words that have become familiar (see e.g. 1:2, 5). Behind all the action, the ebb and flow of history and the fallibility of Israel and its leaders, there stands the most powerful promise of all – the promise of God. That is signalled very clearly, not only in the words from God, but in action as well. The focus changes quickly – 'Joshua took them by surprise' (10:9) to 'the LORD threw them into confusion before Israel' (10:10). Although Israel pursued the enemy and cut them down (10:10), the victory was won by the Lord:

> As they fled before Israel… the LORD hurled huge
> hailstones down on them, and more of them died from
> the hail than were killed by the swords of the Israelites
> (10:11).

Part of the wonder of this intervention by the Lord is that the hailstones were aimed with such accuracy, that only the enemy suffered – this was no normal, indiscriminate storm! Hailstones were not the only weapons used in this victory, the whole of God's created order was enlisted to secure it. At Joshua's request 'the sun stopped in the middle of the day and delayed going down about a full day' (10:13b). There are number of translation difficulties which make it hard to say with absolute certainty what happened on that day (see *Further thoughts on 'the sun stood still' below*). What must not be missed is what Ralph Davis calls 'the miracle of prayer'[5]. When the writer states that 'there has never been a day like it before or since,' he qualifies it to show exactly what he is referring to – 'a day when the LORD listened to a human being' (10:14). A word of encouragement follows: 'Surely the LORD was fighting for Israel!' (10:14). This is the major implication that the narrator wants to draw from that day. When he wraps up the story towards the end of chapter 10, he draws no attention to any astronomical features of the campaign, but to the fact that 'the LORD, the God of Israel, fought for Israel' (10:42). The power of the promise is unabated as Israel honours its treaty with Gibeon. This part of the story ends on a somewhat prosaic note: 'Then Joshua returned with all Israel to the camp at Gilgal' (10:15). In fact the campaign narrative continues in the next section. Once again the writer is probably adding an anticipatory note, to show how conclusive the victory has been.[6]

Further thoughts on… 'the sun stood still'

In any review of the main interpretations of 10:12-14 we must not lose sight of the main point outlined above. David Howard sums the issue up as follows:

---

5. Davis, *Joshua* pp. 84-86.
6. See *ibid* pp. 86-87 esp. n9 for more of this.

> The passage bristles with a host of exegetical and historical questions. Interest in these should not obscure the main thrust of the passage, however, which is that God listened to one man's voice and that he fought for Israel as a result (v. 14).[1]

It is important to remember that a single version of the Bible can only properly offer one translation of the Hebrew text. The range of possible translations need be taken into account – most commentators offer some help with this. Our purpose here is to review briefly the main approaches to this text by evangelical commentators, rather that offer arguments against those who simply dismiss it as ancient mythology or seek to heavily amend the text. There are at least four viewpoints that need to be considered.

1. *Cosmic* This view sees it as an unusual interruption of the normal workings of the cosmos. The sun stood still – that is, the earth stopped rotating – until the victory was won. Despite the objections that might be raised to this in terms of the implications for gravity, the earth's orbit, etc; these difficulties are not beyond the power of the sovereign God to overcome.

2. *Atmospheric* The atmospheric conditions of the day were so ordered by God to benefit the Israelites and to assure them victory. One of the translation issues comes into play here. The verb translated 'stand still' (10:12, NIV), is translated

---

1. Howard, *Joshua* p. 239. The whole section pp. 238-257 sets out five major views.

as 'silenced' elsewhere in the Old Testament. Out of approximately twenty-five occurrences of the verb, at least sixteen refer to being silent. It is particularly used in this way in poetry (e.g. Ps. 4:4, 30:12, 31:17 and Lam. 3:28). If this is the appropriate translation here, the sun being 'silenced' would indicate continuing darkness. The sun being darkened by clouds and the hailstorm is a plausible way of interpreting what is happening. It is possible to argue that the overall effect was that the sun didn't complete its usual/normal course.[2] And it does not lessen an emphasis on God's miraculous intervention on Israel's behalf. The timing is perfect and the hailstones carefully aimed – they do not affect Israel's army.

3. **Symbolic** Although it is not unusual to see both the sun and moon in the sky at the same time, in the Ancient Near East it was considered a symbol of disaster, a bad omen on certain days, as the following Mesopotamian text shows:

> When the moon and sun are seen with each other on the 15th day a powerful enemy will raise his weapons against the land. The enemy will destroy the gate of my city.[3]

It is not being suggested that Joshua bought into this mythology. If, however, he knew his

---

2. See Davis, *Joshua* pp. 87-88 for more on this.

3. John Walton, Joshua 10:12-15 and Mesopotamian Celestial Omen Texts in *Faith, Tradition and History* ed AR Millard et al (Winona Lake, USA: Eisenbrauns, 1994), p. 184.

> enemies did, his request was part of his strategy to win the battle. The fact that the moon did not immediately fade from view in the light of dawn would confuse and frighten the enemy.
>
> 4. *Poetic* Most English translations set out 10:12-13 in a poetic form. There are examples of actual accounts of battles being followed by poetic pictures of the same event (e.g. Exod. 14–15; Judg. 4–5). If this is the case here, then the language concerning the sun and the moon is used figuratively to heighten the description of God's intervention.
>
> None of these approaches is without some difficulty and the preacher or teacher will need to be able to justify the approach he or she takes to those of an enquiring mind among their hearers! At the moment of writing (!), I consider (1) and (2) to fit the text and context, but find (2) the most persuasive.
>
> Whatever conclusion we draw, we must not let them divert us from the main thrust of the text:
>
> > There has never been a day like it before or since, a day when the LORD listened to a human being (10:14).

A victory marked (10:16-27)
The literary technique of the writer comes to the fore again. He takes a step back to flesh out some of the details of the campaign. David Firth helpfully describes the technique like this:

> It is as if, having painted the whole landscape before us, an artist then comes back and starts to fill in elements of

detail so that we can see more clearly what the various parts of the landscape are. In this case, we know that Yahweh is keeping his promises, but what does that look like in detail?[7]

In the first place Joshua recognises that the power of the promise will, and does bring down kings and kingdoms. Trapping the five kings in a cave at Makkedah is not the end of the story – the power of the promise brings total victory. Having secured the five kings for now, Joshua orders the pursuit of their armies. The key to victory does not lie in the strategy he follows but in God's promise:

> But don't stop; pursue your enemies! Attack them from the rear and don't let them reach their cities, for the LORD your God has given them into your hand. (10:19)

The pursuit and defeat of Israel's enemies was effective – they 'defeated them completely, but a few survivors managed to reach their fortified cities' (10:20). The language here is carefully balanced; the victory was overwhelming, but there were a few survivors. Their cities would finally fall to Israel later in the story (see 10:29-39). Throughout the conquest narrative, it is important to note the steady drumbeat of God's sovereign intervention – 'the LORD your God had given them into your hand' (10:19).

With the battle over, Israel returns to the camp 'safely' (literally 'in peace'). Such is the effect of their victory that 'no one uttered a word against the Israelites' (10:21). A number of commentators note the use of this expression, which literally is – 'no one sharpened his tongue against

---

7. David Firth, *The Message of Joshua* (Nottingham, UK: IVP, 2015), p. 124.

Israel' – and its parallel in Exodus 11:7 where 'no dog' is the subject. The implication of the clause in Exodus is that Israel's safety was so assured that not even a dog would bark at them. In using the expression here in Joshua, the narrator may be prompting the Israelites to see, once again, the power of God's promise at work on their behalf.

Finally, the narrator brings this part of the story to a conclusion by recounting two marks of victory, both of which will act as an encouragement and reminder of what God has done for them. The first mark of victory speaks of the total subjugation of the five kings. These kings are released from their trap in the cave and brought before Joshua. The names of their cities are spelled out once more, perhaps, to symbolise the defeat of those places. Then Joshua brings together his army commanders and says to them: 'Come here and put your feet on the necks of these kings' (10:24). This action was a common one in the Ancient Near East, marking the absolute power of the victor over the victim. It is an image that is used in both the Old Testament and New (see Ps. 8:6, 18:39, 110:1; 1 Cor. 15:25-27). Joshua's charge to his commanders echoes God's charge to him:

> Joshua said to them, 'Do not be afraid; do not be discouraged. Be strong and courageous. This is what the LORD will do to all the enemies that you are going to fight.'(10:25)

What God has done in the victories so far, is what He will continue to do on behalf of His people.

There is a second mark of victory, one that is becoming familiar in the narrative. The kings are executed and their bodies are exposed; but before nightfall they are taken down and a heap of stones raised over them. This pile of rocks serve as a further reminder to Israel, and to any Canaanites who care to heed its warning – it speaks of the power of God's promise. It remained there, 'to this day' (10:27).

The South subdued (10:28-43)

The account of the rescue of Gibeon and the defeat of the coalition of five kings is the last detailed record of battles that Israel fought. From this point on the accounts of any battles become more formulaic. Although not all of them have every element in them, there is a discernible pattern.[8] The reason for this is to show the inexorable progress of the campaign in the South. Seven defeats are recorded, probably to show the completeness of the overthrow of the South. According to the list in chapter 12 other cities fell to the Israelites (Geder, Hormah, Arad and Adullam 12:13-15). Here, the narrator has painted the picture he wants to – the South is completely subdued.

There is one note in this story that at first sight seems rather odd – the inclusion of the king of Gezer. There is no mention of his city and its fall. Having documented the fall of Lacish, the writer goes onto say:

> Meanwhile, Horam king of Gezer had come up to help Lacish, but Joshua defeated him and his army – until no survivors were left. (10:33)

Gezer was some distance away to the north and, therefore, not in the immediate theatre of war. We can only presume there was a treaty of some kind between Gezer and Lacish or their respective kings. Some commentators point

---

8. R. L. Hubbard Jr, *Joshua NIVAC* (Grand Rapids, USA: Zondervan, 2009), p. 301.

The Power of the Promise (9–12)

out that in the literary structure of the account of the cities, Gezer stands in the central position. This may be because the Israelites never conquered this city (see 16:10) and, therefore, 'the defeat of its leader and his army was considered a major event.'[9]

Once more, the power of the promise is evident throughout this survey of the victories won by Israel. On two occasions – and by implication a third – the writer says, that the Lord gave the city into the hands of Israel (10:30, 32). Note in 10:30 it says, 'the LORD **also** gave that city... ' – having just defeated Makkedah, the 'also' probably refers back to that city. In his summary statement the narrator says:

> All these kings and their lands Joshua conquered in one campaign, because the LORD, the God of Israel fought for Israel.

So, the South is subdued (10:40).

As we read on in the book of Joshua, we will find that some of these cities have to be taken again (e.g. Hebron and Debir, see 15:13-15). Some of the Canaanites might have fled their cities and gone into hiding, only to return when the army of Israel had moved on to its next objective. This may also explain why the book of Judges later records the fact that a number of Canaanites are still in possession of parts of the land. To dispossess them remains the task of individual tribes of Israel. The most cogent explanation of this situation depends on an analysis of the vocabulary that is used here in chapter 10. Ralph Davis explains that the word used consistently in this section is the verb 'to take'

---

9. Richard Hess, *Joshua* TOTC (Leicester UK: IVP, 1996) p. 204.

(Hebrew *lakad*). This contrasts, he argues, with the word most used in Judges 1, which is 'to drive out/dispossess' (Hebrew *yarash*) and 'denotes effective occupation of territory.' The verb *lakad* appears in verses 28, 32, 35 (NIV *captured*), 37, 39 and 42 (NIV *conquered*).

His conclusion is that:

> Much of the problem of the conquest arises from a failure to distinguish the freight these two verbs carry. What has been "lakaded" may need to be "re-lakaded" later; but what has been "yareshed" has been definitely nailed down.[10]

As the battle to rescue the Gibeonites had been recognised as God's intervention, fighting on behalf of Israel, so, now the subduing of the whole area is credited to the Lord.

Opposition rising (iii) (11:1-5)

The focus of the narrative now swings northward. Opposition to Israel continues to grow and a coalition of kings prepares an attack on them. There is an identical use of words in Hebrew that opens both this and the previous account – 'And it happened, when King 'X' heard...' (cf 10:1 & 11:1). The news of Israel's success provokes a considerable response. Forces from across the region in the north of the country are gathered together (11:2-3). It is an immense army that is designed to repulse the Israelites:

> They came out with all their troops and a large number of horses and chariots – a huge army, as numerous as the sand on the seashore (11:4).

---

10. Davis, *Joshua* p. 89 esp n12.

The Power of the Promise (9–12)

An extremely threatening note is struck here – Israel is ill-equipped to face a 'mechanized army'; they only have foot soldiers to face cavalry and chariots. The initiative for this battle, humanly speaking, comes from this impressive coalition:

> All these kings joined forces and made camp together at the waters of Merom to fight against Israel (11:5).

The narrator has laboured to build a picture here that stirs our imagination to see the enormity of the task for Israel. As Robert Hubbard puts it:

> The reader knows that this scene is not mere "show-of-force" to intimidate Israel. The bigger battle – the dramatic denouement of the entire conquest – is about to begin. The result could be Canaan's last stand or Israel's final triumph.[11]

This battle will truly be a test of the power of God's promise.

The North neutralised (11:6-15)

Once more the Word of the Lord breaks into the narrative:

> The Lord said to Joshua, 'Do not be afraid of them, because by this time tomorrow I will hand all of them, slain, over to Israel. You are to hamstring their horses and burn their chariots.' (11:6)

Despite what seems like overwhelming opposition the power of the promise is seen in the certainty of God's 'game-plan' for the next day:

- 'by this time tomorrow' – the timescale of God's action

---

11. Hubbard, *Joshua* p. 327.

- 'I will hand all of them ... over to Israel' – the nature of God's action
- 'slain' – the outcome of God's action.

While the victory is certain – the Lord achieves it – Israel has a part to play. They will be involved in the 'mopping up' operation and, in particular, are commanded to deal with the chariots and horses. This action will put them beyond the use of their enemies and of Israel themselves. Israel must continue to rely on the power of God's promise to prosper and protect His people.

The interplay between God's sovereignty and human responsibility is evident in this story. It is not such a simplistic view of sovereignty that falls back on a 'let go and let God' attitude. Rather, as Ralph Davis says:

> ... Joshua knows better. His view was not to let go but to grab hold. Divine sovereignty creates confidence, which calls forth effort even to the point of reckless abandon. God's sovereignty is not a doctrine that shackles us but a reality that liberates us; not a cloud that stifles us but an elixir that invigorates.[12]

God's sovereign promise results in action:

> So Joshua and his whole army came against them suddenly at the Waters of Merom and attacked them (11:7).

A possible location for Merom suggests that the wooded uplands surrounding that area would have been ideal cover for the Israelite army to mount a surprise attack on their enemy. This attack was successful because 'the Lord gave them into the hand of Israel' (11:8). All was done

---

12. Davis, *Joshua* p. 93. See Hubbard, *Joshua* p. 328.

in compliance with the Word of God. Israel's pursuit of their enemies, to both the northwest and the northeast means, in the end, that the whole of the northern region is neutralised. Having dealt with the opposing army, Joshua 'turned back' (11:10) to deal with the cities of the coalition. The occupants of each were placed under the ban (*herem*), but only Hazor was completely destroyed. Hazor had long been an important and strategic city. Its king would command respect, and possibly duty, from the surrounding cities and their rulers. As the spearhead of the attack against Israel, it received the severest treatment. The Israelites were allowed to take plunder from the other cities and would eventually occupy them (see Deut. 6:10-11 for a forecast of this). This section closes with a comment about the faithfulness of Joshua (11:15).

Trent Butler makes the following observation:

> His faithfulness thus stands as a goal for all future leaders of Israel. Rather than being lawmakers the kings of Israel are law takers and law keepers.[13]

The same should be said of God's people in every age. Joshua's faithfulness is not to be seen as a quality purely of his own making – its foundation grows out of his trust in the God who is faithful, who makes and keeps His promise.

The campaign completed (11:16-23)

In this final account of the main campaign for the land, Joshua is seen centrestage – 'so Joshua took this/the entire land…' (11:16/23). After all that has been said about God's gift of the land and the fact that He fought for Israel,

---

13. Trent Butler, *Joshua* WBC (Grand Rapids USA, Zondervan, 2014) vol 1 p. 516.

we must not elevate Joshua out of proportion to his role. Primarily, he is the obedient servant of God. This final part of the account must be read in the context of the verse that precedes it:

> As the Lord commanded his servant Moses, so Moses commanded Joshua, and Joshua did it; he left nothing undone of all that the Lord had commanded Moses (11:15).

The chain of command and the final authority behind the conquest can be clearly seen.

We have had cause to comment before on the telescoping of the stories in Joshua. This section is an example of that technique. There is considerable ground covered geographically and a large number of battles that would have had to be fought. The time span is summed up in an almost casual way – 'Joshua waged war against all these kings for a long time' (11:18). The Hebrew is literally 'many days' and the same expression is used in 24:7 of the wilderness wanderings for forty years. This is not to imply an equal length of time for the conquest; but it does suggest a lengthy period.[14] Although the focus is mainly on Joshua, the purpose and activity of the Lord are also clearly seen. With the exception of the Gibeonites (11:19), no other groups entered into a treaty with Israel. Despite the obvious threat and the fear that they experienced, they remained in opposition to God's people – and, therefore, to God (an outworking of Gen. 12:3a).

The key to this opposition becomes clear in 11:20:

---

14. Howard, *Joshua* suggests 5-7 years. See p. 273-278.

> For it was the LORD himself who hardened their hearts
> to wage war against Israel, so that he might destroy them
> totally ...

As we argued earlier this is neither a hasty nor a vindictive act on God's part. Rather, it is a sign that God's patience has run out after four centuries of increasing evil on the part of the Canaanites (cf. Gen. 15:16). Their wilful, evil ways reap their natural consequence – judgement.

In the final episode of this section, the narrator turns his attention to the Anakites. The mention of them and their defeat is an appropriate note on which to end the story of the conquest. It recalls the previous generation's failure to enter the land after Moses had sent spies to explore it from the south. The majority report from those spies was that:

> ... the people who live there are powerful, and the cities
> are fortified and very large. We even saw descendants of
> Anak there ... We seemed like grasshoppers in our own
> eyes, and we looked the same to them (Num. 13:28, 33).

The Israelite response to this news was, 'Wouldn't it be better for us to go back to Egypt?' (Num. 14:3). Their lack of trust in the Lord condemned them to forty years of wandering in the wilderness. Only now do the new generation inherit what was promised (11:23).

So, 'the land had rest from war' (11:23). As we will see, there are still areas to be occupied (13:1); but the major conflicts are over. The emphasis of the story will now turn to the allocation of the land to the tribes of Israel. They have experienced the power of the promise, now they will receive the promise in real terms – as land of their own.

How the East was inherited (12:1-6)

In a sense, chapter 12 acts as a coda to the whole conquest account. It first revisits the possession of the East Bank territories and the allotment given to the two-and-a-half tribes in that region. The second part of the chapter acts as a reminder of how God has brought them to this point by conquering the kings on the west side of the Jordan.

To review the East Bank conquests, the narrator takes us back in time to the days when Moses was still Israel's leader. One reason for doing this is to re-assert the concept of 'all Israel', so prominent in the early chapters of the book. Now that the main part of the land had been subdued, the time is approaching for the men of Reuben and Gad and the half-tribe of Manasseh to return to their land and families (more on this return will be seen in chapters 22—24). Here, the review of the East Bank conquests serves to tie the whole nation together. Despite the various battles that have been fought, there has only been one campaign. God's war against the pagan nations and God's gift of an inheritance to His people must be seen as a unified action by a unified people.

David Howard describes the reference to Sihon and Og, their defeat and possession of their lands as, 'the down payment on the inheritance' of the whole land. He suggests that this record is important:

> ...in confirming the tribes' claims to the lands mentioned here, and in confirming that God was faithful to his promises to give these lands to his people.

The details that are included (12:2-5), he suggests, indicate that God:

... would fulfil his promises, right down to the last village or town and every last border, passing atop this hill over here and descending through that valley over there.[15]

All this was accomplished under Moses, 'the servant of the Lord,' and assured the East Bank tribes of their inheritance (12:5). History again testifies to the power of the promise.

How the West was won (12:7-24)
Turning towards the Mediterranean, the narrator opens this final section with a reprise on the words he has just used concerning Moses. As Moses led Israel at the beginning so Joshua now takes on that role:

- Moses/Joshua and the Israelites **conquered**
- Moses/Joshua **gave** their lands
- as an **inheritance** (12:6-7)

The continuity of purpose under both leaders emphasises the overarching purpose of God. Again there is a 'passing atop this hill over here and descending through that valley over there.' As God had promised Israel: 'I will give you every place where you set your foot,' so the narrator takes them step-by-step through the land. It is here that he includes some of the places that have not been mentioned before in the story (see e.g. 12:13-15).

This record is not just a checklist, to which they simply respond, 'been there – done that'. It also functions as a call to thanksgiving and praise, as they see the great work of their Warrior-King on their behalf. As they review and remember this action of God, it prepares them for battles

---

15. Howard, *Joshua* p. 278.

they may face in the future. Taking an even longer view, Ralph Davis asserts that:

> Every one of Yahweh's victories over his enemies in the process of history is a partial portrayal of his victory over all his enemies at the consummation of history. This is meant to steel and strengthen his suffering people as they long for that grand finale.[16]

Even something so apparently simple as a list in Scripture bears testimony to the power of God's promise – confirmed in the past, active in the present and sufficient for the future.

From text to message

When seen solely from Israel's perspective there is an ebb and flow in the nation's fortunes. They meet with success and failure as they seek to occupy Canaan. The single factor that keeps them on course is God's working in power to fulfil His promise. Despite Israel's inadequacies at various levels, God remains consistent, faithful to His promise and purpose. It will be important in this section not to over-psychologise the reasons for Israel's failures in particular, but to keep the focus firmly on God.

Getting the message clear: the theme

This section opens with a failure in spiritual discernment by Israel's leaders. They cannot undo the promise they have made – it was made before the Lord (9:18-19). If the past cannot be undone, the Sovereign God can still use the mistakes and faults of His fallible people for His own purposes. The treaty between Israel and Gibeon is the catalyst for a rise in the opposition against God's

---

16. Davis, *Joshua* p. 106.

people. The Lord brings victory out of this situation by His supernatural intervention. Although this provokes even more opposition, God brings the whole campaign to His appointed end. Key ideas in this section are:

+ The grace of God in overruling the frailty and fallibility of His people
+ The sovereignty of God in ordering all things according to His will
+ The power of the promise of God directing everything to His appointed end.

Getting the message clear: the aim
The section before us contains and illustrates two different aspects of the life of faith. They are summed up in the following quotations:

+ The Israelites … did not enquire of the LORD (9:14)
+ There has never been a day like it before or since, a day when the LORD listened to a human being (10:14)

The stories in chapter 9 and 10 revolve around these two factors. As interesting and inspiring as these stories are, one of their main thrusts is to foreground the people of God's dependence on the Word of God and the power of God. The other chapters (11 and 12) are also conditioned by a similar note. As opposition rises, the Word of the Lord comes to Joshua again to encourage and reassure him (11:6). On the basis of this promise, he and the Israelites can pursue their campaign, until 'the land had rest from war' (11:23). We need to encourage people:

- to depend on God in the, apparently, ordinary things of life as well as the extraordinary
- to know His will through His Word
- to trust the power of His promise

A way in

Think of a personal example when the flattery of someone else has either led you to make false assumptions about your own ability or blurred your judgement in some way. Relate this to the way that the Gibeonites approached the Israelites.

A contemporary example of a business or institution that established itself on false pretences might also lead into the Gibeonite story.

Alternatively, suggest a range of responses that people might make to a problem. Some will shrug with resignation and not face it, some will be confident in their own ability to solve it. Israel had to face a range of problems:

- Jericho shut up
- Ai offers some resistance
- There will be rising opposition from two confederacies of kings
- The immediate problem is rather more subtle – the Gibeonite deception.

Ideas for application

- Scripture sometimes offers us a picture of the folly of self-reliance (see e.g. Judg. 16; Luke 12:13-21). In his chapter on Joshua 9 (entitled 'The Trouble with

Common Sense') Ralph Davis writes of the need for direction in life from the Lord:

> Not that you have to ask the Lord whether you should get a haircut at four o'clock. The scriptures do not require wilting in the everlasting arms, only leaning on them. But we must beware of that subtle unbelief that assumes "I have this under control".[17]

- Although the making of a treaty with the Gibeonites was a mistake, it was not one that could be airbrushed out of the picture. For them to do so would dishonour God. We have to live with the consequences of our actions – do we do this in a way that honours God and relies on His grace in that situation?

- At times we all have to face opposition for our belief and commitment. We need to prepare for this situation and trust God in it. See John 15:18-27 for both the reason and the remedy.

- Joshua 10:11 portrays God as the Warrior who fights on behalf of His people. We need to be encouraged to see Christ as the Victor in the most decisive cosmic battle and what that means day by day.

- Joshua's prayer may have been exceptional in terms of its outcome, but that should not stop us pleading with God for great things. His prayer was in line with God's purpose and so must ours be. It should be a constant reassurance that 'the LORD listened to a human being' (10:14).

---

17. Davis, *Joshua* p. 78.

- Good leaders are encouragers (10:25). How can we encourage people from this section? If we are focussing on the defeat of the Amorite kings, at the very least we must make clear that opposition to God can never have the last word. That is good news for believers and an encouragement to get right with God for those who aren't.

- The main part of the conquest – the battle for the South – was one campaign (10:42). The fight for the North took a long time (11:18). This is a helpful reminder that the 'campaign' of a believer's life is not a question of a 'quick fix'. Jesus taught the need for persistence (e.g. Luke 18:1-8), and Paul sees the Christian life as both a struggle (Col. 1:29) and a fight (2 Tim. 4:7).

- The Canaanites, even if they did not recognise it, were recipients of the patience of God. Judgement was postponed – but not for ever. 2 Peter 3 is worth pondering as a New Testament perspective on these things.

- The fears of an earlier generation proved to be fruitless. The power of God's promise was more than adequate to deal with even the most fearsome enemy (11:21-22). In Christ we know that even death has died – 'swallowed up in victory' (1 Cor. 15:54).

- Israel remembered the kings they had defeated, they had the opportunity to recognise anew the power of God's promise. How can we – who have 'better promises' and 'better and lasting possessions' (Heb. 8:6, 10:34) – keep the power of God's promise in view, both individually and together?

Suggestions for preaching

Sermon 1
The large amount of material, of various kinds, prevents too detailed an exposition of every episode or idea. A sermon that provides an overview will help familiarise people with the stories and highlight the main ideas.

Independent Israel (9:1-27)

The problem of self-reliance, presuming they can handle the situation, means that the people of God are trapped in an alliance they should not be in. To break their word would be to dishonour God

Dependent Israel (10:1–11:5)

- the battle is the Lord's (key verse 10:8)
- dependence shown in prayer (key verse 10:14)
- dependence shown in obedience (key verse 11:15)

The power of the promise (11:16–12:24)

- the final campaign (11:16-23, key verse 11:23)
- taking stock of the territory won under Moses (12:1-6 and under Joshua (12:7-24)
- the promise fulfilled (cf. 11:23 with 1:13).

To set these ideas in a New Testament context, a consideration of Hebrews 4:6-11 is helpful. The rest Joshua gave the people was not the last word – the rest Jesus offers is.

Sermon 2

Chapter 9 can be treated as a self-contained unit; although the implications of the story have further repercussions in chapter 10. In this unit Israel creates a problem for itself.

An **introduction** should not ignore the importance of **9:1-2** – these verses set the context for the rest of the story, particularly Gibeon's motivation to deceive Israel.

A careless decision 9:3-15

Faced with the apparently convincing evidence of the Gibeonites' long journey, Israel failed to enquire of the Lord and entered a treaty with them.

A difficult discovery 9:16-21

When the deceit is discovered, the leaders of Israel are presented with at least two difficulties – preventing the Gibeonites from being killed and not dishonouring God. A resolution had to be found.

A strange providence 9:22-27

Gibeon becomes the servant of Israel and particularly is to serve at the sanctuary. Lives are saved and knowledge of God made possible.

By this strange providence this pagan group are brought into the heart of God's people and influence. The Psalmist would see this kind of service as a blessing (Ps. 84:10), so does Jesus (Mark 10:42-45) and so does Paul (Col. 1:23). God's strange and gracious providence lifts us out of our rebellion and paganism (see e.g. 1 Cor. 6:9-11).

Sermon 3

Chapter 10 recounts the battle against a coalition of kings in the central area of the land. Once this enemy is defeated,

The Power of the Promise (9–12) 285

the decisive victory means that a united Canaanite front is now less likely. Once more God the Warrior is centrestage.

An **introduction** can show that the kings remain opposed to the work of God **(10:1-6).**

The battle is the Lord's (10:7-11)
The word of assurance (v. 8) is backed up by the Lord's heavy artillery (v. 11)!

A day like no other (10:12-15)
However we interpret the lengthening of the day, we must not miss the main point of the text – the Lord listening to humans (10:14).

A complete victory (10:16-27)
The two 'marks of victory' (see notes above) convey the finality and totality of the victory.

As a **conclusion**, a very brief survey of the southern campaign, should emphasise its final note – 'the Lord... fought for Israel' (10:42)

The finality of God's victory points to the finality of Christ's victory – when His enemies will be made His footstool (Heb. 10:13). This victory opens the way by which God can hear and answer prayer.

Sermon 4
The list of kings **is** part of the inspired Word of God. Our task is to convey what it meant in its context and to its original readers – and then draw lessons for today.

An **introduction** again points to the hostility toward the things of God **(11:1-5).**

Following orders (11:6-15)
What God says (11:6) is what Joshua does (11:9). The emphasis in this section is on obedience (see 11:15).

Final inheritance (11:16-28)
To gain their final inheritance, Israel needed perseverance (11:16), obedience (11:20) and courage (11:21-22, see notes above). But the war did not go on for ever (11:23).

Victory parade (12:1-24)
As rulers of the ancient world would lead both captives and plunder in their victory parade, so chapter 12 does this. And the victory is a comprehensive one.

There are necessary qualities needed in facing the enemy, but the war does not go on for ever. There will be a final victory parade (Eph. 4:8; Col. 2:15) – but we need to make sure we are in the right part of the procession!

Suggestions for teaching

Questions to help understand the passage

1. In what ways do the various forces opposing Israel in this section illustrate the rebellion of Psalm 2:1-3?

2. What is the main failure of Israel in the Gibeonite affair? How does the writer postpone God's response to it?

3. Why is the Israelite oath 'before the LORD' so significant?

4. What is the full implication of Joshua 'saving' the Gibeonites (9:26)?

The Power of the Promise (9-12)   287

5. God does not speak in the Gibeonite episode until just before the battle to save them (10:8). What is the significance of this?

6. How might you address any questions you, or others, have concerning the sun 'standing still'?

7. Why and how at this point of the narrative does Joshua encourage his fellow leaders (10:22-26)?

8. Why do you think that the writer tends to use a formula to describe Israel's victories in the second half of chapter 10? What forms the climax to this section?

9. There is a full description of the forces massed against Israel in 11:1-5. What purpose does this serve in the narrative?

10. How does 11:18 affect your understanding of Israel's campaign for Canaan?

11. Compare 11:21-22 with Numbers 13:28-33. What are the important factors in this comparison?

12. How comprehensive is the list of people and places in chapter 12? Why is it important to include that list at this point in the narrative?

Questions to help apply the text

1. 'We need not only the power of God to overwhelm our obvious enemies but also the wisdom of God to detect our subtle enemies.'[18] How was this true for Israel and how is it true for us?

---

18. Davis, *Joshua* p. 78.

2. How important are the words and promises of God's people?

3. What examples can you suggest from scripture and from your own experience where God uses our mistakes and even our rebellion, although we still have to live with the consequences of our actions?

4. Why do you think the writer seems to make more of Joshua's prayer than the miraculous sign? How do we undervalue prayer?

5. In what ways is Christ's great victory important and effective both for our present and future?

6. How does our culture encourage us to want everything 'now'? How does Israel's story counteract that trend?

7. Do we really see God as our Warrior King? If not, why not?

8. Sometimes we are disabled by our fears – Israel was in Numbers 13. What makes the difference in 11:21-22, and what does that teach us for today?

9. The promise of rest for the people of God comes to fulfilment in 11:23. Read Hebrews 4:6-11 and think about the rest we are promised. Are there any clues in Joshua 11 that will help us work towards our rest?

10. How does knowing that all Christ's enemies will have to acknowledge Him as Lord help us live each day?

6

Receiving the Promise (13–21)

Introduction

We have already asked the question, 'What makes this part of the book important enough for it to be included in Scripture?' The key is to understand its place in the promise of God. As we read it, we see traced out the distribution of the Promised Land. It is God's incredible gift to His people. And it is all because of His promise – a visible, tangible expression of that promise freely given to His people. We noted in Part One (***Lists and more lists***) that Richard Nelson recognised 13:1-7 as a turning point in the book. Robert Hubbard comes to a similar conclusion:

> The years of war are gone, and a new part of the book of Joshua opens. In one sense, this is the most important part because it reports of fulfilment (finally!) of the promise to Abraham: "To your offspring I will give this land" (Gen. 12:7; cf. Josh. 11:23). Yahweh's command to

Joshua initiates the settlement of Canaan (13:7), just as it did the conquest.[1]

It is difficult to imagine that the first readers of these chapters approached them as a dry-as-dust list of real estate. Rather, they saw in them the thrill and anticipation of the announcement of a bequest, or better as a gift, because the benefactor is very much alive and well, and active on their behalf.

Another perspective on the importance of these chapters and why we need to read them is offered by David Firth. He suggests we should do so, recognising their function:

> They are the key evidence that Yahweh has indeed given the land, and more than that, that every clan could understand that the land where they lived was theirs.[2]

This makes them the equivalent of title deeds; deeds that are given to a landless and wandering people. They are symbols of stability, security and peace.

Listening to the text

Context and structure

Despite all that had been accomplished, there still remains a sense of tension in the text. There are two significant markers:

+ 'Joshua took the entire land' (11:23).

---

1. R. L. Hubbard, Jr, *Joshua NIVAC* (Grand Rapids, USA: Zondervan, 2009), p. 396.

2. David Firth, *The Message of Joshua* (Nottingham, UK: IVP, 2015), p. 142.

- 'there are still very large areas of land to be taken over' (13:1).

In between these verses is chapter 12, which itemises the kings and the territories that God has delivered into their hands. The land is subdued, it is theirs, there is no major opposition to face. Even if there remains work to be done, the upcoming allocation of the land must be a cause for thankfulness and rejoicing in God's goodness and faithfulness to His promise. The reality of receiving the promise is that it also points people to the fact that there is more to come.

As Bruce Waltke says:

> At any given point during the process of possessing the land, it can be said God fulfilled his promise. Moreover, each individual fulfilment was a part of the ultimate fulfilment and could be reckoned as such. The New Testament presents the same tension regarding the kingdom of God: it is already here but in its fullest context 'not yet'.[3]

Living with this tension is, then, part of the authentic experience of believers in every age. We receive a foretaste of what is to come – but, it is still to come!

Earlier we viewed the structure of this section of Joshua as a series of concentric circles with God's presence in the middle of His people as its focal point. As we work through the text we will follow the linear progression of the text, showing the links to the corresponding sections and their common themes. The basic outline of the text is as follows:

---

3. Bruce Waltke 'Joshua', *New Bible Commentary* (Nottingham, UK: IVP, 1994), p. 251.

13:1-7	Back to the future (i)
13:8-33	Guaranteed provision (i)
14:1-5	By royal appointment (i)
14:6-15	From start to finish (i)
15:1–17:18	Sharing in the inheritance (i)
18:1-10	In the presence of God
18:11–19:48	Sharing in the inheritance (ii)
19:49-51	From start to finish (ii)
20:1-6	By royal appointment (ii)
20:7–21:42	Guaranteed provision (ii)
21:43-45	Back to the future (ii)

Working though the text

Back to the future (i) (13:1-7)

There can be no doubt that when we move from the first twelve chapters into this part of the book of Joshua (13-21), we move into a different atmosphere. Gone are the battles and most of the details about the actions of Israel and of God on their behalf. The narrative unfolds in a different way and the opening verse (13:1) marks a turning point in the narrative flow. According to Robert Hubbard:

> Syntactically, the opening, subject-first sentence structure (lit. 'Now Joshua was old...') both signals the opening of a new scene and the introduction of a new character, Joshua as an old man.[4]

The text does not give any evidence of a united opposition to Israel; rather it speaks in terms of pockets of resistance to be cleared out.

There is no sense in which the promise of God, that has enabled them to subdue the land, has been left behind.

---

4. Hubbard, *Joshua* p. 396 n1.

Indeed, it is still the motivation and power behind finishing the task, as we shall see. The tension between what has been done and what still needs to be done is evident in this first section.

Gordon McConville says:

> The present chapter, in fact, faces two ways: forward into the narrative of distribution and backward, by way of reflection and comment on the story of the conquest so far.[5]

The future is dependent on what has been achieved in the past.

The Lord's words that open this section (13:1) appear to indicate Joshua's work is over.

As he had taken over from Moses, perhaps now is the time for him to hand the work on to another. Before that can happen and we hear the farewell speeches of Joshua there is a final work to do – the distribution of the land. This may be the last great task of Joshua, because he alone had the authority to accomplish it. To the words of the Lord, 'there are still very large areas of land to be taken over' (13:1), there is added a kind of parenthesis, either by the Lord or by the narrator, detailing that land. It can be summarised in three distinct areas:

- in the South, land occupied by the Philistines (13:2-3)
- a corridor of land along the Mediterranean Sea (13:4)
- the northern hill-country chiefly of Lebanon (13:5).

---

5. Gordon McConville & Stephen Williams, *Joshua, Two Horizons Commentary* (Grand Rapids, USA: Eerdmans, 2010), p. 61.

As the allotment of territory proceeds, it will be the responsibility of the individual tribes to dispossess the people of those regions. Gone are the day of 'all Israel' war. The NIV seems to introduce an exception in that God will deal with the North while Israel deals with the others. A clearer translation is the ESV's, having listed all the areas to be occupied, it brings that list to a close with, 'even all the Sidonians'. This is followed by the Lord's declaration:

> I myself will drive them out before the people of Israel. Only allot the land to Israel for an inheritance, as I have commanded you (13:6, similarly NET).

Here is the big change in Joshua's responsibility, no longer the army commander, now he is in charge of the land distribution. The existence of these pockets of land still to be occupied does not conflict to any great extent with the overall narrative we have seen in earlier chapters. One example of this is the area occupied by the Philistines; a remnant of them were still in the cities of Gaza, Gath and Ashdod after the southern campaign (see 11:22).

There is a subtle change for the people of God as well. No longer will they depend on the central control of one great leader, God will drive out the people of the land before the Israelites (13:6). In this new and more settled situation, with the majority of the land subdued, there is an increased emphasis on the responsibility of the tribes themselves. This idea will surface again as we move through the narrative before us. As we noticed at the very beginning of the book of Joshua, leaders come and go; the only real source of stability is God and His promise.

The section ends with a mandate for action to Joshua:

> Be sure to allocate this land to Israel for an inheritance, as I instructed you, and divide it as an inheritance among the nine tribes and half of the tribe of Manasseh (13:6-7).

The other two-and-a-half tribes already had a promised inheritance. Now, the 'title deeds' will be handed over to them.

This section, with both its look back at the past and look forward into the future, is mirrored at the close of this major section with a summary statement that reflects both the past and the future (21:43-45).

Guaranteed provision (i) (13:8-33)

Following the command to allocate territory to the nine-and-a-half tribes on the West Bank of the Jordan, the focus now moves to the remaining tribes on the East Bank. These tribes do not need to be allocated their land by lot – a guaranteed provision has already been made for them. As we have noted earlier in the story, the tribes of Rueben, Gad and half tribe of Manasseh had been gifted land to the east of the Jordan. This is in line with the agreement made with Moses and a former generation (Deut. 2:26–3:17). As the people of Israel finally approach the Promised Land this agreement was ratified on condition that the fighting men in these tribes would take the lead in the battle for the land (Num. 32). It was an agreement that Joshua called on to begin the campaign (Josh. 1:12-18). So, the moment arrives when these tribes can finally become established in 'the inheritance that Moses had given them east of the Jordan' (13:8).

As will become familiar to us as we work through these chapters, there follows a geographical sketch of the area allocated to the East Bank tribes. The first sketch covers the whole of the territory the two-and-a-half tribes occupy (13:8-13). This will be followed by a more carefully delineated area relating to each tribe:

+ 'the tribe of Reuben according to its clans' 13:15-23
+ 'the tribe of Gad according to its clans' 13:24-28
+ 'half the family of Manasseh according to its clans' 13:29-31.

In the same way the descriptions begin with Moses being the one allocating the lands (13:8), so the list also ends (13:32). This further underlines the importance of Moses in regard to the East Bank settlement.

This is a truly guaranteed provision for these tribes, but their future in the place has a shadow hanging over it. Although this land has been taken, the narrators record the fact that:

> ... the Israelites did not drive out the people of Gesher and Maakah, so they continue to live among the Israelites to this day (13:13).

One of the factors behind the imposition of the ban (*herem*) was to safeguard Israel – to act, as it were, as a 'disinfectant', to avoid pollution from both local politics and religion. The effect of the Geshurites living alongside Israel had repercussions even in David's day. Absalom, whose mother was a Geshurite, led a rebellion against David his father (see 2 Sam. 3:3, 13:37-38 and 15:1-12). The men of Maakah were also involved in an anti-David coalition (2 Sam. 10:6-8). The reluctance to be fully obedient to the Lord's command did not necessarily result in an easier life for Israel.

Another significant note sounded in this section is the double reference to the tribe of Levi. These references bracket the details concerning the two-and-a-half tribes (see 13:14, 33). In the first of these, their inheritance is in and through the service of the Lord. The second simply says: 'the LORD the God of Israel is their inheritance' (13:33). Simple the statement may be, in one sense, but it is also an infinitely richer inheritance. The totality of their needs is provided for in their relationship to, and service of, God Himself.

A reasonably detailed description of the territory possessed, the hills, the plains, the cities and the rivers, would remind the book's first readers of the strong link between geography and theology. God's promise included a place to live and these details show that promise in terms of real locations in real time. And for a landless, homeless people, that met a real need.

When we come to the matching section towards the end of this part of Joshua, the Levites will make a return. They will receive an allotment of cities from the inheritance of Israel – a guaranteed provision for them. In a similar way those places designated as a city of refuge will offer a guaranteed provision to meet the needs of others.

By royal appointment (i) (14:1-5)
These verses act as a prologue to the complete account of the distribution of the land. They foreground the fact that this is the tribes' inheritance. A more literal translation of 14:1 makes this clear:

> Now these are the areas the Israelites inherited in the land of Canaan, which Eleazar the priest, Joshua son of

Nun and the heads of the tribal clans of Israel caused them to inherit.

The account of the allocation will extend over the next six chapters, which is an indication of its importance and centrality to the story. This prologue also makes clear how the allocation for the West Bank tribes will proceed – it will be conducted by lots. The brief nature of this prologue might cause us to overlook some important issues that are raised in it. These include:

- the two people responsible for the allocations are named
- the authority behind the allocation
- a further mention of Levi
- an explanation concerning the number of tribes.

Joshua is given his 'full title' – Joshua son of Nun. The use of his name in this way not only opens and closes the account of the land distribution (see 19:49, 51), but also appears at significant turning points in the whole narrative (see 1:1, 2:1, 6:6, 24:29). Further, it formed a link back into the Pentateuch where his full name is used (see e.g. Exod. 33:11; Num. 11: 28, 14:6; Deut. 1:38, 31:23 etc). The historic continuity reinforces the authority of Joshua and his place in the purposes of God. Eleazar the priest is also mentioned by name. He is the son of Aaron and his successor in the high priest's role. The very mention of his name and his sharing responsibility with Joshua makes it clear that the division of the land is not simply a political or secular exercise. As 18:1 will show us, there was a strong theological element to the allocation. The final division was made at Shiloh where they set up the tent of meeting and it was there that Joshua 'cast lots for them ... in the presence of the LORD' (18:10).

Although, humanly speaking, Joshua and Eleazar were in charge of the allocation of territory, a greater authority stood behind them. Twice in this brief passage we hear that it was done 'as the LORD had commanded Moses' (14:2, 5). The tribe of Levi is again referred to as receiving 'no share of the land but only towns to live in' (14:4). And, as we saw above, the Levites were not without a place of their own, but they are singled out as a special case and we will hear more about this later.

This introductory section also sets right, as it were, the numbering of the tribes. With Levi excluded from the main allocation and Joseph tribes divided into Ephraim and Manasseh, the distribution of the land continues to require twelve distinct allocations.

The method of allocation, its officers and recipients as well as the authority behind it, are all clearly spelled out – it is by royal appointment. The matching section (20:1-6) also speaks of cities that are to be set aside as places of refuge. They are also instituted as such by royal appointment– by divine command.

From start to finish (i) (14:6-15)

Before we reach the larger section – detailing the actual land allocation, the narrator pauses to introduce a more personal story – that of Caleb. It is matched later in the narrative by the allocation of land to Joshua as an individual (19:49-51). These two men, of course, are the only survivors from the previous generation. They brought back an encouraging report concerning Canaan and they believed that with the Lord's help the land could be taken (see Num. 13:30, 14:5-10). Now, they both stand in the Promised Land and again the Word of the Lord has come to pass. As the Lord had said to the wilderness generation:

> Not one of you will enter the land I swore with uplifted hand to make your home, except Caleb son of Jephunneh and Joshua son of Nun (Num. 14: 30).

Here we see them together again and Caleb reminds Joshua of those earlier days (14:6-9).

Who was this man Caleb? Most of the references to him in Scripture are focussed on his role as one of the spies of Numbers 13–14 and in the story before us. Little else is known of him. Something of his heritage is seen in 14:6; he is part of the delegation who come to Joshua from the tribe of Judah (cf. Num. 13:6 & 1 Chron. 4:15). He is also called a Kenezzite. This should not be confused with a non-Israelite group in Canaan; rather his name indicates his ancestry as a 'son of Kenaz'.[6] If little is known of his personal background, there are some features of his character clearly demonstrated in the text.

The first of these is he 'followed the LORD my God wholeheartedly' (14:8). This characteristic is repeated twice more in this episode (14:9, 14). Devotion was not just an inner feeling without any real foundation. It arose from his trust in the Word/promise of God. This foundation is referred to a number of times here:

* 'you know what the LORD said to Moses ... about you and me' (14:6)

---

6. See David Howard Jr, *Joshua NAC* (Nashville, USA: Broadman & Holman, 1998), p. 327.

Receiving the Promise (13–21)

- 'just as the LORD promised' (14:10a)
- 'since the time he [the LORD] said to Moses' (14:10b)
- 'that the LORD promised me' (14:12a)
- 'I will drive them out just as he said' (14:12b).

Ralph Davis' comment is exactly to the point:

> Five times Caleb hammers this point home: his request is nothing but what God had promised him (v. 9). True faith always functions that way, it pleads God's promises; it anchors itself upon the word of God. There can be no other foundation for faith.[7]

It was a promise that was reiterated by Moses (14:9 cf. Num. 14:24 and Deut. 1:36). Now the moment had come to claim it. Caleb may be old – 85 years – but his strength and spirit are undiminished:

> I am still as strong today as the day Moses sent me out; I am just as vigorous to go out to battle now as I was then. Now give me this hill country that the LORD promised me that day (14:11-12).

He did not fear the descendants of Anak forty-five years ago; and he still does not fear them. Some of these people had obviously escaped the purge of the southern part of the land and reoccupied the area around Hebron. This is exactly the area Caleb claims. It is not an act of machismo, to prove a point; it is a wholehearted trust in God whom He has served from the start to the finish. So, Caleb received

---

7. Ralph Davis, *Joshua – No Falling Words* (Fearn, UK: Christian Focus, 2012), p. 117.

'Hebron as his inheritance' (14:13) – now the narrator can say again, 'the land had rest from war' (14:15).

Sharing the inheritance (i) (15:1–17:18)

In broad outline the sharing of the inheritance moves from the south to the north of the land. The tribes do not receive their allotment in the order of the sons of Joseph whose names they bear. Judah is the first to receive their territory. Although Judah was the fourth son of Joseph, born to Leah, he assumed a leading role among the brothers (see e.g. Gen. 43:3-10, 44:16-34) and received a special blessing from his father, Jacob (49:8-12). The tribe was to take the lead every time the nation moved on during the wilderness wanderings. After the death of Joshua, they were the tribe chosen by God to take the lead in fighting the Canaanites (Judg. 1:1-2).

As we read of the area inherited by Judah, we must keep in mind the writer's intention – he is engaging in a form of theological geography. He takes his first readers and us on a tour of the land saying: 'this is where you have trodden, this is how God fulfilled His promise'. David Howard pictures it as the ancient equivalent of what is today called 'virtual reality'.

He goes on to say that it is like:

> ... watching a borderline being drawn in 'real-time' with a computer-generated line, moving up and down, in and out, twisting and turning. The reader is drawn into the actual creation of the line, it seems, and given a 'bumps-and-all' tour of the land.[8]

---

8. Howard, *Joshua* p. 334.

For the reader today, they may seem to be 'just a list of names', for the first readers they were the details of their first real home and the substantial answer to a real and effective promise from God.

The boundaries of Judah's region having been described (15:1-12), the narrator pauses to focus back on one particular member of the tribe – Caleb. Some additional information is added concerning the taking of Hebron and the exploits of Caleb. Having dealt with the Anakites of Hebron, Caleb moves on to take the town of Debir. Othniel rather than Caleb takes the town and also receives Caleb's daughter in marriage (15:16-17). The land that Caleb gives the couple, possibly a wedding gift, also needs water. Aksah, Caleb's daughter, is bold enough to ask for this; he responds by giving her the rights to some springs. The inheritance Caleb has received will pass to his family, but he is prepared to relinquish some of it even now – such is his trust in God's provision.

To drive home the extent of Judah's inheritance, the narrative continues with lists of the towns that are now in their possession (15:22-62). There is, however, an ominous note that closes the list:

> Judah could not dislodge the Jebusites, who were living in Jerusalem; to this day the Jebusites live there with the people of Judah (15:63).

Jerusalem is listed as a city in the region of Benjamin, but, in fact it sat on the border with Judah as well (cf. 15:8 & 18:16). The problem for both tribes was that a non-Israelite people could introduce them to non-Israelite ways. Closeness often leads to compromise.

The allocation of inheritance then moves to the Joseph tribes, beginning with an overview of the whole territory (16:1-4). It then moved on to describe the two tribes' portions of the land in turn. The younger of Joseph's two sons' family group is dealt with first. Their land is part of the central area of Canaan. Once again the problem arises of the Canaanites who still live among them (16:10). After a brief statement about Manasseh's allocation (17:1-2), we are (re)introduced to Zelophehad's daughters. After their father died, leaving no male heirs, the five daughters went to Moses to plead for an allocation of land to preserve their father's name (see Num. 27:1-11). Moses consulted the Lord on the issue and He pronounced in favour of the daughters' request. They now come to Joshua and Eleazar for their inheritance. Their only plea in this case is based on the Word of the Lord – 'The LORD commanded Moses to give us an inheritance among our relatives' (17:4). However strange that may have sounded culturally, the strength of their plea was its foundation – the promise of God.

The list of towns that are part of Manasseh's territory are something of a mixed bag (17:7-11) – other tribes possessed areas and towns within their territory. In the same way, Manasseh had property in the lands of other tribes. And this was not the only cause for concern:

> Yet the Manassites were not able to occupy these towns, for the Canaanites were determined to live in that region. However when the Israelites grew stronger, they subjected the Canaanites to forced labour but did not drive them out completely (17:13).

This is now the third time this note has sounded. Each time it represents a failure on the part of the Israelites to

Receiving the Promise (13–21)

follow the Lord's instructions. The damage this failure will do to their relationship with God will be evident across the pages of the book of Judges – as will be the price they have to pay for that failure. The final episode in this account is of the people of Joseph saying to Joshua:

> Why have you allotted us only one portion of land and one share for an inheritance? We are numerous people and the LORD has blessed us abundantly. (17:14.)

It seems at this point Joshua is on his own, no mention is made of Eleazar. The people of Joseph may have been playing the 'tribalism' card – Joshua is an Ephraimite and surely will sympathise with their complaint. And the complaint is, 'Not enough land.' Their logic seems to them to be impeccable, too many people and too small an inheritance. Is their claim, entitlement to more land, based on the sense of their own importance? They may feel that God's blessing has resulted in their being numerous and so deserving special privileges. The NASB translates the second half of 17:14 as: 'I am a numerous people whom the LORD has thus far blessed.' Obviously, to their eyes, the allocation of the land they had received is not a sign that this blessing continues with them. As we have seen, and we'll see, however, the allocation of each tribe's inheritance is under the sovereign control of God. In the end their dissatisfaction is not with Joshua, but with the Lord. At root, their problem is that they are not content with the promise of God; they are not convinced He will continue to keep it.

Joshua's response is brief and to the point: 'If you are so numerous and blessed, press on into the hill country and carve out some more land for yourselves' (see 17:15).

Their reply repeats their dissatisfaction with what they have and adds a further complaint about the problem of the Canaanites and their chariots (17:16). In Joshua's last word on this subject, he doesn't close his eyes to the difficulties the people face. Yet, his focus is surely not on the problem but on the promise:

> When you go to war against your enemies and see horses and chariots and an army greater than yours, do not be afraid of them, because the LORD your God who brought you out of Egypt will be with you (Deut. 20:1).

The attitude of the Joseph tribes is the opposite of that of Caleb. For him difficulties meant buckling on his sword and trusting God – for the people of Joseph it was to complain that God's provision was not enough. What determines these two different attitudes? They are determined by the approach taken to the promise of God.

In the presence of God (18:1–10)

We have reached a turning point in the narrative. Up until now the camp of Israel has been located at Gilgal. Here we have a new focus, the nation assembles at Shiloh (18:1). And we hear for the first time of the tent of meeting being set up in the camp. Gordon McConville comments on 18:1:

> This opening verse is one of the most theologically pregnant in the book of Joshua. The setting up of the tent of meeting at Shiloh clearly marks a significant step in the progress of Israel towards fulfilling its destiny in the promised land.[9]

---

9. McConville, *Joshua* p. 73.

There is, in fact, only one other reference to the tent of meeting and that occurs at 19:51 signalling the end of the distribution of the land. We should not miss, therefore, the importance of this verse in terms of the whole story of Israel and especially the conquest. McConville's observations on this are worth quoting at length:

> The present verse has a function, therefore, in the whole narrative from Exodus to Kings in its affirmation that under Joshua the people of Israel have entered upon the benefits of their relationship with Yahweh, promised since Sinai. Israel is in its land; they have sought and found the place which would symbolize Yahweh's ownership of the land and his presence to them for worship and inquiry.[10]

We can, I believe, trace this further back into the book of Genesis – to the promise to Abraham and to God's creative purpose in establishing a place to live, a people to live there and a relationship to enjoy. McConville does make a connection with the creation narrative when he points out that the verb in the sentence, 'The land lay subdued before them' (18:1 ESV) is the same verb as God's command to humanity to 'subdue' the earth in Gen 1:28.[11]

It is not simply the reference to the tent of meeting that stresses the importance of this episode with regard to God being present with His people. The very act of casting lots is something done before the Lord and therefore under His control. This is made clear by the threefold repetition of the phrase 'in the presence of the LORD' (18:6, 8, 10). The whole process of describing, mapping and allocating the land by lot is done, as it were, under the eye of God.

---

10. *Ibid* p. 75.

11. *Ibid*.

Another significant factor in these verses is the care that is taken to be completely inclusive. It brings to the fore once again the book's stress on all Israel. In 18:5-7, even if every tribe is not named, they are included. Twice it is acknowledged that there are seven allocations still to be made. Also the territory, already given to Judah and the Joseph tribes, is re-affirmed. Finally the East Bank tribes are said to 'have already received their inheritance' (18:7). As we have noted on previous occasions, the tribe of Levi get a special mention – they have no land allocation, but 'the LORD is their inheritance' (18:7).

Some commentators see Joshua's words in 18:3 as an accusation and challenge to the Israelites:

> How long will you wait before you begin to take possession of the land that the LORD, the God of your ancestors, has given you?

After years of wandering and then of warfare, perhaps they were content with the gains they had made. Joshua knows there is a bigger picture and exhorts them to enter into their full inheritance.

Here, at the centre of this section of the book concerned with receiving the promise, we see not only the final act in dividing up the Promised Land, but also a marvellous fulfilment of God's promise. The setting up of the tent of meeting is the first concrete step in realising God's Word in Deuteronomy 12. Once the people have crossed the Jordan and settled in the land, once they have rest from their enemies (Deut. 12:10):

> Then to the place the LORD your God will choose as a dwelling for his Name – there you are to bring everything

I command you... And there rejoice before the LORD your
God – you, your sons and daughters ... (Deut. 12:11-12).

Although 'the place' will one day be transferred to Jerusalem, here, at Shiloh, the people receive that promise. A similar promise is found at the end of the list of blessings in Leviticus 26:11-12:

I will put my dwelling place among you, and will not abhor you. I will walk among you and be your God, and you will be my people.

This latter text sums up the essence of God's covenantal relationship with His people. It comes to real expression at Shiloh as all is done, 'in the presence of the LORD.'

Sharing the inheritance (ii) (18:11–19:48)
Joshua's words at Shiloh (18:3) are designed to spur a somewhat reluctant group of Israelites – the remaining seven tribes – into action. He also wants to make sure that the process of distribution is fair and transparent. Once the land has been carefully mapped, the distribution can begin. Unlike the first round of allocations (*Sharing the inheritance [1]*), this round takes us on another 'virtual tour' and makes no comment about any residual groups of Canaanites. It is worth keeping Genesis 49 in the background while reviewing these tribal allotments. In both places – the blessing of his sons by Jacob, and the lots of land – the birth order of the sons is not necessarily followed. There are also indications for a few of the tribes as to how their family history will unfold. The division of the land to these seven tribes is worked out in the following way:

Benjamin The territory allotted to this tribe is described in the most detail. Various suggestions have been offered as to why they are given pre-eminence here. These include the position of this land between Judah and the Joseph tribes, Benjamin's position as a favourite son of Jacob and the fact that Jerusalem is included in their territory. There seems to be no conclusive evidence for any of these options. It is clear from both the geographical description and the city list that it was a considerable territory given over to this tribe.

Simeon The distinctive mark of Simeon's inheritance is that it 'lay within the territory of Judah' (19:1). This may simply be based on the size of the tribe, but a deeper reason might be behind this. David Firth suggests that Genesis 49:5-7 may be in the background here. Jacob, in his 'blessing' of Simeon and Levi says:

> Cursed be their anger, so fierce, and their fury so cruel!
> I will scatter them in Jacob and disperse them in Israel
> (Gen. 49:7).

This was said because of their act of violence against Shechem (Gen. 34). Firth comments:

> ... it seems that the concern here is to show how God's purposes are being worked out. If so, we see a profound paradox in which God takes the outworking of human sin and makes it the basis on which he is able to show righteousness.[12]

The Old Testament portrays Simeon as a tribe in decline, the number in the tribe drops dramatically between the first and second census of Numbers (Num. 1 & 26). 1 Chronicles 4:27 also reflects the tribes numerical infer-

---

12. David Firth, *The Message of Joshua* (Nottingham, UK: IVP, 2015), p. 180.

iority; and in Moses' blessing of the tribes, Simeon is noticeable by his absence (Deut. 33).

Zebulun Although the description of Zebulun's land is relatively brief, the tribe occupied a commanding position in the Galilean region. Earlier references to their position in the land (Gen. 49:13 & Deut. 33:18-19) connect them with the sea, Paul Wright suggests that the blessing of Jacob and Moses 'can best be understood as anticipating Zebulun's strategic position ... in the land of Canaan'. And he adds:

> ... the tribal inheritance carried a number of important natural routes connecting the sea coast with points inland, including the Great Trunk Road running between Egypt and Mesopotamia.[13]

Nazareth, although not mentioned in our text, was within their boundaries and later references to this territory (cf. Isa. 9:1 quoted in Matt. 4:12-16) lead Wright to conclude that:

> ... biblical statements regarding Zebulun subsequent to the Pentateuch tend to emphasize Zebulun's role as a people who were important in redemptive history.[14]

Issachar Briefer still is the account of Issachar's territory; it is an area to the southwest of Galilee. There has been a tendency among commentators to suggest that Issachar as a tribe submitted themselves to the service of Canaanite overlords early on in their occupation of the land. This is based on an interpretation of Genesis 49:14-15 that is open

---

13. Paul Wright, 'Zebulun' in *Dictionary of the Old Testament: Pentateuch* (Leicester UK/Downers Grove USA: IVP, 2003), p. 912.

14. Ibid p. 911.

to question. In a broader context Issachar is one of the tribes not mentioned in Judges 1 among the tribes who failed to drive the Canaanites out of their territory. Indeed, Issachar are praised in Deborah's song (Judg. 5:15) for their part in the fight against the oppressors of Israel.[15] Overall there is some ambivalence to the evidence concerning this tribe.

Asher Of the place names that are provided in the list of Asher's territory (19:24-31), the majority of them are cities and the remainder are geographical features. 'The coastal plains of Asher boast some of Israel's richest soil, suitable for producing a hearty menu'.[16] Jacob's blessing may be pertinent here:

> Asher's food will be rich; He will provide delicacies fit for a king (Gen. 49:20).

Judges 1:31 shows that there is some ambivalence concerning the success of Asher – it names at least four cities from which the Asherites failed to drive out Canaanites.

Naphtali The tribe settled in the northwest region of the country. It was probably the most favoured area of Canaan and its beauty and productivity are reflected in Jacob and Moses' blessing on them (Gen. 49:21 & Deut. 33:23). While they were not successful in driving out the Canaanites (Judg. 1:33), they did join Deborah and Barak, (a Naphtalite) in the fight against the king of Hazor (Judg. 5:18). They were also associated with Zebulun in the later prophets – they 'sat in darkness' because of their

---

15. See Victor Hamilton, *The Book of Genesis Chapters 18-50 NICOT* (Grand Rapids USA: Eerdmans, 1995), pp. 664-668.

16. Adolph Harstad, *Joshua Concordia Commentary* (St Louis USA: Concordia Publishing House, 2004) p. 612.

Receiving the Promise (13–21)

northerly position, vulnerable to the attacks of Syria and Assyria (see again Isa. 9:1 & Matt. 4:12-16).

Dan The last lot falls to the tribe of Dan. They are to settle in the coastal region, with Judah to the south and the tribes of Benjamin, Ephraim and Manasseh bordering them. Their territory is indicated by a list of city names, rather than boundaries, which included the land associated with these places. As if in an aside, the narrator adds:

> When the territory of the Danites was lost to them, they went up and attacked Heslem, took it, put it to the sword and occupied it. They settled in Heslem and named it Dan after their ancestor (19:47).

A fuller explanation of this tribal movement is given in Judges 18 and it is not a very flattering story concerning the Danites. Gordon McConville comments:

> The Joshua narrative lacks the express ironies of the Judges account, yet it poses the same question. How can it be said of this territory which is expressly not the one allocated to them as their inheritance by lots that it is "the inheritance of the tribe of Dan" (v. 48)?[17]

A brief survey of the Judges account of the Danites' movements will help fill out the background of the account in Joshua. The main elements are:

- 'they had not yet come into an inheritance among the tribes of Israel' (Judg. 18:1).

- so they sought 'a place of their own where they might settle' (Judg. 18:1).

---

17. McConville, *Joshua* p. 78.

- their spies found an area in the north where 'the people were living in safety … And since their land lacked nothing, they were prosperous' (Judg. 18:7).

- they mounted an attack against the unsuspecting people of the region (Judg. 18:10) and they took it 'with the sword and burned down the city' (Judg. 18:27).

- they rebuilt the city and named it Dan (Judg. 18:28-29).

- they set up an idol there that they had stolen on their journey north with a priest they had 'persuaded' to go with the idol (Judg. 18:30-31).

Two other connections with the tribe of Dan and their city need to be noted:

- Dan was the northernmost city where Jeroboam set up one of his golden calves to subvert the worship of Israel – taking them away from Jerusalem (1 Kings 12:28-29).

- In the New Testament, Dan is excluded from the list of twelve tribes in Revelation 7, presumably because of its notoriety concerning idolatry.

While God's faithfulness to His promise is clearly seen in this whole section, there is evidence enough of the faithlessness of some of Israel in receiving it. This tension is highlighted by McConville, who says: 'The case of Dan posits a sharp discrepancy between the notion of legitimate possession and the actuality of Israel's occupation.'[18]

---

18. *Ibid.*

From start to finish (ii) (19:49-51)

The story of allocating the land by lots comes to a more positive end with the mention of Joshua himself and his inheritance. This brief passage mirrors the earlier one concerning Caleb, Joshua's fellow spy, who brought back a positive report to Moses about Canaan (Num. 13-14). These two men of faith stand in stark contrast to much of the record concerning the tribes in general and the allocation of their inheritance.

The account of Joshua gaining his inheritance is told in a low-key way. Even though he has been the leader of the nation through all this period, bringing them safely into the land, no special ceremony accompanies his allocation. It is all done 'as the LORD had commanded' (19:50). The specific command of God is not recorded in Scripture, but the allocation is in line with God's promise to Caleb and Joshua in Numbers 14:30 (see also Josh. 14:6, where Caleb says to Joshua: 'You know what the LORD said to Moses the man of God at Kadesh Barnea about you and me'). Further, in common with many Israelites, possessing and developing his inheritance required continuing work.

> They gave [Joshua] the town he asked for – Timnath Serah in the hill country of Ephraim. And he built up the town and settled there (19:50).

The record of the allocation of the land by lots is closed off with the concluding statement that implies that the land is a gift from God and that He sovereignly disposes of it. It was: 'Assigned by lot at Shiloh in the presence of the LORD at the entrance to the tent of meeting. And so they've finished dividing the land.' (19:51)

They had truly received the promise of God.

By royal appointment (ii) (20:1-6)

As all of the tribes were given their land and cities 'as the Lord had commanded through Moses' (14:2), so now God sovereignly appoints cities of refuge. These cities come from the inheritance already given and are, in a sense, a gift to the people as a whole. 'They would be a gift because any innocent person could avail himself of the protection offered there.'[19]

This is not a random provision; it is by royal appointment – 'as I [the Lord] instructed you through Moses' (20:3). The overall purpose of these cities is to provide a refuge for someone who had killed accidentally or unintentionally (20:3), until their case can be properly heard. It sets limits on the possibility of a blood-feud and insures that the 'avenger of blood' (20:3) does not act in a hasty or illegal manner. The avenger is a member of the dead person's family who is appointed to exact the appropriate penalty from the offender. This provision shows that there is not a 'one-size-fits-all' to divine law. Even in the case of a killing there are different levels of punishment.

The basic purpose of the law having been made clear, God instructs Joshua and Israel about its process. It has these basic elements:

+ the offender must flee to one of these cities

+ a case must be made before the elders of that city – at the gate, the place of judgement

+ if the elders are satisfied with the case and the need for refuge, they are to grant entry and provide for the offender

---

19. Howard, *Joshua* pp. 381-2.

- there has to be a full trial, if this doesn't happen the offender remains there until the death of the current High Priest[20]
- there is then the right to return to their own town.

The provision of these cities was already detailed earlier in the Pentateuch (see Exod. 21:12-14, Num. 35: 9-29 & Deut. 19:10); now they are to be given full expression – by royal appointment.

Guaranteed provision (ii) (20:7–21:42)
What follows is mainly a list of cities. The first part of it names the cities of refuge and the second the cities to be given to the Levites.

There are six cities of refuge – three on each side of the Jordan. Although the population to the west would have been considerably larger, it was a much more compact geographical region. Whereas the East Bank was more spread out. The principle for the allocation appears to be the ease of access from all parts of the nation rather than population density. Of particular note is the way the lists end (20:7-9), it takes a 'wide-angle' view of the nation:

> Any of the Israelites or any foreigner residing among them who killed someone accidentally could flee to these designated cities ... (20:9)

The purpose and privilege of these cities was open to all, natural born or alien alike – the wider purposes of God's promise, that we have identified on a number of occasions, are still evident as the settlement reaches its conclusion.

---

20. See the commentaries concerning 'the death of High Priest' and its connection with atonement.

> Anyone ... who killed someone accidentally would flee to these designated cities and not be killed by the avenger of blood prior to standing trial before the assembly (20:9).

The narrator turns his attention to the cities that are set aside for the Levites. We have noted in this wider unit that the Levites do not inherit a portion of the land (see e.g. 13:14, 33). This was part of God's ordering of things (see e.g. Num. 18:20-24, Deut. 10:8-9), but to sustain them and keep them in family groups, cities were to be provided for them (see Num. 35:1-3). On the basis of this promise from God, they now come to Joshua and Eleazar at Shiloh where the land has been allocated by lots and said:

> The LORD commanded through Moses that you give us towns to live in, with pasturelands for our livestock (21:2).

The rightness of their claim is recognised and cities are given to them. It is clear from the language used in 21:4-42 that it is at the Lord's direction that these cities are assigned to the Levites. In the same way that other tribes had received their land – by the drawing of lots – so the Levites were given theirs. The repetition of 'were allocated' (at least seven times) makes it clear that this was no arbitrary selection of the cities. There is perhaps a concentration of some cities in the vicinity of Jerusalem, but in general they are spread across the whole nation. As part of their allotment, they are given all the cities of refuge. This may be particularly because of their ministry. When Moses pronounced his final blessing on the tribes, he said of Levi:

> He did not recognise his brothers or acknowledge his own children, but he watched over your word and guarded

your covenant. He teaches your precepts to Jacob and
your law to Israel. (Deut 33:9-10)

In cities where the Law had to be carefully administered and where atonement needed to be made for crimes, the presence of the Levites would be of great importance. As the nation's health and future depended on hearing and obeying the Word of God it was vital that the teachers of the Law live among them. As Calvin acutely observed, although their scattering among the tribes was, at first a punishment for Levi's crime at Shechem, now:

> ... the disgrace of it had been converted to the highest honour by their appointment as a kind of guardians in every district to retain the people in the pure worship of God ... and preventing their countrymen from revolting from piety. This is the reason for stating so carefully how many cities they obtained from each tribe; they were everywhere to keep watch, and preserve the purity of sacred rites unimpaired.[21]

The physical needs of the Levite families were not ignored in this allocation. After each list of tribes, the note is added concerning the number of cities given 'together with their pasture-lands.' To conclude this part of the narrative, the writer adds this summary:

> The towns of the Levites in the territory held by the Israelites were forty-eight in all, together with their pasturelands. Each of these towns had pasturelands surrounding it; this is true for all the towns. (21:41-42)

---

21. John Calvin, *Calvin's Commentaries Vol IV Joshua*, (Grand Rapids USA: Baker Books, 2003), p. 246; where he also notes that they were, in a sense, 'strangers' – separated out for this purpose.

With the completion of this allocation, 'all Israel' has received the promise of God. All have land, sustenance and rest from their enemies – the conquest is complete.

Back to the future (ii) (21:43-45)

We noted at the beginning of this section that the future is dependent on what has been achieved in the past. The final statement echoes that thought. It is not the end of the story but the beginning of a new chapter – Israel now enters the 'rest' provided by God. These three verses provide an overview of 'the story so far':

- 'they took possession of it' (21:43) summarises chapters 13-21

- 'the LORD gave them rest…Not one of their enemies withstood them' (21:44) summarises chapters 1-12

- 'Not one of all the LORD's good promises…failed ' (21:45) summarises the whole story to this point.[22]

In the light of the nature of the material that precedes these verses, the lists of cities and territory, David Firth suggests that:

> Perhaps that is why the book needs to come to this point of doxology, in order to remind us that this is not simply a list of distant towns … rather, it is a ringing declaration of the faithfulness of God.[23]

There is an insistent note sounded in these verses to stress the action of God:

- 'the LORD gave *all* the land he had sworn to give' (21:43)

---

22. See Davis, *Joshua* p. 157.

23. Firth, *Joshua* p. 192; and see Davis, *Joshua* pp. 158-160.

Receiving the Promise (13–21)

- 'the LORD gave them rest… according to *all* he had sworn' (21: 44 NASB)
- 'the LORD gave *all* their enemies into their hands' (21:44)
- 'Not one of *all* the LORD's good promises failed' (21:45)
- '*all* came to pass' (21:45).

These words are designed to lift Israel's (and subsequent readers') eyes to the wonder of what God accomplishes for His people – to attribute to Him the glory for what has been done. It is a further example of the grace of God operative for His people – not the product of human ability or worth (see Deut. 7:7-9).

As the past is celebrated, there is also an anticipation of the future. They are now entering into their promised 'rest'. This is not simply the end of the story; it is where the whole story has been heading. When Joshua spoke to the East Bank tribes before the campaign began, he called on them to honour their promise.

> You are to help them until the LORD gives them rest, as he has done for you, until they too have taken possession of the land that the LORD your God is giving them. After that you may go back and occupy your own land… (1:14-15).

The goal of the conquest is not just the acquisition of land, but the beginning of a whole new life. The future now stretches before them. God has brought them into His place, welded them together as His people – the future stretches before them in which to enjoy the blessing of relationship with God.

We have noted as we have worked through the text that there still remains land to be possessed. The country lies subdued before them, but there are enclaves of Canaanites within it that still have to be displaced. The promise of God has been fulfilled; Israel must continue to meet its responsibility under the promise.

From text to message

There is an obvious difficulty in preaching from Scripture when the text before us seems to be no more than a list. To think like this, however, betrays **our** perspective on the material, not the perspective of the Israelites who first heard these lists.

To repeat the words of Richard Nelson quoted in Part 1:

> … the geographical shape of Israel in the land was not the result of human will or historical contingency, but Yahweh's will and of Israel's obedience.[24]

The sovereign promise of God has to be received by faith and trust in the God who makes the promise. The text before us will show that God keeps His promise but there is at times a mixed response to that promise and how much of it is actually received.

Getting the message clear: the theme

This part of the book opens with a reminder that 'there are still very large areas of the land to be taken over' (13:1). The account of the division of the land into its tribal regions shows that there are battles to be fought. Acknowledging this does not mean that the closing statement of the book is

---

24. Richard Nelson, *Joshua OTL* (Louisville USA, Westminster John Knox Press, 1997) p. 209.

Receiving the Promise (13–21)

discredited – that all has been delivered into Israel's hand. On the basis of what has been received there can be no reason to doubt what will be received. The promise of God is sure. The land is theirs, whatever mopping up operations need to be done. The whole section works to underline the following ideas:

- the certainty of God's promise
- the land as gift and inheritance
- the solidarity of the people – 'all Israel'
- the ultimate blessing of God being with them.

The opening verses of chapter 18 encapsulate the main idea of the whole section – in the presence of God, the people of God receive His great promise, the place He has provided for them.

Getting the message clear: the aim

This was, in their immediate history, verification that God was faithful to His Word; that should have given them continuing confidence in the promise of God whatever else had to be faced. Christians today also can have confidence in God's promise for both the present and future. His faithfulness to His Word has been demonstrated in history – in the person and work of Christ. Although we no longer look for a land, we can find our 'rest' in Christ. And we are not alone as we wait for that final revealing of all God's promise. We, too, are part of the people with a shared inheritance that is wholly gift. The greatest blessing of all for Israel was God's presence with them. In Christ and through the Holy Spirit that is our experience as well.

Those who are 'in Christ' are people of the promise – waiting for the ultimate blessing, of being in God's place, His presence, for all eternity.

A way in

Alan Jacobs has written:

> People make such checklists for themselves only when forced by experience into intellectual humility; proud people don't want to use them. But once those same proud people *are* forced to use them they acquire a dose of that very humility, because they have no choice but to acknowledge that they forget things they need to remember.[25]

So, what things are we in danger of forgetting and how will a list help? Joshua 13–21 doesn't give Israel the opportunity to forget any of the promise and goodness of God.

On what basis do you ask someone else for help? Why them? It might be on the basis of past experience – help you have received. It might be because of their character or obvious power to deliver. It might simply be because they have made you a promise. If you know that all of these are relevant to the person you are asking, you can be confident about the help they will give. Think about the basis on which Caleb made his request for his inheritance. What does that show us?

We have kept the details an estate agent gave us when we first viewed the house in which we now live. To many people the details, the measurements, the description of both the building and the land on which it stands may seem

---

25. Alan Jacobs, *How to Think: A Guide for the Perplexed* (London UK: Profile Books, 2018), p. 157.

as dry as dust. But, to us it represents our home, the first house we have lived in that is wholly and permanently ours. We have never been homeless and yet are very thankful and excited (still!) about living where we do. How much more so would someone, who has been homeless for decades, feel when finally they get a place of their own. Surely, this would have been something of the experience of Israel when they received a land/home of their own.

Ideas for application

- 'The future is dependent on what has been achieved in the past' (p. 293 above). This was true for Israel – the Exodus, the crossing of the Jordan and the defeat of the Canaanites are just some examples in their history. In the light of these events they can face the future with confidence in God and His purposes for them. Christians also have the assurance of past, historic events on which we can base our confidence. Not only is Israel's history our history, but also we have the life, death and resurrection of Christ as the foundation of our hope for the future.

- The promise of God and the obedience of the believer go hand in hand through this narrative. This has not changed today – there is always an appropriate response to make to the initiative and action of God.

- The Word of the Lord established a 'guaranteed provision' for the tribes of Israel; whether their territory was assigned by divine command or by lot. The certainty of a place of 'rest', provided by God is still the hope of believers today – Hebrews 4: 8-11 and 11: 8-16 should be pondered on this subject.

- Although the land was allocated by lot, there is no indication in the text that this has anything to do with chance. The whole process is under the Lord's direction (see e.g. Prov. 16:33); this should be an encouragement to trust the Lord in every situation. He is, after all, the one who has numbered every hair on our head (Matt. 10:30).

- Caleb's 'wholeheartedness' was founded on a trust in God's Word. What he asks from God is what God has promised. This attitude should surely shape the way we think about our lives in general and our prayers in particular.

- It is easy to assume that the details of towns and territories are 'just a list of names', and to ignore the real implication and blessing they conveyed to the first readers. There is always the temptation for the believer to presume on what we might dare to call the 'mundane' things of life that are in fact God's blessings to us.

- One of the issues raised by the Joseph tribes in chapter 17 is the possibility of 'spiritualising' our own needs to make our case for greater consideration from others. Their danger was that of their dissatisfaction with their land being, at root, dissatisfaction with the promise of God – indeed with God Himself. This is not just a problem for Old Testament believers!

- If the analysis of this section suggested above has validity, the presence of the Lord at Shiloh presiding over the allocation of the land is of utmost importance. The presence of God remains the key to the life and health of His people today. As Greg Beale says:

... the church will only expand its witness as it stands in the presence of God, submitted to the power of his Word and praying in brokenness for the nations.[26]

- The record of allocations given in 18:11–19:48 shows something of the reluctance of some tribes to act on the promise of God. The New Testament does not minimise the struggle that faces the Christian believer. We all need help in thinking through what particular temptations cause us to give up on that struggle.

- The appointment of the cities of refuge highlights the need for sin to be atoned for through sacrifice. This can be clearly linked to Christ as our refuge from judgement and the only effective atoning sacrifice.

- One of the implications of the closing verses (21:43-45) is that history leads to doxology. Good exposition, sound theology and a grasp of our Christian history should always lead to praise.

Suggestions for preaching

Sermon 1

With such a large amount of material before us, we can only touch on some of the main ideas. To introduce the whole section and overview could be attempted as follows:

- **Receiving the promise** A look at the big picture – it will include all of the land as it is allocated to all of the people. Every geographical reference and every city name is a reminder of 'every place where you set your

---

26. G. K. Beale and Mitchell Kim, *God Dwells among Us* (Downers Grove USA: IVP, 2014), p. 165.

foot' (1:3). Each place is a cause for thanksgiving and praise to God for His faithfulness

- **Living with the promise** There are different responses to the promise accord, these are epitomised by:
Caleb – wholeheartedness
Joseph tribes – dissatisfaction

- **The certainty of the promise** 21:43-45 summarises the whole conquest and should lead to the praise of God now and confidence in Him for the future.

If all God's promises find their 'Yes in Christ' (2 Cor 1:20), how have we responded to Him?

Sermon 2
This and the following three suggestions focus on the themes based on the concentric circles structure outlined in Part One. Here we concentrate on the certainty of the promise.

Evidence from the past
In both 13:1-3 and 21: 43-45 there is clear acknowledgement of what has been accomplished (even if some land is yet to be taken).

Encouragement for the present
The task of settling the land and becoming established in it (at 'rest') can proceed with confidence (13:6 and 21:43-44 – the basis for life *now*).

Hope for the future
God's action for His people and presence with His people condition all that is to come.

This structure can be used in relation to our life in Christ.

Sermon 3
Here we focus on the land as gift and inheritance.

The inheritance is sovereignly given
Although the land is divided by lot it is not by chance – it is done as the Lord has instructed.

It is freely given
These chapters have no sense of any transactions going on within them. The summary of chapters 13–21 in 21:43 stress that it is all gift (cf. Deut. 6:10-12, 7:7-8).

It is a permanent possession
At the end of most tribal lists there is a statement about the land being theirs in perpetuity – an inheritance is passed on from generation to generation

The New Testament uses the concept of inheritance to describe God's grace to those in Christ. 1 Pet 1:3-5 spells this out.

Sermon 4
The unity of the people of God is in focus here:

'according to their tribal divisions' (18:10)
Whether by previous promise (the East Bank tribes) or by lot – every tribe receives its division of the land. The earlier emphasis on 'all Israel' is found in every tribe having a place of their own

No exceptions
Even the Levites were given their own towns and pasturelands 'as the Lord commanded through Moses' (21:2), despite the penalty the tribe had already incurred.

No exclusions

As foreigners were able to come into the orbit of Israel in the earlier stories (Rahab and the Gibeonites), they were also protected within the justice system. The cities of refuge are open to 'any foreigners residing among you' (20:9).

Unity is a vital element in the life of God's people in the Old Testament, New Testament and today.

Sermon 5

The central unit in this section focuses on the presence of God.

God's presence is indispensable

The people of God depend on the presence of God for their life and survival – Exodus 33:1-17 provides the background for the importance of God's presence. The Ark in the earlier stories represents that presence. Shiloh (18:1) is an acknowledgement of the need of God's presence.

The challenge of God's presence

It is never a call to 'let's go and let God' – it demands a response (18:3-7).

The comfort of God's presence

There is grace for all regardless of who they are – all received land and Levi has its inheritance in the direct service of the Lord Himself.

Today we continue to need God with us – but His presence challenges us to live our lives for Him and offers us the comfort of Spirit to be our helper.

Receiving the Promise (13–21)

Suggestions for teaching

Questions to help understand the passage

1. How do the command and promise of God relate to each other in 13:1-7?

2. What is the background to the way the East Bank tribes receive their territory?

3. What is the principle on which the land is divided (see 14:1-5)?

4. Take note of any expressions that are repeated in 14:6-15. On what basis does Caleb make his request for land?

5. There is an occasional negative note sounded in chapters 15–17. What is it and why is it important?

6. How does the narrator stress God's activity in the allocation of territory in 18:1-10? What does this teach us about the whole process?

7. What distinctive features are there in the record of land allocation in chapters 18 and 19? How do you account for these?

8. Why do you think Joshua receives his inheritance at the end of this record of the allocations?

9. How important are the cities of refuge and why do you think they are among the towns given to the Levites?

10. How do the final three verses (21:43-45) summarise the whole section?

Questions to help apply the text

1. How can we live day by day in the light of our inheritance from God? What is the most important aspect of it for you?

2. If all that we have as Christians comes as a gift from God, how should we respond to all that He asks of us?

3. Caleb made his request on the basis of God's promise. How should that help us in our prayers?

4. One danger for the people of God was the influence the Canaanites who remained in the land would have on them. We can't avoid contact with the surrounding culture, but how can we guard against it?

5. How do we sometimes imitate the tribes of Joseph in their dissatisfaction with God's provision, or even with God Himself?

6. Do we take seriously the promise we have of God's presence with us? How does that show (or not) in our lives?

7. To what extent is God (Father, Son and Holy Spirit) at the centre of our church's life?

8. Is unity in our local congregation a real concern? If not, why not? What things do we need to do to help unity happen?

9. God provided cities of refuge for Israel, places of safety and atonement. How is Jesus providing those things for us today?

10. How can we encourage our leaders in ministering to us the Word and promise of God? Moses and Joshua are seen as men 'under authority', what does that teach us about true leadership?

7

Life in the Promise (22-24)

Introduction

A prominent feature of this final section of the book is a series of speeches by Joshua. They are:

- a commendation of the East Bank tribes (22:1-8)
- a farewell speech to all Israel (23:1-16)
- a renewal of the covenant (24:1-28).

In all three speeches some common themes arise:

- the 'rest' the people now have is God-given
- God has been a Warrior for them
- obedience has been a key factor in the conquest
- it will remain a necessity for the future
- the danger of compromise with the Canaanites
- the unity of the people – shared experience should bind them together.

Having been united against a common enemy and under a single chain of command – God, Moses and Joshua – these final chapters are designed to keep the people of God together. From now on they will live in their own territories but they still need to be one nation – God's people, living life in the promise.

Listening to the text

Content and structure

With the whole history of their joint endeavour in the Conquest behind them, the time for standing down the lead troops, those of the East Bank tribes, has come. They had done what they had promised to Moses and received their allotted lands. With the allocation complete and 'rest on every side' given to them by the Lord (21:44), Joshua sends them home with his blessing (22:6-8). Although the text is silent over Joshua's location through the majority of this section he dismisses these troops from Shiloh (22:9). Presumably he remains there for some time, but when he seeks to renew the covenant with the whole nation, there is a new central location – Shechem (24:1).

The majority of commentators, while recognising chapters 22–24 as a single unit, tend to analyse the literary structure of the text chapter by chapter. As helpful as these analyses are, they do not always show the connections between the major elements of the narrative. The following structure concentrates on the main units of the story and we will attempt to show the interconnection as we work through the text.

22:1-9   A first farewell
22:10-20   A cause for concern

22:21-34	A peaceful resolution
23:1-11	In case you forget
23:12-16	A note of caution
24:1-15	Joshua's final demand
24:16-28	The people's response
24:29-33	Final rest

Working through the text

A first farewell (22:1-9)

Now, all the tribes have been allotted their inheritance and the land has been subdued, it is time for Joshua to release the East Bank tribes from their commitment. He recognises that they have done all that they promised, having followed the commands given by Moses and himself.

> For a long time now – to this very day – you have not deserted your fellow Israelites but have carried out the mission the LORD your God gave you. (22:3)

Calvin observes that:

> They indeed deserve praise for their patient endurance in not allowing weariness of the service to make them request their discharge, but in waiting quietly till Joshua of his own accord sends for them.[1]

If the tribes of Reuben, Gad and the half tribe of Manasseh are going to be separated from the main body of Israel by the natural barrier of the Jordan, Joshua does not want to see a separation at a spiritual level. He, therefore, encourages them to remain obedient to 'the law that Moses the servant of the LORD gave you' and:

---

1. John Calvin, *Calvin's Commentaries Vol IV Joshua*, (Grand Rapids USA: Baker Books, 2003), p. 210.

... to love the LORD your God, to walk in obedience to him, to keep his commandments, to hold fast to him and to serve him with all your heart and with all you soul. (22:5)

The way this verse is constructed shows that the covenant relationship is not simply a question of rule-keeping. Adolph Harstad sets out the structure like this:

'Only take great care to do the commandment and the teaching [*torah*] that Moses the servant of the LORD commanded you:

- to love the LORD your God
- to walk in his ways
- to keep his commandments
- to cling to him
- and /yes to serve him with all your heart, and with all your soul' (22:5).[2]

Each of the five infinitives in this verse are not different ways of doing 'the commandment and teaching of Moses.' They are designed to intensify and exemplify the way the people are to do it. The call to 'love the LORD your God' (repeated in 23:11) echoes the words of Moses in Deuteronomy (Deut. 6:5, 10:12, 11:1 etc.). The context in which they are used in both Joshua and Deuteronomy is of great significance according to Harstad:

> Israel's love for the LORD can only flow from his prior, deep and abiding affection displayed first to his people through his acts of salvation and in his Word.[3]

---

2. Adolph Harstad, *Joshua Concordia Commentary* (St Louis, USA: Concordia Publishing House, 2004), p. 686.

3. *Ibid* p. 681.

Life in the Promise (22-24)

The other four infinitives also strongly echo Deuteronomy:

* to walk – Deuteronomy 8:6, 10:12, 11:22 etc
* to keep – Deuteronomy 4:2, 5:29, 6:2 etc
* to hold fast/cling – Deuteronomy 10:20, 11:22, 13:4 (N.B. Gen. 2:24)
* to serve – Deuteronomy 6:13, 10:12, 11:13 etc

Joshua's appeal is not simply to the head, but to the heart and will – he desires these tribe to remain fully engaged and committed to the Lord. So, these tribes, having seen God's promises fulfilled, are called on to love Him wholeheartedly once they return to their homeland.

With Joshua's blessing, they make their way back. They may have spent a considerable time away from home and family, but they do not go back empty handed. They go with great wealth; 'large herds of livestock, with silver, gold, bronze and iron' (22:8), to share with their fellow Israelites. Some commentators see 22:9 as the start of a new section of the narrative, but it is better to see it as the conclusion of this farewell story. The logic of the narrative would seem to be: Joshua thanks the tribes, exhorts them to walk in the way Moses commanded, blesses them; and:

> So the Reubenites, the Gadites and the half-tribe of Manasseh left the Israelites at Shiloh in Canaan to return to Gilead, their own land which they had acquired in accordance with the command of the LORD through Moses (22:9).

As we have seen before, the narrator sometimes uses a concluding statement to allude to an event that is about to happen, or a fuller explanation of something he has only briefly sketched. Taken with Joshua's concerns for the unity of the people of God, there is a clue in 22:9 that he is preparing us for something yet to come. There is in this verse a distinction made between two geographical regions – 'Shiloh in Canaan' and 'Gilead, their own land'.

Not only is this distinction made but the narrator describes these two groups of people as separate entities – first the two-and-a-half tribes are named and then, it is said that they 'left the Israelites at Shiloh'. The question we may ask here is: Is there already an implicit division of the nation involved? The next narrative unit will show that there may certainly be a cause for concern.

A cause for concern (22:10-20)

The departing tribes, as they approach the River Jordan, stop and build an altar.

> When they came to Geliloth near the Jordan in the land of Canaan, the Reubenites, the Gadites and the half-tribe of Manasseh built an imposing altar there by the Jordan (22:10).

As soon as the news of this construction project reached the main body of Israelites it became a cause of concern to them. It was an issue that roused them to prepare to 'go to war against them' (22:12). A number of significant factors in this story need to be considered, chiefly:

- the location – why here?
- the construction – for what purpose?
- the reaction – what does it mean?

The narrator leaves us in no doubt, at one level, about where this altar is located. The place is named – Geliloth – and

Life in the Promise (22–24)

then its location is qualified three times over: 'on the border of Canaan', 'near the Jordan', 'on the Israelite side' (22:11).

Howard comments:

> Clearly the altar was west of the Jordan, which was not in territory allotted to the Transjordan tribes. That is, they had built a large altar in land belonging to Judah or Benjamin (15:7, 18:17), not their own land east of Jordan.[4]

He also suggests that Gilgal is the possible site in question. So, a question is raised: Is this an act of provocation? The construction of the altar itself also raises a question. It is an 'imposing altar' (22:10). The idiom used suggests it is widely visible and Trent Butler translates this as 'an altar visible for miles.'[5] The purpose of it is unclear just from this verse, but, as we will see, the question in the West Bank tribes' minds is: Is this an altar in rebellion against the Lord? (see 22:16)

The reaction it provokes is an ominous one – 'the whole assembly gathered at Shiloh to go to war against them' (22:12). To speak of the 'whole assembly' seems to assume that the West Bank tribes are true Israel. The narrator constantly separates out the East Bank tribes by name, keeping them distinct from the Israelites (see 22:9, 13, 21). It is likely that the war the Israelites seek to wage is 'holy war'. As they had eradicated pagan nations from the land, they will now have to remove any possible defilement due to the East Bank tribes. The questions asked of the two-and-a-half tribes show what their suspicions are.

---

4. David Howard, Jr, *Joshua* NAC (Nashville, USA: Broadman & Holman, 1998) p. 406.

5. Trent Butler, *Joshua* WBC vol 2 (Grand Rapids USA, Zondervan, 2014), p. 243.

A review of 22:16-20 makes it clear that they suspect:

- breaking faith with the God of Israel (v. 16)
- turning away from the LORD (v. 16)
- in danger of repeating the sin of Peor (v. 17)
- bringing God's wrath on the nation (v. 17)
- turning or rebelling against God (v. 18)
- repeating the sin of Achan (v. 20)

It is clear that they suspect the worst! Fortunately they do not just act on their suspicions. They send a high-powered delegation to investigate. It often used to be said that 'jaw, jaw is better than war, war!' and that is precisely the case here. The delegation consists of important and notable men in Israel. Heading the group is Phineas, son of Eleazar, a man of no mean reputation when it came to sorting out rebellion against God. His action, when the people of Moab wooed the Israelites to follow Baal at Peor, was responsible for turning away God's anger from Israel (see Num. 25 for the story). This group express a right concern about the situation – that it might be a mark of sin that would bring judgement on the whole people. Ralph Davies quotes George Bush as saying:

> Their holy jealousy, therefore, in these circumstances was no more than a proper expression of their intense concern for the glory of God and the honour of his institutions… they evidently go on the presumption that they *may* have been mistaken in the construction of the affair, and that at any rate it was proper that they should not condemn their brethren unheard, but should give them

the opportunity of justifying themselves in the measure if it were possible.[6]

And this policy proved to be the right one to pursue.

A peaceful resolution (22:21-34)

It is clear that there needs to be a resolution of this issue because, along with Phineas, the 'heads of the clans of Israel' need to be able to report back to 'the whole assembly of Israel' (22:12) if war is to be avoided – or if it is to be fought. The initial response of the East Bank tribes suggests that war with the rest of Israel is not their chief concern. Their reply is designed to show that they did not mean any possible offence to God. Before giving an explanation, they make a confession:

> The Mighty One, God, the LORD! The Mighty One, God, the LORD! (22:22)

These three names of God, spoken twice, may be an oath to confirm what they are about to say. Gordon McConville points out that this threefold name of God is used elsewhere in the context of worship (see Ps. 50:1).

In the light of this he adds:

> The series of names, proclaimed here by the Transjordanians, is a strong statement that Yahweh is indeed the only true God and even takes the form of worship. It is therefore a powerful rebuttal of the accusation of Phineas.[7]

---

6. See Ralph Davis, *Joshua – No Falling Words* (Fearn, UK: Christian Focus, 2000) p. 174.

7. Gordon McConville & Stephen Williams *Joshua, Two Horizons Commentary* (Grand Rapids, USA: Eerdmans, 2010), p. 86.

This opening statement of their loyalty to the Lord, is immediately followed by an appeal to Him – 'He knows!' (22:22). They believe that the Lord can and will vindicate them and the rest of Israel will know it (22:22). To underscore the fact that there was no evil intention in the construction of the altar, they make this statement:

> If this has been rebellion or disobedience to the Lord, do not spare us this day. (22:22)

But, more than this:

> If we have built our own altar to turn away from the Lord and to offer burnt offerings and grain offerings, or to sacrifice fellowship offerings on it, may the Lord call us to account. (22:23)

Only people who truly have a clear conscience make statements like this!

Now comes the real reason concerning their motivation for building the altar. They are worried that the day might come when the problem of 'outsiders' vs 'insiders' would rear its ugly head. How do you define national identity? The tendency for the West Bank tribes could be to insist that identity is connected with possession of the land, whereas the East Bank tribes would major on the ties of kinship. Something of this division can be seen in the terms used for each group. The West Bank tribes are the 'whole assembly of Israel' (22:12, 18, 20, 21); the East Bank tribes are constantly referred to by their 'family' names (22:9, 10, 13, 15, 21).

As Daniel Hawk says:

> The crux of the story revolves around different perceptions of how the nation is to be defined and held together.[8]

The perception of the East Bank tribes is that the day might just come when those west of the Jordan say:

> What do you have to do with the LORD, the God of Israel? The LORD has made the Jordan a boundary between us and you – you Reubenites and Gadites (22:24-25).

Whatever the motive, territorial, tribal or some other reason, the possibility of those living in the land rejecting those across the Jordan is a real concern to the East Bank tribes. They have a spiritual concern in this as well: 'So your descendants might cause ours to stop fearing the LORD.' (22:25). The accusers become the accused – if they transmit any attitude of 'territorial superiority' to the next generation, they will be responsible for turning others away from the true faith.

It is only now that the two-and-a-half tribes move on to give the reason behind the building of the altar. Only in the light of what they have said so far, will their action make any real sense to the rest of Israel. So they continue:

> That is why we said, 'let us get ready and build an altar – but not for burnt offerings or sacrifices.' On the contrary, it is to be a witness between us and you and the generations that follow… (22:26-27).

They want to make it clear that this is not an alternative place of sacrifice. Their intention is to gather with the rest of Israel to 'worship the LORD at **his** sanctuary' with their various offerings (22:27). The altar is their way of putting

---

8. L. Daniel Hawk, *Joshua*, Berit Olam (Collegeville USA: Liturgical Press, 2000), p. 229 to whom I owe the ideas of this paragraph.

down a marker, which says. 'Before you can cross the River Jordan and set foot in the east bank, remember we are still all one people under one Lord.' Their argument is that:

> … in the future your descendants will not be able to say to ours, 'You have no share in the LORD' (22:27).

To make sure there is no possibility of either party talking past the other, the East Bank tribes repeat their case (22:28-29), outlining:

- the possibility of division
- the necessity of a witness
- their godly motivation
- their desire to be a full part of the worshipping community.

The moment of danger is now past; the fears of both parties can be silenced. There is no need for war between them and no threat of judgement from God hanging over them. Phineas recognises that the threat of judgement has receded, as he says: 'Now you have rescued the Israelites from the LORD's hand' (22:31).

On his return to the West Bank tribes, Phineas reports on the peaceful resolution of the issue and:

> They were glad to hear the report and praised God. And they talked no more about going to war against them (22:33).

As a final act in this episode those from the East Bank give the altar a name: 'A witness between us – that the LORD is God.' (22:34). The true unity of Israel is not based on a shared land or a common history, but on their relationship with the one true God.

Life in the Promise (22–24) 347

In case you forget (23:1-11)
We come now to Joshua's farewell to the leaders of Israel. It occupies all of chapter 23, but two rather different notes are sounded. The first is in this section, in which Joshua wants them to be careful to remember all that God has done for them – and to live in the light of that knowledge. The second note is one of caution – showing how forgetfulness is the enemy of faith.

The narrator makes sure that we understand Joshua's speech to be his farewell address at the end of his life. He is 'a very old man' (23:1 & 2). This address takes place, 'after a long time had passed' (23:1). David Howard reckons this was about twenty-five years after the distribution of the land.[9] Joshua's status in Israel as the successor to Moses is also indicated here – as he is able to gather the chief people of the nation together to address them (cf. Deut. 32 & 33). It is clear that he considers this to be one of the last opportunities that he will have to encourage the nation to stay faithful to the Lord. He accepts the fact that he is 'about to go the way of all the earth' (23:14). What is it that he wants the people of God to keep uppermost in their minds? It can be summarised as:

+ Remember what God has done
+ Remember what God has given
+ Remember what God has promised (23:3-5).

Each of these is an aspect of the Lord's grace to Israel and each demands the same response – loyalty and love. The people have seen with their own eyes what God has done for them (23:3). They have witnessed the removal

---

9. See Howard, *Joshua* p. 419-420.

of the nations from Canaan as God Himself has fought for them. Here, as with almost everything Joshua says in this section, there are strong echoes of Deuteronomy. The whole progress of the conquest is due to God fighting for His people (Deut. 11:23-25, cf. Josh. 1:3). Closely linked with this is the idea that the land comes as a gift from God. It is not their land because of force of arms – it is theirs by inheritance (23:4). Joshua is not claiming pre-eminence when he says: 'Remember how I have allotted an inheritance for your tribes... the nations I have conquered' (23:4). The book never portrays him in this way; he is always the servant and instrument of God. Although there is an acknowledgment that territory still needs to be occupied, Joshua calls on the people to remember the ongoing promise of God:

> The LORD your God himself will push them out for your sake. He will drive them out before you, and you will take procession of their land, as the LORD your God promised you (23:5).

Again, there are echoes from earlier in the book and also a clear link back to God's promise through Moses (see Deut. 9:3-5).

As Joshua turns to exhort the people more directly in 23:6-11, both the idea of remembering and also the echo of Deuteronomy are still evident. The headline statement in this exhortation is: 'Be careful to obey all that is written in the Book of the Law of Moses' (23:6). There then follows a string of imperatives that show how they can 'be careful'. These can be viewed as follows:

- be careful not to turn away (23:6)
- be careful of the company you keep (23:7)

Life in the Promise (22–24)

- be careful to honour your bond with the Lord (23:8)
- be careful to love the Lord (23:11).

Joshua himself had been urged **not to turn away** when commissioned by God at the very beginning of the conquest (1:7). One of the chief ways of not deviating from the Word of God that had been written down for them, was to:

> See that you do all that I command you, do not add to it or take away from it (Deut. 12:32).

It is to recognise that what God has said is sufficient for all of life and that His provision is all that is needed. To maintain this single-minded devotion to the Law needs strength – 'Be very strong' (23:6) prefaces the whole set of imperatives. To walk in God's way, in obedience to His Word demands effort. God's people do not live in an hermetically sealed environment, so Joshua continues to encourage them to **be careful of the company they keep**. He recognises the grave danger that accommodation to the surrounding culture will bring. One possible example of this accommodation might be in the realm of agriculture. The Israelites have been a nomadic people for a whole generation; now they are learning to adapt to a settled life. They will have seen that Canaanites had successfully farmed the land and so may seek to follow their methods. But, here lies the trap for them. The Canaanites would attribute their success to the work of their fertility gods. The best way to farm for them would start at the shrines of Baal and Asherah. The presence of the Canaanites would easily lead to the influence of their gods. So, Joshua commands:

> Do not associate with these nations that remain among you; do not invoke the names of their gods or swear by

them. You must not serve them or bow down to them. (23:7)

Obedience to the Word of God also arises from the relationship the people have with God Himself. A further imperative underlines this: **be careful to honour the bond with the Lord.** Joshua speaks of an intimate and permanent relationship between God and His people:

> But you are to hold fast to the Lord your God, as you have until now. (23:8)

The word translated by 'hold fast' is a significant one. Its first use in the Old Testament is Genesis 2:24:

> That is why a man leaves his father and mother and is **united** to his wife, and they become one flesh.

This intimate bond is reflected later in the Old Testament narrative in Israel being pictured as the Lord's bride. The word also speaks of indissolubility, of permanence – the prophet Isaiah uses it of metal that has been welded together (Isa. 41:7). It is this kind of relationship Israel enjoys with God. By their obedience to His Word they know that bond.

Before coming to the final imperative, Joshua adds another word of motivation:

> The Lord has driven out before you great and powerful nations; to this day no one has been able to withstand you. One of you routs a thousand, because the Lord your God fights for you, just as he promised (23:9-10).

Once again, Joshua urges them on – the evidence of the past gives them confidence for the future. There is here a further echo of Deuteronomy (see Deut. 32:30 and cf. Lev. 26:7-8).

David Howard comments:

> When God fought for his people, the odds increased by factors of hundreds, even thousands, in their favour.[10]

The final imperative in this section is: 'be very careful to love the LORD your God' (23:11). Moses had made the same demand of Israel when giving them the Law (see Deut. 6:5). In Joshua's speech it represents the high point of what he wants to say. His words have double-edge to them. In the first place, obedience and devotion to the Law of God reaches its fullest expression in obedience and devotion to the one who stand behind these words. It is not simply a question of loving the Law, but of loving the Law-giver. There is, secondly, an attitude and approach that is bound up with this. If the people love the Law-giver, they will seek to do what He wants, what He requires of them. Love for God will feed obedience to Him.

The first part of Joshua's address is to offer encouragement in case the people forget – forget their recent history and their God who stands behind it.

A note of caution (23:12-16)

When Joshua (and scripture in general) places a demand or choice before people he does not leave them in any doubt as to which option to choose. We will see this in more detail in chapter 24. Here, he has called upon them to choose the path of obedience and love to the Law of God, and therefore to God Himself. To make sure there are no doubts as to which way they should go, he now traces the alternative path. He acknowledges that there is the

---

10. David Howard, Jr, *Joshua NAC* (Nashville, USA: Broadman & Holman, 1998), p. 423.

possibility of 'turning aside to the right or to the left' (23:6); but the people need to be clear as to what the outcome of that will be. To drive his point home, he makes it clear as to how 'turning aside' will happen and the disastrous result it will have.

The most obvious deviation from the Law of God will come as Israel makes some accommodation with the other nations. There is a real possibility, which needs to be rejected, of Israel allying themselves 'with the survivors of these nations that remain among you' (23:12). The most obvious way of forming such alliances will be through intermarriage (23:12). Such actions will have consequences (23:13):

- God will withdraw His help
- the other people will not bring peace, but problems
- the final outcome will be that they will lose the land.

Action of this kind is the equivalent of placing oneself outside the people of God, outside the covenant. Joshua had already made this clear (see 23:7). It involves the service of other gods. In this situation, people can no longer expect God to fight for them and secure their inheritance. There will be immediate effects as well. Rather than bringing peace and harmony to the land, it will bring internal strife. Joshua piles on the agony, as it were – snares and traps, whips and thorns (23:13). But, there are long-term results as well – they will lose the land. As if not content to issue this note of caution, Joshua retraces his steps adding further weight to this warning. The stark reality of this warning is prefaced by a personal plea.

Trent Butler describes it as a poignant plea and goes on to paraphrase it:

> Will the people not listen to the voice of an old dying man? Can they not accept his personal testimony? If not, can they not look deep within themselves and accept the reality of what they know? God has failed in nothing. Everything Yahweh said, Yahweh has done.[11]

The keynote statement of the whole book is repeated in 23:14, rather than another review of the history of God's faithfulness in the conquest. In doing this Joshua roots his warning to the people in the known and experienced grace of God. He then makes clear all that turning away from God and His ways implies. As sure as the promises for good have been fulfilled, so the promises of judgement will be. Just as they have been given the land, the violation of the covenant, especially by idolatry, will inevitably result in the loss of the land, (23:15). The people had seen once before the effect of God's anger burning against them (7:1); now Joshua uses the same expression to indicate God's anger against rebellion.

Realism demands that a note of caution has to be delivered to God's people – their history will show its necessity. The warning here sets the scene for what is to come in the time of the Judges, and what Israel's eventual fate will be.

Joshua's final demand (24:1-15)

The location of Joshua's speech in the previous section is not identified, but the final gathering of Israel before his death is. Shechem is to be the place of covenant renewal. This

---

11. Butler, *Joshua* p. 283.

location has already featured in the covenant ceremony of chapter 8 – although it is unnamed there. Gilgal and Shiloh have played an important part in the whole narrative. Now, the focus rests on Shechem.

Jerome Creach notes:

> That geography sometimes serves theological purposes in the book of Joshua is nowhere more evident than chapter 24. Shechem was associated closely with covenant making, a fact that helps explain why Joshua gathered the Israelites there for the ceremony reported in 24:1-28.[12]

The significance of Shechem reaches much further back into the history of Israel, as far back as the foundational promise from God to establish the nation. Important connections with Shechem are:

- Genesis 12:7 – God's revelation to Abraham that he is in the land that will be his people's inheritance
- Genesis 33:19-20 – Jacob bought a plot of land here; this is where his bones will be buried (Josh. 24:32)
- Deuteronomy 11:29-30 – here Israel must rehearse the blessings and curses of the covenant (cf. Josh. 8:30-35)
- Deuteronomy 27:4-5 – it is the place appointed by God for Israel to build an altar in the Promised Land.

Of special significance for what is about to happen in Joshua's day is the fact that it was at Shechem that Jacob called on his family to destroy their foreign gods. Now, Joshua will call on Israel to do the same thing. The Hebrew vocabulary is strikingly similar on both occasions:

---

12. Jerome Creach, *Joshua* (Louisville, USA: John Knox Press, 2003), p. 119.

Life in the Promise (22–24)

> Put away the foreign gods which are among you (Gen. 35:2 NASB).

> Put away the gods which your fathers served beyond the river and in Egypt (Josh. 24:14 NASB).

To the historically alert Israelite, this background would undergird all that is about to be said at Shechem. Although the same groups of leaders, who were previously addressed by Joshua, are again mentioned here, the whole nation has come together at Joshua's command – 'all the tribes of Israel', 'all the people' (24:1-2).

In his final address, Joshua is portrayed as an even more 'Moses-like' leader. He acts as the mouthpiece of God to the people. The Word of God Joshua brings to them shows them that everything they have comes from the hand of God. In the course of twelve verses, there are, at least, fifteen statements which begin with 'I', spelling out God's action on behalf of His people. It puts their history in proper perspective – they would be nothing and nowhere without God. The brevity of the account is startling, but the important elements of salvation history are clear:

- Abraham – taken from idolatry, shown the land and given a family
- Jacob – the descent into Egypt
- Moses and Aaron – the confrontation with the Egyptians
- Escape and rescue from Egypt and its forces
- Wilderness wanderings
- East Bank victories

- Defeat of the seven nations of Canaan
- The gift of the land.

Abraham The emphasis here is on the inauspicious beginnings of the nation. There was nothing in and of Abraham himself that caused God to choose him. He and the other ancestors 'worshipped other gods' (24:2). This is borne out by the wider testimony of scripture – as Abraham was 'brought out' of 'Ur of the Chaldeans' (Gen. 15:7), so Israel was 'brought out of Egypt' (Exod. 20:2, Deut. 5:6) and Isaiah speaks of Abraham as being 'redeemed' by the Lord (Isa. 29:22).[13] The Lord led him through the land that would be his descendants' inheritance; and against all odds gave him the son from whom the nation would grow.

Jacob Having briefly mentioned the line from Abraham to Jacob, the focus now moves from Canaan to Egypt where the family is forced to go because of famine. This sets the scene for the next major episode in Israel's history.

Moses and Aaron The drama of the early chapters of Exodus is related in the briefest possible way: 'I afflicted the Egyptians by what I did there' (24:5).

Escape and rescue The greater emphasis is now placed on the events of the Passover and, particularly, the crossing of the Red Sea. A major note here is the destruction of people's enemies – an important note in the context of the book of Joshua. It reinforces the promise of God to act on His people's behalf and give them victory in the land.

---

13. Calvin, *Joshua* p. 273 comments on 'I took your father Abraham from the land beyond the Euphrates' saying, '... Abraham did not emerge from profound ignorance and the abyss of error by his own virtue, but was drawn out by the hand of God.'

Life in the Promise (22–24)

Wilderness wanderings Forty years of wandering is summed up in just ten words: 'Then you lived in the wilderness for a long time' (24:7). This brevity serves to remind us that, as David Firth says:

> ... the point of the exodus was always that Israel should enter the land. It is easy to read of the exodus and see it as an end in itself, but as Joshua makes clear it had to be understood as part of the larger story of salvation.[14]

East Bank victories The story of the possession of the land begins with the victories over the people 'east of the Jordan' (24:8). The emphasis here is on the people and tribes who 'fought against you' (24:8-9); but it is also on the fact that the Lord fought for Israel. The concentration of the first-person statements by the Lord makes this absolutely clear:

- I brought you to the land
- I gave them into your hands
- I destroyed them before you
- I would not listen to Balaam
- I delivered you out of his hand (24:8-10).

Balaam's attempts to curse Israel are turned into blessings by God; another way of fulfilling the promise of Genesis 12:3a.

Defeat of the seven nations The seven nations of Canaan were first listed in 3:10 (although they appear in a different order). The list is not necessarily exhaustive; it is designed to show completeness.

---

14. David Firth, *The Message of Joshua* (Nottingham, UK: IVP, 2015), p. 219.

As David Howard comments:

> The book comes full circle now in affirming that God has done what he promised: he has delivered the Canaanites into the Israelites' hands (v. 11), and he had driven them out (v. 12).[15]

The defeat of these nations is again shown to be the work of God:

> I sent the hornet ahead of you, which drove them out before you ... You did not do it with your own sword and bow. (24:12)

The text speaks specifically of 'the hornet' in the singular, rather than the plural, which might indicate a literal plague of hornets. The words may be translated as 'terror' (see NET) and that makes a great deal of sense in the context of a whole book (see 2:9-11, 24; 5:1 etc).[16]

The gift of the land The culmination of this review of covenant history is a statement concerning the fulfilment of the covenant promise:

> So I gave you a land on which you did not toil and cities you did not build; and you live in them and eat from the vineyards and olive groves that you did not plant. (24:13)

This conclusion revisits a constant theme throughout the book – the land comes as a gift from God. It is not earned or merited; it comes from the Lord's grace. All that is needed for life in the land, and by implication, life with God, is provided from the hand of God.

---

15. Howard, *Joshua* p. 432.

16. See Butler, *Joshua* vol 2, p. 295.

Life in the Promise (22–24)

Covenant history having been reviewed, and the grace of God in that covenant reaffirmed, Joshua now brings God's covenant demands before the people.

> Now fear the LORD and serve him with all faithfulness. Throw away the gods your ancestors worshipped beyond the River Euphrates and in Egypt, and serve the LORD (24:14).

The call is for absolute obedience and service to the one true God who is the God who has saved and preserved them to this day. They have seen and experienced His provision at every level of life and they are now called to devote their lives to Him and His service. And this call is necessary because idolatry, the worship of false gods, has been a perennial problem. Joshua points to the fact that it has plagued the nation from the time of the ancestors, through the time in Egypt (see e.g. Ezek. 20:6-8, 23:3, 8) and right into the present ('the gods of the Amorites' 24:15).

It is clear from Joshua's words in 24:14-15 that there can be no such thing as 'atheism' or 'agnosticism'; there will be worship of something. The question is not will you serve a god, but which god will you serve. The choice is, as Ralph Davis puts it, between 'Yahweh the real historical God' or 'the ancestral Mesopotamian gods' or 'the contemporary Amorite gods'. He goes on to say:

> The conservatives who were fond of tradition, of what has stood the test of time, who yearned for the "faith of our fathers", might vote for Mesopotamia. The liberals with their yearn for relevance, for being in step with the times, might prefer to identify (as an act of goodwill) with the

current local milieu and enter into dialogue and worship with the Amorites.[17]

This is not however a case of what we would call today 'non-directive counselling' – Joshua makes it clear by example that there is only one choice:

> But as for me and my household, we will serve the Lord. (24:15).

In this he stands in line with the biblical tradition of not only showing what the true choices are, but also, which is the right one to make. He follows in the footsteps of Moses:

> This day I call the heavens and the earth as witnesses against you that I have set before you life and death, blessings and curses. Now choose life ... (Deut. 30:19).

The people's response (24:16-28)
The verb 'to serve' has a high profile throughout chapter 24. The chapter opens with the comment that the ancestors 'served other gods' (24:2 NASB). In verses 14 and 15 Joshua uses the verb seven times (see NASB and ESV). Now the people respond that they will not 'serve other gods' (24:16), but 'will serve the Lord, because he is our God' (24:18). It seems that they have understood the implications of the history lesson they have been given. They acknowledge:

- the rescue from Egypt and slavery
- the great signs they have seen God perform
- the protection God has given
- the victory God has given (24:17-18a).

---

17. Davis, *Joshua* p. 199.

They will imitate Joshua and his household and serve the Lord (24:18b).

At first sight Joshua's reply seems devastating: 'You are not able to serve the LORD' (24:19). Surely, this is what Joshua has been aiming to get them to do – to commit to serving the Lord. And now he says it is impossible! If Joshua had intended this to be an absolute and final statement, this should have been an end to the matter. The text, however, makes clear that he continues to challenge the people of Israel to total commitment to the Lord. Finally he makes a covenant for them.

Trent Butler offers a helpful perspective when he cautions us to read this in its proper context:

> The issue at stake in the entire chapter is the service of other gods, presented as a present reality for Israel. [18]

The attractive thing about the other gods is that they 'make fewer demands than Yahweh'. The gods of the other nations were there to be manipulated for the nation's own ends. This is a danger for Israel.

Butler suggests:

> They see God as the one who is bound to protect them along their way, so they can protect him by serving him. Joshua demands a service with a deeper motivation. He wants service based on the nature of God himself. [19]

Having displayed the grace of God in action through Israel's history, he declares two more characteristics of God in his response: 'He is a holy God; he is a jealous God' (24:19).

---

18. Butler, *Joshua* vol. 2 p. 324.
19. *Ibid.*

It is often said that the fundamental idea expressed by 'holiness' is that of separation, of separateness. While this has value, it is an inadequate description, because it immediately raises the question 'Separate from what?' That is, it is a negative idea, concerned with what it is not. In Scripture, it rather expresses what God **is** – the absolute, independent distinctiveness of His nature. When used of His people it speaks of their distinctiveness, how they should stand out for what they are rather than what they are not (see e.g. Lev. 20:26; Num. 6:5, Jer. 2:3 etc). The moral perfection of God's character is expressed in the form of Law for His people. Through the Law, the Lord also says 'I want you to be like me.'

We have already seen in the book of Joshua one response to the holiness of God as Joshua prostrates himself and takes off his sandals – a sign of reverence and submission. Isaiah's experience in the temple (Isa. 6:1-13) reinforces both the need for reverence and submission:

> What makes him tremble is not the consciousness of his humanity in the presence of divine power but the consciousness of his sin in the presence of moral purity.[20]

God's jealousy, the other aspect of His character spoken of by Joshua, is inextricably linked to His holiness. Jealousy is the active outreach of holiness against anything that offends it. It is the demand for exclusive devotion, maintaining God's own rights to the exclusion of others (see Exod. 34:14). Jealousy imposes God's holiness on people, for holiness is not simply the opposite of evil – it is the positive

---

20. H. H. Rowley, *The Faith of Israel* (London, UK: SCM Press, 1956), p. 66.

Life in the Promise (22–24)

threat to the continued existence of all those who oppose it.[21]

It is not a surprise, therefore, that Joshua wants to warn the people of the serious steps they are about to take. The people have seen many of the blessings of relationship with God – but they also need to know the dangers of turning away from Him.

> He is a holy God; he is a jealous God. He will not forgive your rebellion and your sins. If you forsake the Lord and serve foreign gods, he will turn and bring disaster on you and make an end to you, after he has been good to you. (24:19-20)

Joshua's seemingly harsh words are designed to make the people stop short of an easy declaration of loyalty and make them consider afresh the God with whom they have to deal. Despite Joshua's caution, the people are willing to make that commitment to God: 'No! We will serve the Lord.' (24:21). Once again Joshua wants the commitment they are making to be absolutely clear to them:

> You are witnesses against yourselves that you have chosen to serve the Lord. (24:22).

In the ancient world of that day, a covenant required witnesses. Normally the covenanting parties called on their respective sets of gods as those witnesses. This obviously cannot happen for Israel, so Joshua called on the people to be their own witnesses. Robert Hubbard sees a clear element of mutual responsibility in this:

---

21. This way of viewing God's holiness is derived from lectures by Alec Motyer.

> ... here Joshua declares that the assembled crowd ... are witnesses against each other in the present matter. That "witnesses" is plural implies that their testimony is individual not corporate. Each person attests the participation of the others in the covenant and each is responsible to hold others accountable for keeping it.[22]

There is no doubt in the people's minds as to what Joshua means; they reply: 'Yes we are witnesses' (24:22). This agreement by the people does not settle the matter in Joshua's mind. He makes a further demand on them:

> Now then ... throw away the foreign gods that are among you and yield your hearts to the LORD, the God of Israel. (24:23)

Words are fine, but Joshua also wants action – the strength of their commitment will be shown in a complete rejection of other gods. Ominously, their response falls short of this; they reply: 'We will serve the LORD and obey him' (24:24). What they do not say or do is significant here, as their later history will show. The similar incident, we mentioned earlier, in Genesis 35 combined both word and deed as the idols were buried – here, that action is not repeated. Commentators also point to the significance of the word 'yield', which normally refers to an exclusive commitment.

Joshua has brought the people as far as he can in their public commitment to Lord. He now makes a covenant for the people binding them to the Lord and His Law (24:25). 'Joshua recorded these things in the Book of Law of God' (24:26). The primary witness of God and to God is, once again, the Book. To save the people from forgetfulness,

---

22. Hubbard, *Joshua* p. 559.

he erects a further witness, a large stone, that he sets up in Shechem 'under the oak tree near the holy place of the Lord' (24:26). The purpose of this stone is to 'be a witness against us' (24:27). It is one further reminder of all that the Lord has said and done. For this and future generations, 'it will be a witness against you if you are untrue to your God' (24:27). Having impressed on the people the seriousness of what they are doing, particularly in the light of who God is, and the peril of going back on their commitment; Joshua 'dismissed the people, each to their own inheritance' (24:28).

Final rest (24:29-33)

The book closes with three burials: Joshua's, Eleazar's and the bones of Joseph. Not only is Joshua given his full name – Joshua the son of Nun – but also an additional title, 'the servant of the Lord' (24:29). Up to this point in the biblical narrative, this has been a title used exclusively of Moses. Indeed, Joshua starts out as 'the servant of Moses' (see 1:1 NASB), but now after a long and faithful life, he is invested with this title of great honour. His burial takes place in his allotted inheritance. A testimony to his leadership is included:

> Israel served the Lord throughout the lifetime of Joshua and of the elders who outlived him and who had experienced everything the Lord had done for Israel (24:31).

Yet here again, an ominous note is sounded – the faithfulness of one generation is not necessarily passed on to the next. For Joshua's generation the grace of God in their rescue, protection and the provision of the land was a reality they had experienced. Future generations, as they became detached from that history, would pay the price for not keeping those truths alive among them.

With the burial of Joseph's bones, another element of the ancient promise is fulfilled. In the plot of land, which Jacob had purchased so many years before, his bones are now interred. It marks God's faithfulness towards those who have lived in His promise. Finally the book closes with the death and burial of Eleazar. He has been the other leading figure in the allocation of territory to the tribes of Israel. His work, like Joshua's, is now completed. The people of God should now enjoy life in the promise – they have their place, they are united as a people and their relationship with God is established by covenant.

Further thoughts on ... Joshua 24

The majority of commentators consider Joshua 24 to be a covenant renewal ceremony. It is not a strict detailing of every element of the covenant, rather a report of the situation in which the renewal took place, and the main features of that renewal. It is now commonplace to view covenants in the light of the wider Ancient Near Eastern context. They were generally composed of six elements. In their simplest form they can be summarised like this:

Parties
Prologue
Provisions
Preservation
Permanence
Penalties

Parties – *preamble* – those involved in making the covenant, often the major figure takes the lead in this. *This is who I am.*

Prologue – *historical prologue* – an account of what has been done especially by the greater for the lesser party. *This is what I have done.*

Provisions – *stipulations* – the greater party spells out their expectations of the lesser party. *This is how to live in the covenant.*

Preservation – *deposit/rereading* – how and where copies of the covenant are to be kept and (often) when they should be re-read. *This is how to remember.*

Permanence – *witnesses* – witnesses are called to guarantee the terms and the keeping of the covenant. *This makes it certain.*

Penalties – *sanctions* – both blessings and curses are included to safeguard the covenant. *This is the outcome.*

The order of the first three elements does not vary in Scripture – it starts with God and what He has done before it moves to the stipulations, the response people must make. It underlines the priority of grace over works. In Joshua 24 all the elements of the covenant are present:

- Parties   the Lord   (v. 2a)
- Prologue   the history   (vv. 2b-13)
- Previsions   what is required   (vv. 14-15)
- Preservation   the book   (v. 26)
- Permanence   witnesses   (v. 22, 26b-27)
- Penalties   curses   (vv. 19-20)

> The final chapter of the book closes this part of the narrative with renewed emphasis on the grace and commitment of God to His people only then does it call for their response.

From text to message

Although the demand of Joshua 24:14-15 is a favourite text for preachers, it is often used completely adrift from its context. The narrator has carefully constructed this final section (chapters 22-24) to show the great principles by which life in the land of promise should be lived. Chapters 22 and 23, in particular, are not like the attic of many homes – the place where you put everything you don't have room for elsewhere, or you are simply not sure what to do with it. There is a progression through these chapters, which shows how life in the Promised Land must be lived. The people need to:

- remember the goodness of God
- preserve the unity of the people
- not presume on the grace of God
- be wary of the surrounding culture
- hold fast to the covenant.

These things should characterise their life in the land of promise from this time on.

Getting the message clear: the theme

In the course of Joshua's farewell address, he repeats the great theme of the book:

> You know with all your heart and soul that not one of all the good promises the LORD gave you has failed. Every promise has been fulfilled; not one has failed. (23:14)

As Joshua is aware that his time on earth is to come to an end, he reminds them of this great fact. And he does it in the context of instructing them concerning the things that will make life in the promise a continuing reality. Those things we have outlined above. Bringing them together with the reminder of the book's great theme, the main idea in this section of the narrative can be stated as follows:

> All that the Lord has done for His people (fought for them, given them the land, etc.) now enables them to live together in the land of promise, in loyalty to the Lord and to one another.

The gift of God, the unity of the people and the covenant bond make possible life in the promise.

Getting the message clear: the aim

The lessons that God's people of old needed to learn to enable them to live in the promise (that is: the place God gives, as the people called together by Him and living in a right way before Him) remain vital lessons for God's people in every age. As we have seen, we cannot treat lightly the goodness and grace of God and we must not presume on His holy and jealous character. It is not a light matter to be in a relationship with this God. We need, therefore, to encourage believers to keep in perspective the gift and grace of God in Christ, the unity we have in Him and the accountability we have to Him as we live in the light of His greater promises.

A way in

A common trait is that we like to 'pigeon-hole' others – to put them in a category to help us understand, or even to control them. It may be a simple category – '(s)he is all head and no heart.' Or it may be rather more sophisticated. Charles Handy, in his book 'Understanding Voluntary Organisations' offered the following more 'classical' categories:

- *Zeus people are personalities* – they are 'people' people. Often with large address books!

- *Apollo people are logical people* – they like things done rationally/logically; 'decently and in order'.

- *Athenians enjoy problems and teams* – they may strive for perfection, but, at the very least, they want them done well and on the basis of consensus.

- *Dionysians do not really belong in organisations at all* – they are generally loners, valuing freedom and the right to make their own decisions.[23]

In any group of God's people all and more of these will be found. The group will only function properly if there is clarity and mutual understanding between these groups. This is certainly what was needed between the East and West bank tribes in Joshua 22.

The kind of 'head' or 'heart' categories mentioned above are often seen as mutually exclusive, as if there was an impenetrable wall between intellect and emotions. Joshua's appeal to the people at the end of the book shows that the

---

23. C. Handy, *Understanding Voluntary Organisations* (London, UK: Penguin, 1988), pp. 100-101.

two are actually inseparable. The people need both the facts of what God has done for them and the attachment of both will and emotions to Him for His goodness.

Ideas for application

- Concerning Joshua's commendation and blessing to the East Bank tribes, Matthew Henry wrote:

  > Though it was by the favour of God and his power that Israel got possession of this land, and he must have all the glory, yet Joshua thought there was a thankful acknowledgment due to their brethren who assisted them, and whose sword and bow were employed for them. God must be chiefly eyed in our praises, yet instruments must not be altogether overlooked.[24]

  There is, in those words, both a rebuke and an encouragement to today's church.

- The opening part of Joshua's speech (22:1-9) can be considered as an Old Testament counterpart of 1 John 4:19: 'We love because he first loved us'. This is always the Bible's way of viewing relationship with God.

- The old movie adage 'Shoot first, ask questions later!' seems to be the West Bank tribes' attitude (22:12). Divisions and fights are inevitable among the people of God if we do not take time to listen.

- Can 'territorial superiority' happen even today among the people of God? Yes, it can! The 'we were here first' or 'this is our territory' spirit is alive and well.

---

24. Quoted in Davis, *Joshua* p. 168.

- The East Bank tribes' response in 22:22-23 is the response of a clear conscience. Similarly only a clear conscience can allow Paul to say, 'You know how I lived among you' (see Acts 20:18 and 1 Thess. 1:5).

- '… they talked no more about going to war' (22:33). The truth is fundamental to unity.

- In Joshua's farewell speech in chapter 23, what God has done for the people again takes centre stage. The call to trust God is based on the fact that He is trustworthy.

- Remember the vocabulary of intimacy is being used when Joshua encourages the people to 'hold fast' to God (23:8). How do we express that in our individual and corporate life?

- Israel faced both the temptations to presume on the grace of God and to compromise with the surrounding culture. Think through the ways in which this is true for you and your situation.

- In chapter 24 Joshua outlines briefly some of Israel's history – and it wasn't always glorious! Adolf Harstad comments:

  > Christians who speak with personal pride of coming from a long line of believers should go back a bit further. We also will find our ancestors steeped in dark superstition [see Eph. 2:12] … God alone deserves our boasting for calling us to salvation by the Gospel of Jesus Christ.[25]

---

25. Harstad, *Joshua* p. 769.

Life in the Promise (22–24)

- Joshua was very aware of the danger of settling for 'lip-service' rather than 'whole-life-service'. In particular he did not want the Israelites just to renounce their idols, but to throw them away. This should not be used to castigate our pet hates but to show the seriousness of the one we serve; especially in the light of the great cost He has borne for us. Luke 14:25-27 is worth reflecting on concerning this.

- 'Israel served the Lord throughout the lifetime of Joshua and of the elders who outlived him' (24:31). Every generation needs to be taught the truth of God and make their own commitment.

Suggestions for preaching

Sermon 1
Without attempting to deal with every aspect of these three chapters, an overview sermon can open up some of its major themes.

One people
At the heart of chapter 22 is the unity of God's people – they may be divided geographically but their unity is based on their shared experience of God at work for them all.

One God
Chapter 23 focuses on the one God who gave them the land, who is also the one God that they must serve.

One heart
Joshua's final demand to the people is to serve God with undivided hearts.

The New Testament clearly echoes each of these themes.

Sermon 2

The relationship between the two sets of tribes is in the foreground here. The following outline seeks to make clear both the rightful concerns of each group and the essence of their unity.

Mission accomplished (22:1-9)

- Joshua commends the East Bank tribes for their obedience (22:2), their support of the West Bank peoples (22:3) and completing their mission from God (22:3).
- They are sent on their way with an exhortation (22:5) and a blessing (22:6-8).

Seeking the truth (22:10-20)

- News of the East Bank tribes altar demands a response (22:10-12).
- A delegation is sent to seek the truth (22:13-16).
- The seriousness of the situation is recognised (22:16-20).

Guarding the future (22:21-34)

- A clear answer (22:21-23).
- A real concern (22:24-29).
- The future secured (22:30-34).

The unity of the people of God is vital to their life and mission. Paul recognised this when he wrote to the Philippians asking them to stand together and stand for the Gospel (see Phil. 1:27).

Life in the Promise (22-24)

Sermon 3

Much of Joshua's farewell speech to Israel (chapter 23) expresses his warning to the nation about what might face them if they turn away from God. The essence of what he says can be outlined as follows:

Don't forget (23:1-5)

- Remember what God has done (23:1-3).
- Remember what God has given (23:4).
- Remember what God will do for you (23:5).

Don't defect (23:6-11)

- Be careful to follow the Law (23:6).
- Be careful not to compromise (23:7-8).
- Be careful to love the Lord (23:9-11).

Don't be surprised (23:12-16)

- If the people of the land bring you down (23:12-13).
- If the LORD brings you down (23:14-16).

Forgetfulness of the foundational truths of the Gospel lead many astray. Paul had much to say on this in 2 Timothy for example. The centrality of the Word (the Law) is the key to persevering in the life of faith.

Sermon 4

In his challenge to the people at Shechem (chapter 24) Joshua spells out the issues in covenantal terms. The main elements of the covenant are represented in his words to the

Israelites. An approach to preaching the major elements could look like this:[26]

Living under the grace of God (24:1-13)

- Joshua details how the nation has seen God at work, keeping His promise.

Living at the pace of God (24:1-13)

- Abraham was promised many descendants and got… Isaac (24:3). No instant fulfilment.
- Between 24:4 and 5 there are four hundred years; then 'you lived in the wilderness a long time' (24:7).
- It is not about speed but about faithfulness.

Living before the face of God (24:14-33)

- The Reformers used this phrase because it summed up for them the privilege and the seriousness of the life of faith.
- The privilege – heirs to God's inheritance, life in the promise.
- The seriousness – realising who we are dealing with – the holy and jealous God.

As Christians, we live under the grace of God (Gal. 2:20-21), at the pace of God – suffering and persevering are as much a part of the Christian life as victory (see Heb. 11:32-37) – and with the privilege and seriousness of being God's people (Mark 8:34-38).

---

26. See Davis, *Joshua* particularly pp. 188-190.

Life in the Promise (22–24)

Suggestions for teaching

Questions to help understand the passage

1. Note the verbs in 22:1-6 that are used concerning what God requires from the people.

2. How have the East Bank tribes responded to the commands of both God and Moses?

3. Why do you think the West Bank tribes responded to the altar the other tribes built as strongly as they did? Reflect on the sins they mention from their history in 22:15-20. What was the nature of those sins and what were the consequences?

4. Why did the East Bank tribes want the altar as a marker and a reminder?

5. What are the main elements of Joshua's reminders to all the people in 23:3-4? What confidence does this give for their future (23:5)?

6. What echoes of earlier scripture can you find in 23:6-11?

7. What are the main dangers of compromise for Israel in 23:12-13?

8. How is God faithful to His promise of both blessing and cursing (23:15-16)? What does that tell us about both salvation and judgement?

9. Trace the main points of Israel's history recorded in 24:2-13. Why do you think these were selected?

10. What is Joshua trying to do in his dialogue with the people in 24:14-24?

Questions to help apply the text

1. Joshua clearly acknowledges the contribution the East Bank tribes have made in securing the land. How do we acknowledge and encourage others in the service of God and His people?

2. How are our love for God and our obedience connected? What will this mean in everyday life?

3. What is often the first response we make when we think someone is in the wrong? What should it be?

4. How do we sometimes create unnecessary divisions? And how do we avoid that happening?

5. In what ways does a knowledge of what God has done help us to face the future?

6. There are always pressures on God's people to compromise. What are the particular issues that put you under that pressure at the moment?

7. Think about the consequences of turning away from God in your own life. How has that situation changed?

8. What do you do to make sure you keep remembering the great facts of your faith? Bob Dylan once sang, 'You gotta serve somebody' – if you are not serving God then what or who do you serve? What temptations do we face as Christians in this area?

9. Why is it so important to count the cost of our commitment to Christ?

Further Reading

The book of Joshua is well served by a wide variety of expositions and more technical commentaries. The expositions will help you to earth your understanding of the text and also help you illustrate and apply it. These should, of course, only be consulted after you have grappled with the text itself!

I have not listed below all the resources I have consulted in the preparation of this book. The authors listed may not agree with all my interpretations of Joshua, or with my adaptations of their ideas, but they have provided vital stimulation in my preparation. I am extremely grateful to them all for opening up new vistas on the text.

Expositions of Joshua

John Calvin, *Calvin's Commentaries Vol IV Joshua*, (Grand Rapids USA: Baker Books, 2003)

Ralph Davis, *Joshua – No Falling Words* (Fearn, UK: Christian Focus, 2000)

Rhett Dodson, *Every Promise of Your Word* (Edinburgh, UK: Banner of Truth 2016)

David Firth, *The Message of Joshua* BST (Nottingham, UK: IVP 2015)

David Jackman, *Joshua, People of God's purpose* (Wheaton USA: Crossway 2014)

Commentaries

Trent Butler, *Joshua* WBC (Grand Rapids USA, Zondervan 2014) 2 vols

Adolph Harstad, *Joshua – Concordia Commentary* (St Louis USA: Concordia Publishing House 2004)

Daniel Hawk, *Joshua, Berit Olam* (Collegeville USA: Liturgical Press 2000)

David Howard Jr, *Joshua NAC* (Nashville, USA: Broadman & Holman 1998)

Robert Hubbard Jr, *Joshua NIVAC* (Grand Rapids, USA: Zondervan 2009)

Gordon McConville & Stephen Williams, *Joshua, Two Horizons Commentary* (Grand Rapids, USA: Eerdmans 2010)

Richard Nelson, *Joshua OTL* (Louisville USA, Westminster John Knox Press, 1997)

Pekka Pitkanen, *Joshua Apollos OT Commentary* (Nottingham UK: Apollos, 2010)

Bruce Waltke, 'Joshua' in *New Bible Commentary* (Nottingham, UK: IVP 1994)

Marten Woudstra, *Joshua NICOT* (Grand Rapids USA: Eerdmans, 1981)

Other resources

To think through the question of violence in the book, the following are recommended:

G. K. Beale, *The Morality of God in the Old Testament* (Philadelphia, Phillipsburg USA: Westminster Seminary Press, P & R Publishing, 2013)

Paul Copan, *Is God a Moral Monster?* (Grand Rapids, USA: Baker 2011)

Paul Copan & Matthew Flanagan, *Did God Really Command Genocide?* (Grand Rapids, USA: Baker 2014)

Tremper Longman III, 'The Case for Spiritual Continuity' in *Show Them No Mercy* (Grand Rapids, USA: Zondervan, 2003)

Melvin Tinker, *Mass Destruction* (Welwyn Garden City, UK: EP Books 2017)

C. J. H. Wright, *The God I Don't Understand* (Grand Rapids, USA: Zondervan, 2008)

PT Resources

Resources for Preachers and Bible Teachers

PT Resources, a ministry of The Proclamation Trust, provides a range of multimedia resources for preachers and Bible teachers.

Teach the Bible Series (Christian Focus & PT Resources)
The Teaching the Bible Series, published jointly with *Christian Focus Publications*, is written by preachers, for preachers, and is specifically geared to the purpose of God's Word – its proclamation as living truth. Books in the series aim to help the reader move beyond simply understanding a text to communicating and applying it.

Current titles include: *Teaching 1 Peter, Teaching 1 Timothy, Teaching Acts, Teaching Amos, Teaching Ephesians, Teaching Isaiah, Teaching John, Teaching Matthew, Teaching Numbers, Teaching Romans, Teaching Daniel, Teaching 1 and 2 Kings, Teaching the Christian Hope* and *Spirit of Truth*.

Forthcoming titles include: *Teaching James, Teaching Matthew, Teaching Mark* and *Teaching Leviticus*.

Get Preaching

Get Preaching is a series produced by the Proclamation Trust looking at a single issue integral to or associated with preaching. Whilst there are many comprehensive and even exhaustive books on preaching there are no titles that are solely focussed on a single area of the art, craft and science of preaching. That is where *Get Preaching* finds its niche. The idea behind *Get Preaching* is in two directions. *Get* preaching, as in understanding preaching, but also get *preaching* as in the hope that these books will equip, excite and encourage people to undertake the task of preaching.

The first titles in this seres are: *Get Preaching: Why Expository Preaching? Get Preaching: Preaching the Cross* & *Get Preaching: All-Age Services*

Practical Preacher series

PT Resources publish a number of books addressing practical issues for preachers. These include *The Priority of Preaching, Bible Delight, Hearing the Spirit* and *The Ministry Medical*. Forthcoming titles include a ministry checklist based on the book of 2 Timothy.

Online resources

We publish a large number of audio resources online, all of which are free to download. These are searchable through our website by speaker, date, topic and Bible book. The resources include:

- sermon series; examples of great preaching which not only demonstrate faithful principles but which will refresh and encourage the heart of the preacher.

- instructions; audio which helps the teacher or preacher understand, open up and teach individual books of the Bible by getting to grips with their central message and purpose.

- conference recordings; audio from all our conferences including the annual Evangelical Ministry Assembly. These talks discuss ministry and preaching issues.

An increasing number of resources are also available in video download form.

Equipped

Equipped to Preach the Word is a teaching series of 24 units, designed to provide a foundation for the work of expository Bible preaching and teaching. It comprises three modules, each of eight units, entitled *Equipped by the Lord* (module 1), *Equipped with the Skills* (module 2) and *Equipped with the Scriptures* (module 3).

The course can be accessed free at www.proctrust.org.uk/equipped.

Teaching the Bible Series

OLD TESTAMENT

TEACHING NUMBERS – ADRIAN REYNOLDS 978-1-78191-156-3

TEACHING JOSHUA – DOUG JOHNSON 978-1-5271-0335-1

TEACHING 1 KINGS – BOB FYALL 978-1-78191-605-6

TEACHING 2 KINGS – BOB FYALL 978-1-5271-0157-9

TEACHING EZRA – ADRIAN REYNOLDS 978-1-78191-752-7

TEACHING RUTH & ESTHER – CHRISTOPHER ASH 978-1-5271-0007-7

TEACHING PSALMS VOL. 1 – CHRISTOPHER ASH 978-1-5271-0004-6

TEACHING PSALMS VOL. 2 – CHRISTOPHER ASH 978-1-5271-0005-3

TEACHING ISAIAH – DAVID JACKMAN 978-1-84550-565-3

TEACHING DANIEL – ROBIN SYDSERFF, BOB FYALL 978-1-84550-457-1

TEACHING AMOS – BOB FYALL 978-1-84550-142-6

NEW TESTAMENT

TEACHING MATTHEW – DAVID JACKMAN, WILLIAM PHILIP
978-1-84550-480-9

TEACHING ACTS – DAVID COOK 978-1-84550-255-3

TEACHING ROMANS VOL. 1 – CHRISTOPHER ASH 978-1-84550-455-7

TEACHING ROMANS VOL. 2 – CHRISTOPHER ASH 978-1-84550-456-4

TEACHING EPHESIANS – SIMON AUSTEN 978-1-84550-684-1

TEACHING 1 & 2 THESSALONIANS – ANGUS MACLEAY 978-1-78191-325-3

TEACHING 1 TIMOTHY – ANGUS MACLEAY 978-1-84550-808-1

TEACHING 2 TIMOTHY – JONATHAN GRIFFITHS 978-1-78191-389-5

TEACHING 1 PETER – ANGUS MACLEAY 978-1-84550-347-5

TEACHING 1, 2, 3 JOHN – MERVYN ELOFF 978-1-78191-832-6

TOPICAL

BURNING HEARTS – JOSH MOODY 978-1-78191-403-8

BIBLE DELIGHT – CHRISTOPHER ASH 978-1-84550-360-4

HEARING THE SPIRIT – CHRISTOPHER ASH 978-1-84550-725-1

SPIRIT OF TRUTH – DAVID JACKMAN 978-1-84550-057-3

TEACHING THE CHRISTIAN HOPE – DAVID JACKMAN 978-1-85792-518-0

THE MINISTRY MEDICAL – JONATHAN GRIFFITHS 978-1-78191-232-4

THE PRIORITY OF PREACHING – CHRISTOPHER ASH 978-1-84550-464-9

About the Proclamation Trust

We exist to promote church-based expository Bible ministry and especially to equip and encourage Biblical expository preachers because we recognise the primary role of preaching in God's sovereign purposes in the world through the local church.

Biblical (the message)

We believe the Bible is God's written Word and that, by the work of the Holy Spirit, as it is faithfully preached God's voice is truly heard.

Expository (the method)

Central to the preacher's task is correctly handling the Bible, seeking to discern the mind of the Spirit in the passage being expounded through prayerful study of the text in the light of its context in the biblical book and the Bible as a whole. This divine message must then be preached in dependence on the Holy Spirit to the minds, hearts and wills of the contemporary hearers.

Preachers (the messengers)

The public proclamation of God's Word by suitably gifted leaders is fundamental to a ministry that honours God, builds the church and reaches the world. God uses weak jars of clay in this task who need encouragement to persevere in their biblical convictions, ministry of God's Word and godly walk with Christ.

We achieve this through:

- PT Cornhill: a one-year full-time or two-year part-time church based training course
- PT Conferences: offering practical encouragement for Bible preachers, teachers and ministers' wives
- PT Resources: including books, online resources, the PT blog (www.theproclaimer.org.uk) and podcasts

Christian Focus Publications

Our mission statement –

STAYING FAITHFUL

In dependence upon God we seek to impact the world through literature faithful to His infallible Word, the Bible. Our aim is to ensure that the Lord Jesus Christ is presented as the only hope to obtain forgiveness of sin, live a useful life and look forward to heaven with Him.

Our Books are published in four imprints:

CHRISTIAN FOCUS

popular works including biographies, commentaries, basic doctrine and Christian living.

CHRISTIAN HERITAGE

books representing some of the best material from the rich heritage of the church.

MENTOR

books written at a level suitable for Bible College and seminary students, pastors, and other serious readers. The imprint includes commentaries, doctrinal studies, examination of current issues and church history.

CF4•K

children's books for quality Bible teaching and for all age groups: Sunday school curriculum, puzzle and activity books; personal and family devotional titles, biographies and inspirational stories – Because you are never too young to know Jesus!

Christian Focus Publications Ltd,
Geanies House, Fearn, Ross-shire,
IV20 1TW, Scotland, United Kingdom.
www.christianfocus.com